# THE KU KLUX KLAN IN CANADA

# THE KU KLUX KLAN IN CANADA

*A Century of Promoting Racism and Hate in the Peaceable Kingdom*

ALLAN BARTLEY

FORMAC PUBLISHING COMPANY LIMITED
HALIFAX

*For my wife, daughters and mother. Thank you for your patience and the gift of curiosity.*



Formac Publishing Company Limited recognizes the support of the Province of Nova Scotia through Film and Creative Industries Nova Scotia. We are pleased to work in partnership with the Province of Nova Scotia to develop and promote our creative industries for the benefit of all Nova Scotians. We acknowledge the support of the Canada Council for the Arts which last year invested $157 million to bring the arts to Canadians throughout the country.

Cover design: Tyler Cleroux
Cover image: Library and Archives Canada

Library and Archives Canada Cataloguing in Publication
Title: The Ku Klux Klan in Canada : a century of promoting racism and hate in the peaceable kingdom / Allan Bartley.
Names: Bartley, Allan, 1950- author.
Description: Includes bibliographical references and index.
Identifiers: Canadiana (print) 20200162160 | Canadiana (ebook) 20200162195 | ISBN 9781459506138 (softcover) | ISBN 9781459506145 (EPUB)
Subjects: LCSH: Ku Klux Klan (1915- ) | LCSH: Racism—Canada—History—20th century. | LCSH: Canada— Race relations—History—20th century.
Classification: LCC HS2339.K6 B37 2020 | DDC 322.4/209710904—dc23

Formac Publishing Company Limited
5502 Atlantic Street
Halifax, Nova Scotia, Canada
B3H 1G4
www.formac.ca

Printed and bound in Canada.

**Photo Credits:**
Alberta Provincial Archives: page 112; City of Edmonton Archives: page 115; City of Toronto Archives: page 102, 107, 108, 109; Community Archives of Belleville and Hastings County: page 106, 113, 114; *The Daily Gleaner*: page 106; Elgin County Archives: page 103, 104, 105; Glenbow Museum: page 111; Red Deer Archives: page 110; Vancouver City Archives: page 100, 101.

# CONTENTS

# PREFACE

Hate has a name. Hate has a face. Hate has an address. It lives in Canada. The Ku Klux Klan's more than one-hundred-year presence in Canada demonstrates how hate lived and flourished and still endures in the nation sometimes known as the Peaceable Kingdom. Our neighbours were partly to blame, but Canadians can also blame themselves.

"Because we believe that it can't happen here, we are too hesitant to talk about the way in which some people — and politicians — are already admiring the reflection they see when they look south," novelist Alexi Zentner wrote in the *Globe and Mail* in the summer of 2019.[1] "We think of virulent hatred as a thing that comes from the history books. And yet, the history books are coming to life again."

The challenges of writing a book on the history of the Ku Klux Klan in Canada go beyond creating a narrative. There is the concern that to write about hate is to condone it. To write about the leaders and their followers runs the risk of glorifying them or ridiculing them or magnifying or minimizing their ideas and impact. The odious reality of the Ku Klux Klan and its imitators over the decades speaks for itself. We need to confront that reality.

The book examines motivations for both leaders and followers. For many leaders, the Ku Klux Klan was a money-making enterprise. For many members, the organization provided a platform to express hate and resentments they would not express as individuals. For some, it offered a chance to be the centre of attention — a moment of recognition that they could parlay into something better for themselves. For others, it allowed them to commit acts of brutality that they would not have engaged in on their own. For victims of the fear, threats, slights, intimidation, beatings and more, the Ku Klux Klan was and is the face of hatred.

This narrative seeks to capture the flow of history; it does not detail all the realities stemming from hate over a century. The Ku Klux Klan will endure as an idea in Canada so long as any stunted human spirit can scrawl KKK on a wall and walk away with impunity. In the course of history, and in moments like ours, these degradations of humanity live again and thrive under many different guises. But Canadian society has a better chance than many of lifting human spirits beyond crude expressions and acts of hate — if we expose and beat back the organizations and groups and individuals who promote such ideas when they appear.

Hate has a name, a face and an address. We need to know these things so that we can confront hate wherever it lives — in the Peaceable Kingdom or elsewhere. From there we move forward.

# PART I

# Chapter 1
# MOVIE NIGHT

The Gayety Burlesque on Yonge Street offered the Sporting Widows Ladies' Band to entertain Toronto audiences in September 1915. Up the street, Loews Theatre featured high-class vaudeville acts starring the McDonald Trio, Jack Taylor, Hallan & Hayes, Cook & Stevens and more. The Hippodrome at City Hall Square had three shows daily with "unique and complete photo-plays and feature film attractions." But over at the prestige-laden Royal Alexandra Theatre on King Street, something completely different was on offer. The display ads blared:

> *Eighth Wonder of the World, Took 8 Months to Produce. 18,000 People. 3,000 Horses. Cost $560,000. The Basil Corporation Presents D.W. Griffith's The BIRTH of a NATION. The Most Stupendous Dramatic Spectacle the Brain of Man has yet Visioned and Revealed. Night Prices 50c to $1.50. All Matinees 50c to $1.00.*

The ideas and images of the Ku Klux Klan came to Canada in September 1915 through the new medium of silent film. For the next decade, the spectacle of *The Birth of A Nation* nurtured an organization dedicated to white racial supremacy, the suppression of Black people, Jews, Catholics, Asians, Chinese, eastern Europeans and just about anybody who looked, sounded or seemed different from the white Protestant majority in Canada and the United States. The trend continued throughout the century that followed, with exploitation of new media of all kinds (film, radio, television, Internet) coming to define how hate was projected, narrated, organized and delivered by the Ku Klux Klan — an organization foreign to Canada but one that found fertile soil to take root.

But in 1915, only a year into the national trauma of the First World War, with its slaughter and sorrows, apprehensive Canadians welcomed the diversion offered by the new moving picture coming out of the United States. *The Birth of A Nation* opened in theatres across the country that fall, drawing crowds everywhere. And everywhere the advertising meticulously prepared by Hollywood publicity teams lauded the "Eighth Wonder of the World."

The reception at the Royal Alexandra in Toronto was repeated at Vancouver's Main Street Avenue Theatre and Montreal's theatres during that looming fall of 1915.[1] Crowds lined up around the block to buy tickets. There were continuous showings for weeks on end. The film's artistic and technical innovations animated discussions in the street and filled columns of newsprint.

"The features of the first part are the battle scenes, especially that showing the dash of the Confederate troops for the trenches of the Federals, which might suggest the trench warfare in Flanders during the present war," critic Edwin Parkhurst wrote in the *Globe* the day after the film opened in Toronto.[2] "So great has been the success of this attraction that it is not always possible to accommodate the crowds," marvelled Parkhurst. "A line of intending purchasers of seats is at the box office throughout each day."[3]

White Canadians in particular couldn't get enough of the story depicting the aftermath of the Confederate states' defeat. The United States Civil War continued to be a living presence a half-century after the conflict that killed more than six hundred thousand Americans and devastated the life and economy of the southern states. Reunions of American Civil War veterans, including those from the Confederacy, were regularly reported in the Canadian media, particularly around the fiftieth anniversary of the war's end in 1915.[4] The Confederacy had had many Canadian supporters in the 1860s, and their children and grandchildren flocked to see *The Birth of A Nation.*

In Toronto, local police magistrate Colonel George Denison, never shy about seeking publicity for his life and adventures, attended the 1916 reunion of the United Confederate Veterans association in Birmingham, Alabama. The *Globe* newspaper was happy to provide a platform for his southern travels.[5] Denison had a personal link with Confederate officers who had operated undercover in Canada during the Civil War.[6]

The Royal Alexandra's manager, long-time Toronto entertainment entrepreneur Lawrence (Lol) Solmon, saw the crowds, saw the opportunity and paid the next scheduled act to stay away so he could extend the movie's run into the autumn. Lol didn't like moving pictures himself and rarely booked them into the up-scale Royal Alex, but he knew good business when he saw it.

What was the attraction? There was the novelty of a full-length motion picture that ran more than two hours, a bold innovation at the time. There was the drama of the images that showed Atlanta, Georgia, burning at the hands of the northern Union Army, the escape of refugees from the city and the assassination of U.S. President Abraham Lincoln by a Confederate sympathizer barely a month after the end of the war in April 1865. Flaming fiery crosses ignited the screen even though they had never been a feature of the real Klan in the 1860s.

The movie told the story of defeated Confederates who terrorized newly freed Black people throughout the southern United States, riding into their communities at night dressed in white robes and hoods. They sought, so the myth went, "revenge" for the defeated Confederacy.

In fact, the violent terror unleashed by white paramilitary groups came in response to progress made by Black people in the years following the war. In the devastated southern states just after the war, Black former slaves were turned out of the plantations and left with little means to pursue new lives built on their status as free citizens. Remarkably, they took full advantage of all opportunities and managed to make significant gains within a short period — pursuing education, starting businesses, voting, running for and being elected to public office. The displaced white southern elites — plantation owners, political leaders, merchants — bitterly resented all these signs of progress, as the recently enslaved population asserted its humanity and began to take its place as full participants in society.

They also resented the "carpetbaggers" who swooped in to take advantage of political and commercial confusion. The despised carpetbaggers were northern opportunists who flooded the south looking to make fortunes by buying or leasing once-prosperous cotton plantations and other distressed businesses. They were so-called because they were believed to have thrown their few belongings into luggage made from cheap carpet material and headed south at the news of the Confederacy's defeat.

The so-called "scalawags" were seen as even worse — traitors to the Confederacy. They were generally white southerners who supported the Republican Party — the party that emancipated the slaves — thereby depriving the south of its cheap labour and the basis for its prosperous cotton-based economy, not much of which was left after the war.

Criminality of all kinds flourished in the absence of effective law enforcement. The occupying Union armies were focused on dismembering any last forms of organized resistance with little effort made to police the peace. The white southern population resented the occupying northern soldiers and a suddenly free Black population that only a few months before had been slaves of the Confederacy.

The rise of democratically elected Black officials in new state and local governments threatened the old white authority structures. In late 1865, bands of demobilized Confederate soldiers joined together to terrorize the newly enfranchised Black population and thus maintain white control over them, using a combination of violent threats and actual acts of violence. They called themselves the Ku Klux Klan for reasons that remained obscure — Greek myths, Scottish rites, British Israelism,[7] all these and more served over time as explanations for the peculiar name.

For more than two years in Kentucky (where the Klan had been started) and neighbouring states, the Klan inflicted its brand of criminal brutality on Black citizens, scalawags, carpetbaggers and anybody else in their way. Finally, even some southern whites complained that things had gone "too far" under the Klan's reign of terror. Responding to calls for restraint from the white population, Nathan Bedford Forrest, a former Confederate general and the Klan's first grand wizard, formally disbanded the group in 1868. However, remnants continued to operate for years across the south, and a half-century later the Ku Klux Klan and its imitators provided the inspiration for *The Birth of A Nation*.

The movie thrilled Canadians who had little to celebrate and much to mourn as the reality of sacrifice grew more bitter heading into the wartime winter of 1915–16. The country was still absorbing news of the heavy losses its soldiers had taken in the spring of 1915 at Ypres, Belgium, when the Germans unleashed poison chlorine gas on the Canadians. Despite terrible casualties, they had held the line. The bloody battle of Festubert had followed. And now, the 2nd Canadian Division had just arrived in France for what promised to be a grim and deadly winter in the trenches.

Diversions from the war news were popular. And so popular was *The Birth of A Nation* that a second run opened at Yonge Street's Massey Hall on Christmas Day of 1915 "with a matinee and then twice daily."[8] The same thing happened in Vancouver and at theatres across the country.

The almost exclusively white crowds went wild. "The music and the gradual development of the play stimulated great interest in the audience which found an outlet in spontaneous applause at every appearance of the rescuing Ku Klux Klan riders towards the latter end of play," intoned the admiring Edwin Parkhurst, whose specialty was, admittedly, classical music.[9]

White Torontonians were not alone in their enthusiasm. Return engagements were booked in cities and small towns across the country. In New Glasgow, Nova Scotia, for example, the Roseland Theatre brought the show back on an annual basis. The British-born Parkhurst never failed to remind his readers that "this is an exact replica of the production now playing at the Liberty Theatre in New York, where it is in its seven hundred performances."

The film's second run continued into January 1916 in Toronto and across North America. It returned in March 1917 as the Royal Alex's Lol Solmon acceded to popular demand by booking yet another engagement "of that greatest of all Griffith's spectacles."[10] The film came back again in late December 1917, the fifth time in Toronto and this time at Massey Hall with predictions that the film would "go on forever."[11]

And so it seemed. *The Birth of A Nation* was indeed the entertainment phenomenon of the era. The film was the work of American movie maker David Wark Griffith. He had started in the embryonic American west coast film industry early in the century as a bit player and writer, eventually moving on to technical production and directing. *The Birth of A Nation* was his breakthrough movie.

Griffith took as the inspiration for his new film a book and play called *The Clansman* by Thomas Dixon, a white southerner who harboured a nostalgic hankering for his romanticized image of the old way of life in an idealized south. Dixon's father had been a member of the original Ku Klux Klan immediately after the Civil War, and the organization featured prominently in his book and play. As a young child, Dixon witnessed the lynching of a Black man by the Klan, and his memory of this event found its way into *The Clansman.*[12] The book had a receptive audience, as did the play that followed based on the same story.

The stage play toured America in 1905 and 1906, raising racial tensions with its depiction of threatened white womanhood, valiant Klansmen riding to the rescue and restoration of natural (i.e., white-controlled) order. The play's scheduled appearance in Atlanta in October 1906 came in the wake of September race riots sparked by the rumoured rapes of white women in and around the city. More than a dozen Black people were killed in the ensuing violence. The play was seen as a further incitement to racial unrest, and the performance was postponed until later in the year.

The Hollywood opening of the film version of *The Birth of A Nation* at Clune's Auditorium in early February 1915 was accompanied by all the lurid publicity the burgeoning film industry could muster. The New York opening at the Liberty Theatre a few weeks later involved a similar spectacle.[13] Ushers were dressed as Confederate soldiers, usherettes as southern belles. Actors decked out in white robes and hoods stood silent guard on horseback outside the theatre.

In the settled environment of Los Angeles, the night riders of Hollywood cut a theatrical swath that gave the film a profile for future sales. This was noteworthy at the time, but Hollywood being Hollywood, industry attention soon moved on to the next novelty and sensation. The Atlanta opening of the film ten months later however — in the heart of the Old Confederacy — was a whole different story.

A decade after *The Clansman* played in Atlanta, racial tensions in Georgia lingered and had even sharpened. By the time the film version opened in Atlanta in 1915, it had been shown in dozens of cities across the Old Confederacy, pumping awareness and white pride in its wake.[14]

The arrival of the film inspired William Simmons of Atlanta, a born salesman and inveterate joiner of fraternal organizations, to act on his dream of creating a twentieth-century version of the Klan. Like Dixon, Simmons presented as a tall, clean-shaven, two-hundred-pound example of viral Methodist manhood. He was born in rural Alabama in 1880. His father, like Dixon's father, had been a member of the original Ku Klux Klan. Unlike his father, who was a physician, Simmons aspired to a military career, and he joined the First Alabama Volunteer Infantry at the outset of the ten-week Spanish-American War in the spring of 1898. He never rose above the rank of private in the brief conflict, which saw limited fighting in Cuba and the Philippines as the Spanish Empire collapsed. In later years, his military service provided a valued selling point, but Simmons found he simply couldn't abide the military life.

Over the next decade, Simmons became a history teacher, then a garter salesman and then a travelling Methodist minister following a circuit through rural Alabama. Reuben Maury, a future Pulitzer-prize-winning journalist, described Simmons as a Methodist meeting shouter "and whatnot besides."[15] In these few words, Maury captured the essence of fundamentalist Methodist ministries that encouraged participants to shout out during services ("Praise the Lord!" "Hallelujah!" "Amen") and engage in the "jerks" (convulsions of stamping, clapping, moaning, trembling and crying as evidence of religious ecstasy).

Simmons found he had a talent for organizing fraternal organizations. He saw social merit in these organizations, which brought (mostly) men together in groups to share common ideas and goals. The early twentieth century in the United States saw a proliferation of such groups, much like the Rotarians, Kinsmen and Civitans of later eras. They included the Odd Fellows, the Knights of Pythias, the Masons, the Knights Templar, the Heralds of Liberty and the Woodsmen of the World. Simmons was a member of them all, and more. By the time he moved to Atlanta, before the First World War, Simmons was a paid organizer with the Woodsmen of the World with the honorary title of "Colonel" in the organization. He would carry the rank with him for the rest of his life notwithstanding his modest career as a private in the First Alabama Infantry.

Recovering from a serious car accident in 1911, Simmons had time to think about the regalia, the ceremonies and the opportunities that a revived Ku Klux Klan would provide for an accomplished fraternal organizer like himself. The caustic Maury again:

> *Simmons dreamed of a mighty and militant lodge which should in some manner repeat and outdo the noble deeds of the Ku Klux Klan of 1866, organized by southern white men to blackjack the carpet-bagger into decency and frighten foul Yankee notions of equality out of the head of the negro.*[16]

Simmons put together a business plan. He acquired a Georgia state charter and began recruiting in the Atlanta area. His efforts piggybacked on the advance publicity for *The Birth of A Nation*. Riders dressed in Klan uniforms rode horses through Atlanta streets to advertise the film's opening. Advertisements in local papers announced the return of "The World's Greatest Secret Social Patriotic Fraternal Beneficiary Order."[17] The ad carried a sketch drawn by Simmons of a hooded horseman brandishing a flaming torch. "A High Class order for men of intelligence and character," promised the advertising copy.

Meanwhile, the thirty-five-year-old Simmons began fleshing out the myth and the rituals that would animate "future members." The swearing-in ceremony relied on bibles, flags, flames and an oath:

> *I swear that I will most zealously and valiantly shield and preserve, by any and all justifiable means and methods, the sacred constitutional rights and privileges of free public schools, free speech, free press, separation of church and state, liberty, white supremacy, just laws and the pursuit of happiness, against any encroachment, of any nature, by any person or persons, political party or parties, religious sect or people, native, naturalized, or foreign of any race, color, creed, lineage, or tongue whatsoever.*

Reuben Maury summed it up as follows:

> *Bound by this oath a Klansman could hate the negroes if he lived down south, the Catholics in all the cities, the foreigners in the industrial towns, the I.W.W.* [the Industrial Workers of the World union — the so-called Wobblies] *in the West, the Jews in New York and the bootleggers and harlots of whom he was not a personal friend anywhere.*[18]

It was indeed an all-round, spare none declaration of dyspepsia and prejudice that served its intended purpose of attracting Protestants predisposed to hate somebody — Catholics, Jews, unions, Blacks, Asians.

On the margins of the film's opening, Simmons organized a cross burning on Stone Mountain, a landmark of the Confederacy overlooking downtown Atlanta, to mark the launch of his new organization. The fiery cross, a minor aspect of the original Klan's existence, became fixed in the public mind as a symbol of the group. It also became a very real tool in the new group's arsenal of terror. In the years immediately after *The Birth of A Nation* was shown in Atlanta, the revived Ku Klux Klan burned down five Black churches in the state of Georgia alone.

Out of legitimate concern for racial peace, a handful of American states and cities banned *The Birth of A Nation*. The newly formed National Association for the Advancement of Colored People (NAACP) led the fight against the film. The NAACP's predecessor group, the Niagara Movement, had its founding meeting at Fort Erie, Ontario, near Niagara Falls in 1905. The delegates had travelled across the border after they were refused meeting space in Buffalo, New York. In the years since, with leadership drawn from the Black community and support from progressive whites, the NAACP became the institutional voice of Black America. Without a national organization like the NAACP to speak on its behalf at the time, the Black community in Canada relied on local groups, organizations and prominent individuals to fight for fair and equitable treatment.

*The Birth of a Nation* arrived in a Canada where, like in the United States, racism, bigotry and prejudice were ingrained and widespread. Schools in Ontario and Nova Scotia were divided along racial lines. So-called "coon bands" of white musicians in Black face were considered popular entertainment. Itinerant Black minstrel troupes were a favourite. Touring Black baseball teams drew large crowds. As historian Robin Winks recounts, Black people were barred from the Boy Scouts and the YMCA in Windsor, Ontario, although in Toronto they were free to join both. In many small towns, Black people were welcome in community orchestras, but in Owen Sound, Ontario, they were not; they created their own separate orchestra.

The greatest fear of Canada's white legislators was not Black immigration from Africa or the Caribbean, but from the United States. Reports began circulating in 1910 that Black settlers from the American south were looking to move onto free land in the Canadian west. Conservative Member of Parliament William Thoburn from the eastern Ontario riding of Lanark North warned of the inevitable influx of thousands of Black Americans if even a few hundred were allowed to take up land. "Would it not be preferable to preserve for the sons of Canada the lands they propose to give to n-----s?" he asked the House of Commons.[19] In the end, Privy Council Order 1911-1324 was promulgated by the federal cabinet in August 1911 under the authority of the 1910 *Immigration Act*. The administrative order barred from Canada "any immigrants belonging to the Negro race, which is deemed unsuitable to the climate and requirements of Canada."[20]

This kind of targeted racism was not an exception. Venerable Queen's University in Kingston, Ontario, expelled fifteen Black medical students in 1918 after "military hospital soldiers and patients in the community objected to receiving care from Black students."[21] In Edmonton in 1924, the city commissioner tried to ban Black residents from all parks and swimming pools, only to have the ban overturned by city council. In Saint John, New Brunswick, in 1915, all restaurants and theatres were closed to Black patrons. In some places, Black citizens held public office freely, while in others they were told not to even run for public office. Barbers in Saint John, Edmonton and Victoria refused to cut Black customers' hair, but in Vancouver, Winnipeg and Montreal they did. In Halifax, Black military veterans were buried in segregated plots in Camp Hill Cemetery. The Palace Theatre in Windsor, Ontario, placed Black customers in a segregated section dubbed the "Crows Nest."[22] In short, Canadian racism was rife and ubiquitous though inconsistently applied.

British justice — and Canada's elite saw the country as an integral part of Britain's empire — supposedly protected the rights of all. The British

Empire had outlawed slavery in 1835 after two centuries of promoting and protecting the institution of trade in human beings. Therefore, this group argued that if flaws in Canadian society led to discrimination, they were the exception rather than the rule, notwithstanding that mostly white, mostly English-speaking figures held virtually all positions of power. Successful citizens from minority groups were held up as models of integration and evidence of the benign governance of British/Canadian institutions.

The arrival of *The Birth of A Nation* provoked resistance and action from Canada's Black communities scattered across the country. A few weeks after the film arrived in Toronto in 1915, a small group of Black demonstrators complained about the film's negative portrayal of Black people.[23] They lobbied the Premier of Ontario and members of the provincial legislature against allowing the film, but these efforts failed. In Ottawa, the film was shown at the Central Canada Exhibition in mid-September 1915, but the *Ottawa Citizen* was quick to denounce the screening since its intent was clearly to "excite prejudice against, if not hatred of, the negro race."[24] In June 1918, when the film was about to make its fourth run in Calgary, a delegation of Black residents asked the city to ban it. "The delegates argue that the play holds the Negro up to ridicule," reported a local newspaper. The city did nothing, nor did the Alberta cinema censors.[25]

The Ontario film censor board also refused to ban the film because, said chief censor George Armstrong, the film had "no objectionable features from the national standpoint." In the board's view, the film was all about "one period of history in the United States, with which period neither England nor Canada had any part." The censor's lack of historical awareness raised no fuss at all from the wider white community. The film continued to pull crowds into the Royal Alexandra Theatre in Toronto.

The story was different in Montreal and points east. Montreal was historically sensitive to issues of language, race and religion, with its cosmopolitan mix of francophones, anglophones, immigrants and refugees from around the world. With a Black population drawn mostly from the United States and the Caribbean, a film expressing racist views could not be ignored, particularly in a city where Black residents could legally be denied access to theatres.[26] The city's Black population had institutions and organizations in place to protect its interests, including churches and unions.

*The Birth of A Nation* was scheduled to open at the Princess Theatre on Ste-Catherine Street in late September 1915. A meeting organized by the primarily Black Union Congregational Church passed a resolution on September 23 condemning D.W. Griffith and his film. The same night, a fire broke out at the Princess Theatre. The roof was destroyed along with the top gallery and theatrical sets. Police speculated this was a case of arson by someone opposed to showing the film.[27] Faulty wiring was the more prosaic explanation for the fire.[28] Without access to the burned-out Princess, the film was shown at the nearby Orpheum and St. Denis theatres. It attracted the same crowds as in other cities in the face of clear disapproval of local Black leaders.

Farther east, opposition from the Black community had more impact. Nova Scotia had a significant Black population, including descendants of United Empire Loyalist refugees who had escaped slavery, and workers drawn from the West Indies to jobs in factories and coal mines. In wartime Halifax, a film that could raise tensions between races was seen as a distinct threat to public order and the war effort. A local coalition of Black and white residents argued successfully that showing *The Birth of A Nation* "was not in the best interests of the coloured citizens, nor of the citizens in general." This was a position that satisfied the legitimate grievances of the Black community, comforted authorities concerned about local disturbances and acknowledged the need to support the war effort.

The ban came at a critical moment in race relations in Nova Scotia. The Canadian military had grudgingly consented to create a long-sought battalion of Black volunteers, the No. 2 Construction Battalion of the Canadian Expeditionary Force. The battalion was the only segregated unit in the army, and went part way to blunting the resentment amongst Black volunteers who were turned away from most military recruitment stations. But rather than engage in combat, the battalion's members served as a labour force to dig trenches, bury the dead and cut trees. The Nova Scotia film censor's decision to bar showings of *The Birth of A Nation* in the province was seen as helping reduce race tensions in the province.[29]

The reaction to the film was sharply different in neighbouring New Brunswick, which also had a Black population that included many descendants of Black Loyalists. It was the same province where a war-time commanding officer had refused to enroll twenty Black recruits because he believed white soldiers should not "have to mingle with Negroes."[30] There, the provincial film censor approved the film despite opposition. In the port city of Saint John, the Black congregation of St. Philips African Methodist Episcopal Church appealed to Mayor James Frink and city commissioners to either ban the film or compel the censor to cut contentious scenes. The pastor at St. Philips was Rev. J.H. Franklin. He had lived in the state of Georgia and knew U.S.-style racism first-hand. He warned that *The Birth of a Nation* was a "poison" that would infect the Maritimes.[31]

Franklin didn't stop with the local authorities. He approached a local member of the provincial Legislative Assembly, John Baxter, who was also the province's attorney general and a future chief justice of the New Brunswick Supreme Court. A special showing of *The Birth of A Nation* was organized on April 12, 1916, at the Opera House on Union Street, where the film was scheduled to open that night. The audience was composed of Franklin and his lawyer, the attorney general, and the province's board of censors. Franklin asked that cuts be made. The censors refused, and the film was shown in its original form that night. A day or two later, the Opera House manager and stage manager called the police after they claimed to have seen two Black men trying to break into the theatre in the middle of the night.

White audiences in New Brunswick could watch one of their own in the film. Sam De Grasse was born in Bathurst, New Brunswick, in 1875, a town reputed to have a dusk-to-dawn curfew barring Black people from the streets.[32] De Grasse moved to the States, trained as a dentist and was in practice in Providence, Rhode Island, when he married a British actress. His brother Joe was already working in the booming new movie industry. Sam decided to try his luck in 1912, moving to New York and then on to Hollywood. He picked up a series of minor roles, including playing Senator Charles Sumner in *The Birth of A Nation*, before going on to a career with roles in more than one hundred silent films.[33] As one member of a literal cast of thousands, he received no on-screen credit for his appearance in *The Birth of a Nation*.

* * *

As the years rolled by, the film continued to be shown on a regular basis across the country. Toronto, Vancouver, Calgary, Edmonton, Saskatoon and smaller cities from coast to coast regularly hosted *The Birth of A Nation*. It gave every appearance, as the *Globe* had threatened, of going on forever. In the United States, the same phenomenon occurred, increasingly enlivened by the appearance of Ku Klux Klan members as the organization enjoyed a renaissance. Klan bands entertained the movie crowds, Klansmen joined the audiences and stood at regular intervals to point at the screen. Outside, hooded horsemen reinforced the image of a resurgent racist organization with a menacing political and social agenda.

William Simmons initially struggled to build his new organization. Four years after Simmons established the Klan in 1915, the membership remained small, localized in a few communities in Georgia and Alabama and rested entirely on Simmons's ability to sell memberships. In Atlanta in 1919, for example, the Klan's membership was less than that of the B'nai B'rith organization that guarded the interests of the local Jewish community.[34] A boost was needed if the new Klan was to have a future.

The moment came when Simmons joined forces with the publicity genius of Edward Young Clarke and Elizabeth Tyler of Atlanta. The duo of Clarke ("a bushy-haired bespectacled little man") and Tyler ("a rotund widow") had extensive experience organizing and publicizing fraternal organizations. The Anti-Saloon League, a Methodist-based lobbying group dedicated to temperance and prohibiting alcohol, was a valued client. This experience aligned nicely with the Klan's carefully crafted message that it was dedicated to sobriety, spiritual uplift and all things moral. With the colourful backing of bourbon-sipping Colonel Simmons, the team marketed the concept of a revived and rededicated, dynamic and profitable fraternal group. The new Klan publicized its aspirations to clean up public morals and political life in America — and make it harder to get a proper drink, despite Simmons's increasing dependence on alcohol.

Clarke and Tyler took the new Klan to levels not dreamed of by Simmons. Recruiters were given designated sales territories and quotas. Edward Clarke in Atlanta oversaw national and eventually international recruiting efforts. Simmons was formally designated the imperial wizard. He presided over the Klan's imperial palace in Atlanta, all the while becoming more dependent on alcohol.[35]

The Klan saw its revenues grow as recruiters across the United States ramped up their promotional efforts. The public responded by buying ten-dollar memberships, of which four dollars stayed with the recruiting kleagle.[36] As David Chalmers, historian of the Ku Klux Klan, observed:

> *For a brief intense period in the 1920s, the Ku Klux Klan was the great social lodge of the old stock, white native-born, Protestant middle classes of America's towns and many of its rapidly growing cities. Like the other lodges, the Klan offered recreation and a sense of belonging, and it had something more. It had a message.*[37]

The Klan treasury swelled, and with it the aspirations of Simmons, Clarke and Tyler. An organizational structure was created and titles assigned, usually with little or no relation to the original nineteenth-century Klan. The head of the Invisible Empire of the Knights of the Ku Klux Klan was called the imperial wizard. The invisible empire had an imperial palace with imperial officials. A local group was a klavern and was presided over by an exalted cyclops. The klaliff was the vice-president of the klavern. The kligrapp was the secretary. The klokard was a lecturer. The kleagles were the recruiters. Edward Clarke in Atlanta was the imperial kleagle. The klokan conducted inquiries or research or investigations on behalf of the leadership to protect the integrity of the group and its rites and rituals. There were many other titles that proliferated over time in an organization whose brand revolved around the letter "K."

The imperial treasury invested heavily in real estate. In addition to the imperial palace in Atlanta, the Klan began buying college properties, movie theatres, film production facilities and regalia factories. There was an insurance arm, a publishing arm, a propaganda arm. A growing cadre of Klan functionaries elaborated the myth of the Klan and its "moral mission to clean up America's public life and institutions." The Klan commissioned the creation of movies, which were then shown in Klan-owned theatres across the United States. Real estate acquisition became a feature of local

Klan organizations with regional palaces sprouting up in places like Maine, Texas, Colorado and Oregon.

With their mission of purging America of "undesirable influences," national and local Klan leaders realized that real power resided in political office. How else to make the laws, direct enforcement and set the rules that would effectively reserve America for the white race? The Klan's goal, Kleagle Anderson Wright testified to a congressional committee in 1921, was to organize electoral forces to "all vote one way" at the direction of the imperial wizard and put "their own men in office."[38] Klan members began winning elections in states like Texas, Oklahoma, Arkansas, Colorado and Oregon. Klan-sponsored senators were sent to Washington, D.C.; occasionally a state governor owed victory or defeat to the Klan.

Concerns were raised in Washington about the Klan's growing political influence and associated violence, particularly in southern states. The Klan's propensity to attack its enemies was evident in Oklahoma, Arkansas, Texas, and other states. The targets were Black people, white people who were seen as friendly to Black people, union members, bootleggers and anyone whose opposition to the Klan sparked the group's animosity. The violence took many forms. Beatings, floggings, arsons, shootings, castrations, cutting off of ears, tar and featherings and lynchings all were common. Victims were hauled up on ropes to dangle from tree limbs, threatened, sometimes left alive but often hung to death.

There were specialized Klan "whipping squads" in Oklahoma. Klan violence in the state was so common that it took the form of "one flogging for every night of the year."[39] Oklahoma Governor John Walter imposed martial law on the state in an attempt to curtail the widespread violence. In retaliation, the Klan spearheaded a move to impeach him.

A U.S. congressional committee held hearings on the Klan in late 1921. Colonel Simmons welcomed the interest and relished his appearance as a witness. He seized the opportunity to expand on what he saw as the Klan's role in protecting American society and government from foreign influences. His testimony was an advertising opportunity not to be missed. In the end, the committee's findings were innocuous, and the publicity generated by Simmons's appearance boosted Klan recruitment.[40]

In the coming years, the Klan's influence on local, state and national elections continued unabated. Looking outside the United States, the congressional investigators were right to be concerned. In Germany and Italy during the same era, extremists with similar beliefs to the Klan used similar tactics in their campaigns to achieve political power. A second investigation in 1924 by the U.S. Senate Committee on Privileges and Elections examined the Klan's political fundraising activities from Texas to Indiana to Washington. Witnesses took the opportunity to air internal Klan squabbles by testifying about how the Klan raised money to support candidates in electoral battles.[41] These hearings prompted some Klan officials to leave the United States for the obscurity of Canada, particularly the province of Saskatchewan.

By this point, Colonel Simmons, for all his bombast and colourful pomposity, was no match for those in his circle with eyes on larger stakes. He was seldom sober. He lost his two key collaborators when a New York newspaper published a story that "Clarke and Mrs. Tyler had been arrested, not quite fully clothed, in a police raid on a bawdy house in 1919."[42] Mrs. Tyler left the Klan to remarry. Her colleague, Edward Clarke, later described by senior Klan official Charles Lewis Fowler as "the Napoleon of modern organizers, the man who through unjust suffering has grown into a great Statesman, a patriot, friend of men, and genius of the hour" was indicted on a morals charge.[43]

Simmons was manoeuvred out the door by Texas dentist Hiram Evans, who took over the imperial palace in Atlanta in 1923 after working in the propaganda department with Charles Lewis Fowler, a former Baptist minister. Simmons remained in a ceremonial role, but the real power — and money — went to Evans and his followers. Fraternal good will dissolved; bitterness was in the air. Allegations were made and denied. Lawsuits flew back and forth. Kleagles across the country took sides. These included Simmons's supporters like Charles Lewis Fowler, who eventually sought shelter in Canada. Evans banned both Simmons and Clarke from the Klan.[44] Deprived of his leadership role, Colonel Simmons spent his later years in an Atlanta movie theatre sipping bourbon, chewing cloves and watching endless showings of *The Birth of A Nation*.[45] He eventually moved back to Alabama, where he died in obscurity in 1945.

Meanwhile, the Klan and its new leaders moved on to greater excesses. They acquired great wealth, wielded extensive political power and encouraged the activities of local groups, which practiced violence and terrorism — arsons, beatings, lynchings and the murder of Black people, Jews and anyone deemed to pose a threat to their ideal of a white, Protestant America. Klan members burned crosses, torched churches, pointed guns, intimidated the weak, lynched Black men and bootleggers and drove around in the night in white costumes.

Newspapers like the *Globe* warned that Americans would "serve safety and wisdom by scrutinizing this renewed Ku Klux Klan."[46] Canadian authorities took the position that common sense and British justice would protect Canadians from the chaos and vitriol of America. Canada comfortably watched the spectacle from afar as Canadians continued to absorb the messages of *The Birth of A Nation*.

And then the Klan came north.

Over the century to follow, the Ku Klux Klan in Canada went from being an organization in the 1920s, to the idea of an organization without coherence in the 1980s, to a symbol of bigotry and hatred that existed largely in cyberspace in the early decades of the twenty-first century. In the process, the Klan attracted or created or replicated followers with beliefs based on hatred, racism and white supremacy. The Klan provided an institutional home for racists and served as an incubator for new and virulent extremist groups and their members. The Ku Klux Klan of Canada demonstrated the influence of American ideas, amplified domestic disputes and raised a voice of intolerance, animosity and hatred. The results were threats, intimidation, violence and a shelter and home for racists in Canada.

# Chapter 2
# THE KLAN COMES TO CANADA

The Ku Klux Klan appeared in Canada as early as 1921 when recruiting kleagles ventured north of the border, seeking to sell memberships and regalia. They showed up most prominently in Ontario, British Columbia, Alberta and the Maritimes. They arrived after *The Birth of a Nation* had created a market for a new kind of hate. In the absence of a national Ku Klux Klan organization, the recruiting was idiosyncratic, uncoordinated and based on American practices.

The typical Klan outreach involved a discreet advertisement in a local newspaper inviting those interested to attend a meeting at a specific time and place. Often there was a connection with the Orange Lodge: the pitch came to or from members of the Loyal Orange Lodge, or the meeting was held at an Orange Lodge Hall, or the message came via a lodge member inviting his brothers to a meeting. The Orange Lodge, with its adherence to the British Crown, rabid Protestantism and robust hate of the Roman Catholic Church, served as both a supporter and rival of the Ku Klux Klan in Canada.

The known kleagle recruiters we can identify now were almost certainly outnumbered by unknown kleagles, whose activities were not recorded. In some cases, the kleagle had a Canadian connection. Some were Canadian-born, some had family in Canada and some had served in the Canadian military during the First World War. In southwestern Ontario, kleagle Roy Hignett had served in the Canadian army. James Henry Hawkins, the organizer from Virginia who toured Ontario and Saskatchewan, claimed he had a Canadian wife. Eugene Farnsworth, whose Klan reach extended from the state of Maine into New Brunswick, actually had a Canadian wife, a Canadian sister and three Canadian brothers and only missed being Canadian himself by virtue of time, place and biology.

The Canadian-American border was remarkably porous during the height of the Klan era. In New Brunswick, Klan members freely visited back and forth with klaverns in neighbouring Maine. American kleagles came and went with only rarely a written trace of their passage. Those who are known were visible because the Klan itself required publicity to promote sales. A canny kleagle knew that without some public exposure the prospects in Canada or elsewhere would be relatively meagre. In this regard, the continuous showings of *The Birth of A Nation* helped sustain a fertile recruiting climate.

Secrecy had its benefits and disadvantages. All Klan members in the United States — and subsequently in Canada — were sworn to secrecy about the organization, its activities and most importantly, its membership. The result is a dearth of records from the Klan itself and a profound gap in individual and collective memories about Canadians' experiences as members of the invisible empire. Kleagles in places as far apart as Vancouver, Calgary and London, Ontario, threatened actual and potential members with violence if their identity was revealed. Clandestine meetings, controlled access, passwords and more spoke to the Klan's penchant for secrecy.

On the other hand, kleagles like Roy Hignett made themselves readily available to newspapers to tell the Klan story as they sought out new members. Cross burnings, which took place across the country, offered a form of dramatic advertising. Huge rallies and field days — famously known as "open air demonstrations" — created the impression of a growing and potentially powerful political and social force. But the high level of secrecy at the core of the Ku Klux Klan makes it difficult to gain an intimate understanding of the organization in early twentieth century Canada.

One recruiting tactic, however, was well documented. The Ku Klux Klan played to existing divisions in communities. The kleagles fanned the friction and suspicions to create conditions where some would come to view the Ku Klux Klan as a necessary institution to "protect" white people and Protestants, while intimidating those who were not. Historically, the Ku Klux Klan originated from racial divisions, but religious animosities became particularly useful to the group in the Canadian context. Tensions between classes — the government and the governed, the powerful and the weak — also presented opportunities that itinerant kleagles exploited. The recruiting kleagles sniffed out these divisions and manipulated them.

Religion, race and language were familiar grounds for social conflict in early-twentieth-century Canada. Outside of Quebec, Protestant faiths generally made up the majority, and the dominant role of the Roman Catholic Church within Quebec provoked suspicion elsewhere in the country. Outside of Quebec, the French language was viewed as a subversion of "British" values.

These tensions were aggravated by the political climate. The comfortable and predictable national picture of Liberal and Conservative party rivalry was shattered after the First World War. A surging populist movement, the United Farmers, emerged in Canada's vibrant agricultural community. It evolved into the Progressive Party, a dynamic grouping bringing together farmers with labour and socialist ideas that threatened the status quo.

Transformed into a political movement, the United Farmers of Ontario won the 1919 provincial election. Other United Farmers parties won power in Alberta and Manitoba. At the national level, the Progressive Party eroded the two-party hold on federal elections, winning enough seats to hold the balance of power in Parliament. Traditional party loyalties were at risk, and the repercussions were felt in quasi-political groupings like the Loyal Orange Lodge where language, religion and race were rallying cries.

Surprisingly absent from the Ku Klux Klan's list of enemies during the 1920s was Canada's Indigenous population. First Nations peoples, confined to reserves with no political rights, rarely figured among the groups targeted by the Klan. In Saskatchewan, where the Métis Rebellion of 1885 had been suppressed by the Canadian militia only forty years before the Klan's arrival in Canada, the existence of a large population of Indigenous peoples was barely acknowledged. "The Klan . . . never mentioned Aboriginal peoples," noted historian James Pitsula. "It was as though they did not exist; they were thought to be a 'vanishing' race of no interest or relevance."[1]

Two months after the end of the 1885 rebellion, the Department of Indian Affairs instituted a so-called pass system that helped ensure Indigenous peoples were largely invisible to the outside world. An Indigenous person could not leave the reserve without a pass signed by the local Indian agent. If they were caught off the reserve without a pass, they could be arrested by police and returned to the reserve as a prisoner. Further, the limited voting rights granted to properly-qualified First Nations members under the 1885 *Indian Act* had been removed by the end of the nineteenth century.

The Ku Klux Klan's primary targets in the Canadian west were the new immigrants, often Catholic or Jewish. And, as author James Gray noted, the Chinese population was the subject everywhere of political, verbal and physical attacks by the Ku Klux Klan.

Canada's Black population had been near 50,000 before the start of the U.S. Civil War in 1861. By the 1920s, the number had dropped to about 20,000. One cause for the decline was the racism endemic to Canadian society. Black people who fled slavery confronted the reality of racism in Canada after the Civil War and chose to return to friends and family and homes in the United States.[2] The result was a noticeable but diminished Black presence in Canada. The legacy of the flight of escaped American slaves could still be seen, but Black Canadians continued to experience ongoing discrimination and racism. Everywhere in Canada, there were formal and informal forms of discrimination that reflected the social and legal norms of a divided society.

During the period of the Klan's organizing in Canada, *The Birth of A Nation* made the rounds of Canadian movie theatres in a recurring series of performances after its initial showings in 1915 and 1916. "*The Birth of A Nation* is, without a doubt, the most popular film that has yet been produced," noted the *Globe* when the film was shown in Toronto — yet again — in 1920. "It probably stands without a rival in the amount of people engaged, the splendor of the battle scenes, and the thrilling intensity of the work of the Ku Klux Klan."[3] The film was back again in 1923 and 1924 — accompanied by a series of cross burnings across southern Ontario, Alberta and the Maritimes.

## Ontario

The presence of Ku Klux Klan recruiters in Ontario was reported in 1922, although there were almost certainly itinerant kleagle organizers who passed through the international border before then to check out Canadian prospects. A Roman Catholic priest in Welland, on the Niagara Peninsula, wrote to Prime Minister Mackenzie King late that year to complain about the visit to his town by a "Mr. Marten" who was intent on organizing a Canadian Klan along the border.[4]

This was probably J.P. Martin, an American kleagle who recruited in the Buffalo area during 1922 and occasionally ventured across the border to test the Canadian market.[5] An astute kleagle like Martin would have seen in Ontario many reasons to be optimistic. The racial segregation, religious conflict and electoral disarray in the province were themes the Ku Klux Klan was experienced in exploiting for its own purposes.

The Ontario of the 1920s was en route to becoming the economic and cultural centre of Canada. The heart of the province was the city of Toronto, which came out of the First World War with a strong industrial base, thriving corporate elite and distinct sense of self. Long a destination for immigrants, the city was increasingly home to Jews, eastern Europeans and Italians. The English, Scots and Irish still came, and so did Black people from the Caribbean and the United States. There was a dynamic sense of change that threatened the established order of Old Toronto.

If anything in Toronto represented the established order, it was the Conservative Party that dominated provincial and national affairs, aided and abetted by the Loyal Orange Lodge — whose membership and intent was often indistinguishable from the Conservative Party. The provincial Conservative Party led by Howard Ferguson, a well-known member of the Orange Lodge, beat back the populist United Farmers and surged back to power in 1923 as the Klan kleagles began appearing in the province on a regular basis. The Ferguson Conservatives won seventy-two seats in the election, thirty-eight of which were held by Orange Lodge members.[6] No political decision of import was taken without checking with Orange Lodge leaders and members.

The civic government of Toronto was also firmly in the hands of the Orange Lodge. "The mayor of Toronto and most of the aldermen were either Orangemen or had the support of the Orange lodges," wrote Cyril Levitt and William Shaffir in their survey of Toronto's political scene in the 1920s.[7] With almost sixty lodges across the city in 1920, the Orange Order could muster thousands of members to support declarations of loyalty to Britain and the Empire, the Crown and Protestantism. The Orange Lodge had a firm and robust presence across the rest of the province as well, with more than half of the lodges in the entire country. The next most Orange province was Saskatchewan with almost ten per cent of Canada's lodges.[8] The presence of strong Orange Lodges proved to be a harbinger of Ku Klux Klan recruiting success.

Toronto was a segregated city, notes Lincoln Alexander, the first Black Canadian member of Parliament and former lieutenant-governor of Ontario. "Back then in Toronto, there were certain places that, if you went as a Black, you had to be foolish," he recalled. "The scene in Toronto at that time wasn't violent, though you had to know your place and govern yourself accordingly."[9] Stanley Grizzle, an early union organizer among Black railway porters, also lived in Toronto in the 1920s and 1930s. "I never once saw a Black nurse, secretary, politician, teacher, policeman, fireman, civil servant, clerk in a department store, trade union or business leader," he recalled.[10]

Ray Lewis, a future Canadian Olympic runner and member of the Order of Canada, was born and brought up in Hamilton, a city of 100,000 at the western end of Lake Ontario. The era Ray Lewis inhabited was likewise conditioned by race. "The rules of social life in the 1920s and 1930s were strictly enforced — whites and Blacks could play together on the same team, they could go to the same school, but they would rarely, if ever, socialize," Lewis wrote later. "I could not allow myself to be seen with a white girl, or else I would run the risk of being beaten up by an angry mob. The same would go for white people who tried to socialize with Blacks. Society would not allow it."[11]

Supper clubs in Hamilton, Burlington and surrounding towns barred Black patrons from dancing in their ballrooms. Ray Lewis's brother Howard was thrown out of a Hamilton pool hall for being Black. At the Brant Inn in nearby Burlington, famous American jazz musicians like Louis Armstrong and Count Basie could play for white audiences but weren't allowed to stay in the hotel. They had to live off-premises in a rooming house. Ray Lewis described trying to be served in many restaurants in Hamilton:

> *If you were Black, waiters and waitresses would head into the kitchen and try to wait you out if you sought service in a whites-only restaurant. Or they would circle around the restaurant, topping up coffee for other patrons, doing anything*

> *to avoid coming to your table, hoping that you would get tired and leave.*[12]

Conditions were similar for Jews in southern Ontario and elsewhere. They were effectively barred from jobs with the city of Toronto and the provincial government, banks and large department stores. Access to careers in medicine, engineering and education was tightly held; Jews were frequently excluded. And there were the signs in and around Toronto: "No Entrance for Jews," or "Jews and Dogs Not Allowed" or "Gentiles Only." Further north in the Muskoka vacation region, the signs often read "Patronage exclusively Gentile."[13]

The itinerant kleagles arrived in Ontario in 1922 as newspapers were telling the story of Matthew Bullock, a twenty-four-year-old Black American First World War veteran, who had fled to Canada the year before.[14] The details of his flight were reported extensively and set the scene for the expansion of the Ku Klux Klan across the international border into a country rife with racial, religious and political divisions.

* * *

Matthew Bullock and his younger brother Plummer bought ten cents worth of apples at J.P. Williams's general store in the town of Norlina, North Carolina, on January 23, 1921. The fruit was bad, and the brothers asked for their money back from the store clerk, Rabey Traylor. A crowd of whites took offence at the brothers' impertinence. They were chased by a gang of white men and cornered by the nearby railway tracks. Townspeople began arriving with their guns. Shots were exchanged.

Norlina was a poor community in the middle of a poor county a few kilometres from the Virginia state line. With a population that was roughly half Black and half white, the region had a post–Civil War tradition of electing Black officials. With the end of the First World War, the county had seen more prosperity — and the resurgent presence of the Ku Klux Klan. The gunfight in the Airline Seaboard Railway yard in Norlina was the outcome of rising racial tensions exacerbated by the expectations of returned Black veterans that life would be different in postwar America.

Police arrived to break up the confrontation. A white witness later alleged that Matthew Bullock, wearing "a holster that looked like a large army pistol, shot Rabey Traylor in the stomach."[15] More than 100 shots were said to have been fired in the confrontation, which saw eight men wounded. Fourteen Black men were arrested and charged with inciting a riot. They included Plummer Bullock and his friend Alfred Smith. They were taken off to the jail in nearby Warrenton.

A white mob eventually broke into the jail, seized Plummer and Alfred at gunpoint and took them away. The boys were dragged through the main street of Warrenton in the middle of the mob, then set free and hunted down in the nearby bush, killed and their bodies set on fire. Their charred remains were found the next morning hanging from trees, riddled with bullets and mutilated. It was a Ku Klux Klan lynching and associated brutality.

Plummer Bullock's brother Matthew Bullock had escaped from the Norlina railway yard before the police arrived. He sought out his father, a Baptist minister, who urged his son to head north in the family car. Fast. Matthew Bullock drove through the night unaware of what had happened to his brother and his friend. He stopped in Batavia, New York, before pushing on to Buffalo where he hid out until early March. His first attempt to cross the border failed. He was turned back by Canadian officials who invoked the ban issued a decade earlier on immigration by Black people from the United States. Bullock then made another attempt — later mythologized by supporters as a nighttime crossing of the Niagara River over the ice — that saw him arrive in Canada on March 31, 1921.

He made his way to Hamilton, where he dropped out of sight, used the name James Jones and worked as a plasterer. There was no incentive for Bullock to return to the United States. A devastating attack in Tulsa, Oklahoma, a centre of Black autonomy and economic success, in late May 1921 left hundreds of Black people dead, almost a thousand injured, ten thousand rendered homeless and thirty-five square blocks of the city burned out. The enormity of the destruction and slaughter was reported at the time, but then was largely denied and kept secret for decades by authorities. For Black communities in the United States who knew what happened, Tulsa was a warning of the deadly threats to their existence. For Matthew Bullock, it may have reinforced his understanding that there was no safety at home.

Bullock might have stayed anonymous forever in Hamilton, except that in early 1922, likely as a result of writing letters to his family, he was tracked down by local police, arrested and charged with vagrancy. Once his citizenship status was determined, the immigration department ordered him deported for illegally entering the country. The North Carolina authorities learned he was in Canadian custody and sought his extradition in connection with charges related to the Norlina incident.

The result was a months-long dispute between Canada and the United States, each invoking jurisdiction and arguing various levels of hypocrisy. The local Black community rallied to defend Bullock under the leadership of Rev. John D. Howell of St. Paul's African Methodist Episcopal Church in Hamilton. St. Paul's was a central institution of Hamilton's Black community, tracing its roots back to 1835 when slavery was banned in the British Empire. St. Paul's had served as a place of refuge for Black slaves fleeing from the United States. (Ray Lewis and his family were members of the St. Paul's congregation.)

Rev. John Howell was a Black pastor from Arkansas, where the Klan was in the midst of a massive recruiting spurt in 1921–22.[16] At the same time in neighbouring Texas, a local newspaper reported that Klansmen "have beaten and blackened more people in the last six months than all the other states combined." The Tulsa massacre in neighbouring Oklahoma offered a further reminder of how dangerous the American South was for Black people.

Rev. Howell contacted newspapers in both Canada and the United States to ensure coverage of the Bullock case, and he succeeded. The United States government invoked American sovereignty; the governor of North Carolina fulminated against the Canadians. The lynching of Bullock's brother allowed Canadians the vicarious thrill of Klan violence, something seen in scenes from *The Birth of A Nation*. In defence of its immigration process, the Canadian government invoked the merits of "British" justice and the need for due process in handling the case. "Canadian moral superiority, a mainstay of patriotic sentiment which repeatedly defined the Dominion as embodying many fine things that eluded the Republic, had full play throughout the affair," concluded historian John Weaver in his study of the case.

In the end, in March 1922, the immigration department set aside Matthew Bullock's deportation order on the grounds that he could not expect justice in a North Carolina court. He was released from jail draped in a Union Jack.[17] Canadians took mighty satisfaction from Bullock's victory, but within days of leaving custody, the young American began to fear for his safety. The Ku Klux Klan in North Carolina threatened to come north, kidnap Bullock and return him to the state for trial. Ku Klux Klan headquarters in Atlanta issued a statement that they had no knowledge of any such kidnapping plot.[18]

Matthew Bullock's father arrived to help. The pair moved to Toronto where Matthew was taken in charge by the African Methodist Church on Elm Street. A job was found for Matthew at Union Station, the central railway depot, a few blocks away. Rev. William Guy, the pastor at African Methodist, arranged for police protection for the young man. "We are not taking any chances and will do anything in our power to protect Matthew Bullock," he told the press.[19] Guy had been active in organizing support for Bullock ever since his arrest in Hamilton earlier in the year.

A few weeks later, Matthew Bullock was said to have left Canada for Europe and rumoured to have settled in Britain, beyond the reach of the Ku Klux Klan.[20] This may have been a false lead deliberately planted to throw American authorities and the Klan off his trail. What is certain is that Matthew Bullock eventually returned to North Carolina and spent the rest of his life living near Norlina.[21]

***

The first sustained Ku Klux Klan recruiting initiatives came in early 1923 with travelling kleagles making their way across southwest Ontario. Initial recruiting results were mixed.[22] In some districts, potential Klan members showed up at inaugural meetings decked out in their own homemade white hoods, perhaps influenced by *The Birth of A Nation*.[23] Kleagles combined recruiting with renting and selling Klan robes and regalia to new members. The initiative shown by Canadians making personal hoods would cut into their potential income if it continued.

A spate of letters to authorities claiming to come from the KKK were reported in communities as far afield as Thorold in the Niagara Peninsula and Fort William (now Thunder Bay) in the far northwest of the province. No evidence definitively linked these letters to Klan members, but the reports created the impression of a growing Klan presence in Ontario. Faced with this evidence, Ontario Attorney General William Raney stated in early 1923 that the Klan was not welcome.

Newspapers generally denounced the upstart Klan for its American presumptuousness.[24] In Ottawa, the local newspaper put down its marker in opposition to the Ku Klux Klan. A lead editorial in the *Citizen* pronounced:

> *There should be no place in this country for such a body which appeals to racial and religious feeling, and, because of its hidden character, to people who desire to do injury to their fellows in the secrecy and darkness, and under the protection of an "invisible and mysterious" organization.*[25]

* * *

George Wenige, the American-born mayor of London, Ontario, pledged to rid his city of the Ku Klux Klan's "verminous missionaries." The mayor, who had arrived in London a few years earlier as part of a cyclist act in a travelling circus, had reason to be concerned. An unnamed Klan organizer was reported to be at work in London in December 1922. A source who spoke to a reporter about the recruitment effort said he was threatened with "severe consequences" if he divulged the kleagle's name.[26]

A couple of months later, the *London Advertiser* newspaper published a series of lurid articles about the Ku Klux Klan based on interviews with a Klan organizer named Irwin, a.k.a. Roy Hignett. He described himself as an American from Indiana who had joined the Canadian Expeditionary Force and was wounded in France in 1916 while serving with the 13th Royal Highlanders of Montreal.

Irwin was a thirty-year-old Lancashire-born English immigrant to the United States whose family had settled in Pawtucket, Rhode Island. He travelled to Halifax in the fall of 1914 to enlist in the 25th Battalion, Canadian Expeditionary Force. The banty Hignett — scarcely 5′7″ and 135 pounds — stated his occupation as machinist. Sworn in, treated for gonorrhea and shipped off to England the following spring, he had a short war. After five months in the trenches, he was hit by shrapnel from a rifle grenade in late January 1916 at Kimmel, Belgium. Hignett was invalided home with a wound in his right elbow that caused the arm to rest in a permanently straight position. Doctors judged him one-quarter disabled. He was discharged with a small pension and the thanks of the Crown.[27] What he did for the next eight years is a mystery.

When he showed up in southern Ontario claiming origins in the Klan hotbed of Indiana, he oozed credibility. Hignett carried documents identifying himself as a Klan kleagle and so impressed reporters that they reprinted verbatim much of what he told them, complete with photographs and copies of his military service records. Hignett claimed to draw his Klan authority directly from the parent American organization, since there was no equivalent Canadian group or organizational structure.

A London newspaper published a story in March 1923 identifying him as William L. Higgett, an American sent from Papeville, Georgia, with the title of grand serpent to organize the Klan in Ontario. Hignett denied it all. "I do not come from Papeville, Ga., and was never in that town in my life," he wrote later in a published letter. "There is no such office in the organization as 'Grand Serpent.' I am not here on missionary work. The Knights of the Ku Klux Klan have no plans for extension to Canada." He was in London, he said, "resting tired nerves."[28]

The local Crown attorney was consulted. He took the view that no legal action against Klan organizers was possible unless the law was breached in some manner. On one matter, at least, Hignett's denials were accurate. There was no such place in the state of Georgia as Papeville, so Hignett could not have been there. The reporters may have confused the name with Hapeville, a community due south of Atlanta. There are, of course, no records of how many Klan memberships, if any, Hignett sold during his stay in London.

However, his presence in London was followed by Klan activities targeting London's small Black population. A local resident recalled that in the summer of 1924 Klan meetings were held in a large wooded area near the village of Dorchester, east of London. "They [the Klan] put up signs along the road to tell their men where to go," recalled a local resident several decades later. A cross was regularly burned at the fairgrounds over the summer to intimidate the village's few Black inhabitants.

One documented Klan action occurred when the home of a local resident was surrounded by hooded Klansmen who believed the man's wife was Black. The man "walked out and kicked two of the men and took them to the road and told them to go or he would call the police," recalled an onlooker. In another incident, Klan organizers threatened to burn a cross outside the house of a man from nearby Bryanstown, just north of London, said to be involved with a Black woman. "Everybody at Bryanstown was waiting for the KKK with guns," recalled a participant.[29] The threat never materialized, and everybody went home.

* * *

There was no question about the success of Klan recruiter Almond Charles Monteith, who focused his activities in the Hamilton area. It was a city rife with racial prejudice, as the experiences of Ray Lewis and his family attested. The Hamilton police force, concluded historian John Weaver, was inherently racist, with Black people, Italians and Chinese as particular targets.[30]

The police viewed Chinese laundries as possible sites for opium trafficking and prostitution. Chinese restaurants were suspected of late-night meeting places with the booths rumoured to be used for immoral purposes. The Hamilton police proposed that Chinese Canadians should adopt "reasonable" names to help with identity checks.[31]

Monteith did well in Hamilton until the provincial police intervened. Two Ontario Provincial Police officers arrested Monteith at the Orange Lodge Hall on James Street in November 1924.[32] It's not clear what drew the police to the Orange Hall, but Detectives Gillespie and Bleakley interrupted Monteith just as he was about to administer an oath inducting two women into the Klan. Monteith readily admitted that he was a Klan organizer.

Monteith said he was from Niagara Falls, New York, but later confirmed he was a Canadian from the Ontario side of the falls, where he was a bus driver. He was no stranger to the area. He was born in Dulwich near London, where his father had a farm. Over the years he had wandered back and forth across the Canada–U.S. border, leaving wives and children in his wake. Monteith probably joined the Ku Klux Klan on the American side of the Niagara River sometime during the summer and fall of 1923 when klaverns were established up and down the American side of the Niagara Frontier.[33]

Police charged him with carrying a loaded revolver to the Hamilton ceremony. He was also carrying a detective's badge purporting to show he was "attached to the Police Department of Niagara Falls (Ontario)." The chief of police in Niagara Falls denied any link with Monteith. Monteith's lawyers claimed that he was a private detective and therefore had a right to carry a gun.[34] The police court judge released him on one thousand dollars bail.

The police scooped up a list with the names of thirty-two men and women who Monteith had signed up as KKK members. There was correspondence and thirty-six white robes and hoods. His records included an expense account with amounts totalling two hundred dollars for two burning crosses. The police refused to release the list of names carried by Monteith. They did admit to reporters, however, that some of the names were those of prominent citizens. This would turn out to be a precursor to later events.

The police were keenly interested to know if Monteith had been behind three or four burning crosses seen on the edge of the Niagara Escarpment overlooking the city in the previous few weeks,[35] but Monteith refused to answer questions. The cause of the police interest went beyond flaming crosses. They were also investigating two gruesome murders.

The badly mutilated body of cab driver Fred Genesee was found only two days before the Klan meeting near where one of the crosses had burned. Eight days before that, the decomposed body of James Baytoizae had been found five kilometres away, near the site of another burning cross. Newspapers reported police speculation that the Klan might have been involved, although organized crime in the person of bootleggers was also suspected.[36] It was thought that the Klan had some involvement in the killings. South of the border, the Ku Klux Klan was notorious for "enforcing" liquor laws and putting bootleggers out of business — sometimes permanently — in its quest to "purify" America's morals. The burning crosses were, of course, a Klan signature.

Ku Klux Klan officials in Niagara Falls, New York, denied any association with Monteith. So did Orange Lodge officers in Hamilton, who claimed the first they knew about his activities at their meeting hall was a call from the police. Monteith was subsequently found guilty on the gun charge and placed in the city jail. The day after his conviction, one of the arresting detectives received a written death threat, allegedly from the Klan.[37] The scene was set for future dealings between the Ku Klux Klan and the police in Ontario.

## Maritimes

The Maritime provinces of New Brunswick and Nova Scotia were included in the Ku Klux Klan territory of organizer Eugene Farnsworth of Maine from 1922 to 1924.

Eugene Farnsworth was born in 1868 in Columbia Falls in far northeast Maine, about a hundred kilometres from the Canadian border. His family moved to St. Stephen, just across the border, where he lived until he was fourteen. Farnsworth's three brothers and a sister were born in Canada. The family then moved to Massachusetts, where young Farnsworth fell into a series of careers.

He was a barber. He was a Salvation Army bandsman. He took up hypnotism. After marrying Fannie Jacobs of St. John, New Brunswick, he created a travelling magic show with Fannie and a small troupe that performed across New England. "In Rhode Island in 1901, Farnsworth performed an illusion that required an assistant to balance boulders on his stomach while a member of the audience tried to break them," wrote historian Raney Bench.[38] "The act went terribly wrong; the boulder slipped and crushed Farnsworth's assistant. Farnsworth was tried for manslaughter." The judge was persuaded to release Farnsworth, who quickly moved on. Back in Massachusetts, he went to work as a general assignment photographer for the *Boston Herald.*

For the next few years, he travelled widely for the *Herald* and for his own photographic projects. In Massachusetts by late 1917, he decided to try his hand in the booming movie business. In January 1918, he teamed up with Isaac Wolper of Boston to form the Mastercraft Photo-Play Corporation. Wolper was general manager and vice-president.[39] Farnsworth, with his background in show business (albeit tainted by the death of an assistant), was president. They opened a studio in Boston with all the optimism of filmmakers convinced they could replicate the success of *The Birth of a Nation.*

Their first project was a film adaptation of yet another book by Thomas Dixon, author of *The Clansman*. The book was a cautionary tale about the dangers of socialism entitled *The One Woman*. In the wake of the 1917 Russian Revolution, America was coming alive to the threat of communists and socialists, yet the timing of *The One Woman* was off. As the company's officers talked boldly of moving their operations to Hollywood from Boston, the film dropped off the pages of the magazines breathlessly covering the new entertainment industry. The film earned a mere $21,000 before both it and Mastercraft disappeared.[40]

Farnsworth dropped out of sight in Puerto Rico and points south, preparing a photographic reportage on head hunters somewhere in South America. But he soon returned to New England. In 1922, Farnsworth surfaced in Boston as president of an anti-Irish, anti-Catholic, anti-immigrant group called the Loyal Coalition, which aimed to oppose "un-American beliefs" brought to the United States by newcomers (invariably Catholics). By the end of the year, he had realized the easier road to riches was to become a Ku Klux Klan kleagle with a sales territory that spanned New England and stretched across the border into New Brunswick.

Farnsworth came to the Ku Klux Klan straight out of show business via barbering, journalism and itinerant "educational research."[41] He had the personality, charm and show-biz flair that drew a crowd and moved membership sales. His father had been a soldier in the Union Army during the Civil War, so Farnsworth could claim direct historical connections with the events that gave rise to the original Ku Klux Klan.

With his twinkling eyes, goatee and swept-back silver hair, the dapper Farnsworth cut a swath through his home state of Maine. His first Klan speech in January 1923 marked Farnsworth's unchallenged leadership of the Klan for the next eighteen months. A state-wide speaking tour drew huge crowds of up to five thousand people, with Klan memberships on sale at the backs of the meeting halls. Audiences responded to his assertions that the Klan was there to support "Protestant Christianity first, last, and all the time."[42]

The state of Maine was in the throes of a debate over religion whose themes were familiar to generations of Canadians but were only now coming to the fore in the United States. The Roman Catholic Church was taking an increasingly prominent role in community life. The Church had been present for generations, but an influx of Catholic immigrants from Europe,

Ireland and Canada fueled the view that Protestants — white, American-born Protestants — were losing their dominant place.

Black people, Jews, Asians and other foreigners could be put in their place, but it seemed that the Catholic Church was taking over. There was a movement to provide state funding to private Catholic schools. There was debate over which version of the Bible was to be used in public schools. Farnsworth pointed to Catholics and Jews taking seats on public school boards. He warned that French Canadians were flooding into the state to take jobs, introduce the French language and prop up the Catholic Church. With a little encouragement, Mainers were ripe to join an organization that promised to do something about it all.

The Ku Klux Klan in Maine grew from about 23,000 in 1923 to more than 150,000 members in 1925, the year the organization also made its biggest gains in neighbouring New Brunswick. The leadership began pushing a political agenda (pro-Protestant, anti-Catholic, anti-French) with early successes at the local municipal level, school boards and state-level elections. Farnsworth was everywhere, speaking on Protestantism, the Roman Catholic Church and the purity of parochial schools. He moved into a mansion in Portland, Maine.

He ventured into Canada in September 1923, travelling as far as Toronto to encourage Protestants to join the Klan. "We propose not to punish with tar and feathers, but to avenge wrongs," he told Toronto audiences. "We propose not to indulge in law breaking, but in distributing retribution. We call upon all good, native-born Protestants to join us in our work."[43] With success came what were to become recurring Klan problems about money (who got what) and organization (who bossed whom). After a series of controversies involving money and authority, Farnsworth was forced to resign in April 1924 as king kleagle of Maine. He died two years later from cancer.[44]

His legacy, though, lived on in neighbouring New Brunswick where *The Birth of A Nation* had demonstrated ten years earlier that there was a rich market for bigotry in pursuit of profit. The messages delivered by the film and travelling kleagles such as Eugene Farnsworth found a ready listener in the person of James Simpson Lord of St. Stephen, New Brunswick, the same town where Farnsworth had spent his early years. By late 1924, Klan figures in New York were in contact with an unnamed New Brunswicker, almost certainly Jim Lord, who was actively recruiting in the province. The following year, the Ku Klux Klan flourished in New Brunswick. By the end of that year, Lord was named leader of the Ku Klux Klan for the province. He was an enigmatic figure destined to play key roles in the life of the Ku Klux Klan in Canada.

Lord was born on Deer Island, New Brunswick, in 1877. Dubbed "Dirty Jim" by his political rivals, Lord was born into a family committed to the teachings of the Free Will Christian Baptist Church in a part of New Brunswick where religious sects engaged in serious rivalries. On Deer Island, the Free Will Baptists — with their belief that the Bible was the literal word of God — were in constant conflict in the late nineteenth century with the encroaching Methodists and a sect called the Disciples.[45] This was a world where religion mattered deeply. Lord acquired some education, moved to St. Stephen as an adult, and by the early 1920s worked as a successful insurance agent.

The neighbouring province of Nova Scotia also featured racial and religious strife. In Halifax, as criminologist Michael Boudreau noted, Black people, Chinese and other minorities were regularly targeted by police and mob violence. In 1918, a white mob in Halifax tried to lynch a Black man after he was accused of attacking a white child. In an unusual reversal of expectations, a half-dozen police officers waded into the mob while they were looking for a rope and rescued the man. A decade later, an alleged stabbing on Citadel Hill by a "coloured slasher" launched a much-publicized police search for the "Negro Knifer." In the intervening years, there were regular attacks on Chinese businesses by organized gangs of vandals.[46] This was a climate where the Klan could thrive.

## British Columbia

The racial and political climate of British Columbia in the early 1920s, as in other parts of the country, was conducive to bigotry and hate. The primary targets here were the highly visible Chinese, Japanese and East Indian communities. Blacks, Jews and Catholics were less useful on the west coast for Ku Klux Klan purposes. There was a small Black population. Jewish and Catholic institutions were largely invisible. Their faith followers were mostly white and drew little attention. But Asian residents were targeted as visible minorities.[47]

Henry Stevens, the Conservative member of Parliament for Vancouver Centre during these years, described Chinese, Japanese and Indian immigration as "an unmitigated curse, and foul from the bottom up."[48] He was not alone in his views. Another British Columbia MP, William Galliher, a Liberal from Kootenay, told the House of Commons in 1908 that B.C. should be preserved as "a white man's country," a phrase that resonated with governments and voters over the years.[49]

The first wave of Chinese immigration had arrived in the province in the early 1880s, with fifteen thousand indentured labourers hired by the Canadian Pacific Railway to complete the transcontinental rail line. With the railway completed, the Conservative government of Prime Minister Sir John A. Macdonald imposed a fifty-dollar head tax to discourage Chinese immigrants and their families from coming to Canada. Furthermore, the Chinese were denied the vote. Fifteen years later, the head tax was raised to one hundred dollars, then five hundred dollars. These trends culminated on July 1, 1923, with the implementation of the *Chinese Exclusion Act,* which banned all Chinese (with limited exceptions) from entering Canada for the next twenty-four years.

Chinese Canadians were subject to a wide range of official and unofficial restrictions in British Columbia. They were barred from most skilled or public-facing jobs, including those in banks, department stores or hospitals. They were excluded from professions including law, dentistry and pharmacy. They were forbidden to work underground in the coal mines. The wages of Chinese workers were legislated to be less than for white workers. They could not work on provincial or municipally funded contracts. With many occupations denied them, Chinese immigrants worked as seamen or sawmill hands, maids and houseboys, opened small greengrocer shops or laundries or restaurants or sold vegetables from pushcarts. Their food, housing, customs and culture were disparaged in newspapers and public debate.[50]

This highly institutionalized system of racial discrimination against Asians in British Columbia meant that the Ku Klux Klan could offer little that was new. Vancouver, in particular, already saw regular violent white mobs targeting Chinese, Japanese and Indian immigrants. In one memorable example, tensions between the white community and

Asian immigrants peaked in the summer of 1907 after the arrival of four ships bringing Japanese immigrants. After weeks of agitation by anti-Asian groups, a white mob attacked shops and people in Vancouver's Chinatown and Japantown in early September 1907, looting property, burning buildings and beating the inhabitants. The province's institutions and organizations in the early twentieth century were already working hard — and effectively — to execute racist and discriminatory policies and practices targeting non-white residents.

Ku Klux Klan recruiting in British Columbia began as *ad hoc* visits in 1921 by anonymous kleagles moving across the border from the U.S. They typically brought with them KKK enrolment forms that required signatories to pledge allegiance to the United States. The early uptake was minimal, however the same could not be said of the neighbouring American states of Oregon and Washington, where Major Luther Powell, a Ku Klux Klan recruitment star, was hard at work.

Originally from Cameron, Missouri, Luther Powell enjoyed enormous success building klaverns across the American west from California to Idaho, Montana to Oregon. A gregarious man who belonged to the Masons and the Orange Lodge, Powell was in the model of Klan founder William Simmons. Unlike Simmons, Powell had earned his military rank serving as an artilleryman in the 32nd Regiment of the U.S. Army in the Philippines during the short-lived Spanish-American War of 1899.

After that war, Powell migrated to Shreveport, Louisiana, with his wife and two daughters. A born salesman, he soon found his future as a Klan organizer. Following significant success in Louisiana, forty-two-year-old Powell began selling Klan memberships in California in 1920 before moving on to Oregon. He became a legend as an organizer in Portland, Oregon, where a klavern honoured him by naming itself the Luther Powell Klan No. 1.[51] Powell carried with him the accent of the Old South and the persuasiveness of a travelling salesman.

In Jackson County, Oregon, Powell signed up one hundred Klan members in a few days. The new klavern sought to make an impression on public life. As recorded by historian David Chalmers, "A convicted Negro bootlegger was warned to depart from town by the device of pulling on rope around his neck until his toes just barely dragged on the ground."[52]

The Roman Catholic Church also provided a regular target in rural parts of the state. Cross burnings on church grounds and U.S. flags nailed to church steeples were common and familiar tactics.

Powell lost a bitter organizational fight in Oregon to Fred Gifford, who went on to become leader of the Oregon Ku Klux Klan. Gifford's control of the state organization was marked by accusations of financial improprieties. The Skyline Corporation was formed in 1922 to raise money for a new Klan headquarters in Portland. Gifford took a 3 per cent commission on the one million dollars raised for the project from Klan investors. The building never materialized, and the money disappeared. Oil stocks sold by Gifford through his control of a local Klan affiliate called the Riders of the Red Robe were declared worthless.[53] The whiff of embezzlement and fraud settled over the Oregon Klan.

Pushed out by Gifford, Powell shifted his efforts north to Seattle in 1922 and began organizing klaverns in Washington State and Idaho. Powell reached the pinnacle of his Klan career in Seattle. As king kleagle of Washington and Idaho states, he signed up thousands of Klansmen and Klanswomen, founded a weekly magazine and became notorious for organizing a klavern of navy sailors aboard the *USS Tennessee* in Puget Sound. His growing revenue stream reflected his successes. Ku Klux Klan organizer Fred Gifford in Oregon watched all this with interest. In late 1923, Gifford appointed an associate to be grand dragon of Washington State, again putting him into direct conflict with Powell by virtue of horning in on the major's membership sales.

"While Powell was able to organize dozens of Klan chapters in less than a year, his personality undermined his accomplishments," wrote historian Trevor Griffey. "He was a controversial character prone to outlandish exaggeration and constant squabbles for power with other Klan leaders, especially in Oregon." Powell could not withstand the pressure from Fred Gifford and his Oregon crew and was again pushed out. Powell turned his eyes north, announcing plans to begin recruiting Klan members in Alaska and Hawaii, plans that apparently never went anywhere. And then he focused on Canada.

Canadian authorities already suspected a Klan presence in Vancouver. In the spring of 1924, city police were reported to be investigating a Klan organizer who had arrived "from a city in the middle western states."[54]

This may have been R.G. Wallace, who would join up with Luther Powell in Vancouver later in 1925. Before then, in late 1924, Dr. Keith Allen, a former associate of Fred Gifford in Oregon, arrived in the city supposedly "to form a chapter of 'the Catholic-hating Royal Riders of the Red Robe.'"[55]

It was not clear why the bespectacled Dr. Allen, who had served as an investigator for Gifford, would come to Vancouver to recruit for the Royal Riders, a group that existed only in the United States for the purpose of rallying foreign-born Americans to a Klan affiliate. In retrospect, it looked more like a strategic exit from the troubled Oregon Klan. Regardless, Dr. Allen (the source of his doctorate is unknown) had transferred his loyalties to Powell and his efforts to furthering Klan interests in Canada. The likely plan was to put a Klan presence firmly in place on the Lower Mainland to reap the benefits of the local market.

Frank Brown, the member of the Legislative Assembly for Burnaby on the Lower Mainland, challenged the Klan's presence in the province and sought to thwart any electoral ambitions it might have. Describing the Klan as "a fraudulent, alien, terrorist organization" whose history was "one of murder, violent assault, and unspeakable crime," he moved a resolution in the provincial Legislative Assembly "to restrain this seditious movement and bar its membership from all elected or official positions under the Crown." The motion foreshadowed electoral ambitions the B.C. Klan had yet to announce but it was clearly informed by Klan initiatives in the United States and elsewhere in Canada.

The Speaker of the Assembly ruled the motion out of order but not before members had their say. Some argued the motion would breach free speech. Some members were accused of belonging to the Klan. Another MLA found fault with the Klan for putting "Catholics and Negroes on the same plane." He did, though, think the Klan had value if it worked on "running the Japanese and Chinamen and Hindus out of British Columbia."[56]

## Alberta

Ku Klux Klan organizers based in Vancouver travelled into Alberta in 1922 and early 1923. The fluid and fleeting nature of kleagle activities make it difficult to confirm who they were or where they came from. It is certain, though, that in April 1923, Catholic institutions and police in Calgary started receiving threatening letters claiming to be from the Klan. City newspapers cited reports that Klan organizer "Walter Higneot" of Georgia had made trips to Calgary and Edmonton to sign up members. This may have been a confused reference to Irwin Roy Hignett, a.k.a. William Higgett, the kleagle who had surfaced in southwestern Ontario the previous month. During this time frame, however, Roy Hignett was giving newspaper interviews in London, Ontario, and "resting his nerves" so it was unlikely he travelled to Alberta.

Calgary's highly regarded police chief, David Ritchie, stated that threats to local Catholics were the work of "a crank," there was no basis to rumours of local Ku Klux Klan activity and, furthermore, "any one found acting in a suspicious manner around any Catholic churches or institutions" in Calgary would be arrested. A long-serving police officer who had won the Military Cross during the war, Ritchie's words offered reassurance, if somewhat misinformed, to concerned citizens.[57]

Reassurance was hard to find as Klan organizers — apparently from Vancouver but nobody really knew for sure — began selling memberships in towns and cities across the province.[58] Historian James Gray identified Rev. Harry Humble, pastor of the United Church at Milo, southeast of Calgary, as the lead peddler of Klan memberships in the spring of 1924. Harry Humble was born in Yorkshire, England, in 1894. He drove a truck for the British army during the First World War before being "blown up by a shell" in France in October 1917.[59] He and his family arrived in Hanna, Alberta, in March 1923 to take up a farmstead. Over the next few years, Humble carved out a reputation as an evangelist travelling through Saskatchewan and Alberta.[60] He later became an insurance agent in Hanna. In these roles, he had the same kind of background as Klan organizers elsewhere, so it's likely that he combined his religious vocation with recruiting for the Klan and building his insurance business.

Humble and an unknown colleague made the rounds of communities — Calgary, Vulcan, Taber, Medicine Hat, Rose Bud, Big Valley, Drumheller, Lethbridge, Red Deer, Milo and as far north as Edmonton. By December 1924, the Klan was reported to have some three hundred members in Calgary, along with members in three nearby towns.[61] The usual ten-dollar membership fee was charged, and some ten thousand dollars was apparently collected by Humble and his associate for memberships, robes and regalia. Harry Humble then disappeared with the money.

As word spread through the Alberta towns where Humble had sold Klan memberships, tempers rose in righteous indignation. A Klan official — possibly "Dr." Keith Allen from Vancouver — made his way to Calgary and a series of smaller centres to hear member concerns. These sessions were described as intense. The Calgary confrontation was called "the greatest showdown ever witnessed." The Vancouver official cancelled the Calgary group's charter, banished the troublesome members and "slammed his valise shut and proceeded to leave." Whoa back, called the local Alberta leadership. "The door was locked and exit denied," according to historian Peter Baergen.

The "showdown" that followed had lasting repercussions. It appeared the Klan organization in Alberta was ten thousand dollars in debt (probably thanks in part to the absent Rev. Humble). Meanwhile, the rumour floated that leading Klan figures in Vancouver were taking salaries of $450 a month from membership fees. The Calgary membership was furious, as were members in smaller towns around the province. Alberta chapters voted *en masse* to sever their links with Ku Klux Klan operations in Vancouver or elsewhere.

The Klan had a proven ability to generate income for its organizers, while providing the white Protestant population with a structure for sharing its racist views and using violence and threats of violence to terrorize and harass Black people, Asians and other targeted Albertans. But the Alberta experience also demonstrated what could happen when Ku Klux Klan kleagles were left to their own devices, without supervision, collecting substantial sums of money. As happened in almost every region where the Klan operated during the 1920s, the opportunity to skim cash, abscond with cash or simply embezzle proved irresistible to the average kleagle. The membership regularly began asking awkward questions that led to accusations, recriminations and public squabbles. A more organized approach was clearly needed.

# Chapter 3
# KLAN RISING (1925)

The opening of a Ku Klux Klan office in downtown Toronto in January 1925 marked the official creation of a national organization dedicated to hate in Canada. This allowed the establishment of an administrative structure that set the tone for local Klan activities across Canada — with notable exceptions like Alberta and later Saskatchewan. The incoherence of the early years of the Ku Klux Klan in Canada gave way to recognized national leaders, common recruiting methods and common enemies. As always and as everywhere in the Klan world, the leadership's main goal was making money by marketing hatred and racial violence.

The Ku Klux Klan of Canada set up shop in Suite 503-4 of the Excelsior Life Building at 36 Toronto Street, in the heart of the business district. It was a prestige Toronto business address, surrounded by pillars of the Canadian establishment. Most of the tenants at the Excelsior were insurance executives, accountants, barristers, industry associations and advertising agencies; the tenants of Suite 503-4 were decidedly different. The new neighbours were two middle-aged Americans, a floating population of chancers and scam artists, and a few Canadians with high ambitions.

The Americans were an ill-fit at the Excelsior, but there they were, comfortably lodged on a discreet downtown street with a Masonic lodge and a Presbyterian church just steps away from the front door. Four blocks away was the Iroquois Hotel at the corner of King and York Streets. The leaders of the new Ku Klux Klan of Canada met there in its comfortable wood-panelled surroundings to plan the future in January 1925.

The new tenants in the Excelsior Building were keen to keep a low profile in the early months of their stay in Toronto, but in time the other tenants came to know them as Dr. Charles Lewis Fowler and Dr. James Henry Hawkins, imperial kligrapp and imperial klaliff respectively, of the Imperial Knights of the Ku Klux Klan of Canada. The sources of their doctorates were obscure, but they wielded the titles with authority.

Fowler was hiding out in Canada from the New York City police; Hawkins probably should have been. Fowler was a prominent Klan propagandist who had devoted several years to creating the myths used to sell memberships across the United States. His legal problems were a by-product of trying to promote the Klan's mythology in the political circles of New York City. Hawkins presented himself as a doctor of optometry from Virginia and a southern gentleman of the old school. One Canadian journalist questioned whether he was a gentleman from anywhere. Men had hitched their futures and livelihoods to an organization with a dubious reputation that matched their own personal histories. The Ku Klux Klan claimed to have branches in Australia, New Zealand, Mexico and elsewhere, but Canada was the Klan's most successful attempt at creating a national organization outside of the United States.[1]

The Ku Klux Klan's formal arrival in Canada in 1925 originated in the mind of a Toronto businessman, Richard Cowan. As reported by journalist Patrick Richards in *Saturday Night* magazine, he conceived the idea of setting up a Canadian branch of the KKK that, although affiliated to the American organization, would retain a significant percentage of the membership fees for the benefit of local Canadian leaders.

Cowan was a stockbroker who had worked in London (Ontario) and Winnipeg before moving to New York in 1920 to join a Wall Street investment firm, Harvey A. Willis & Co.[2] As a result, he had an ideal perch to see the significant growth of the Klan in New York and across the United States during the early 1920s. Back in Toronto, he considered the business opportunity the Klan represented. He interested a few local notables, including Rev. Otho Elliott, a well-known local Baptist clergyman, in supporting the creation of a Canadian-based Klan organization.

Cowan travelled to New York in the fall of 1924, where he met with

James Henry Hawkins of Newport, Virginia, and Rev. Dr. Charles Lewis Fowler, both men with long histories in the reborn Klan of the 1920s.[3] "A mutual agreement signed before leaving New York . . . proves beyond a doubt that they looked upon the new body merely as a means for making a lot of money easily and quickly,"[4] Richards reported later. The agreement signed on December 1, 1924 stipulated that the trio would share equally in the profits to be derived from signing up new members of a Canadian Klan.

The organized drive into Canada was planned and deliberate and would probably have happened even without Cowan's initiative, given the proven potential for Klan growth in Ontario, British Columbia and the Maritimes. In late 1924, Fowler was already reaching out to an unnamed New Brunswick contact, almost certainly Jim Lord, who was recruiting in the province. "The men up there are wild for the organization," Fowler wrote to Hawkins in early December 1924.[5] The quick surge in New Brunswick membership seemed to support this assessment. Fowler reported further,

> *We shall have no trouble at all along the border land. The entire territory from Nova Scotia which is richly and predominantly Protestant and all along Via Quebec, Montreal, Ottawa and Toronto should be fine territory and should make it possible for us to gather in large numbers at once.*

And the sooner the better as far as Fowler was concerned, since he had compelling reasons to get out of New York City as soon as possible.

Hawkins and Fowler both had extensive backgrounds with the Klan. Born in Doddridge County, West Virginia, in 1876, James Henry Hawkins initially worked as a teacher, eventually became a lawyer in Alabama and finally settled on optometry in Virginia. He practised in a series of small towns on the tidewater peninsula between Richmond, the old Confederate capital, and Norfolk on the Atlantic coast.

While living in Alabama, Hawkins worked as the head of a charity that he claimed cared for orphans and dependent children. In April 1908, at age thirty-two, Hawkins married Barbara Helen Barclay, twenty-one, in Birmingham, Alabama. Barbara was born in the Black Hills of South Dakota, which a 1910 census taker assumed meant she was Indigenous.[6] She was not.

Her father was born in England; her mother, Mary, was born in Canada and left for the United States with her family when she was a toddler. This was the only Canadian connection Hawkins possessed, but it was enough. During his years in Canada, he spoke often and glowingly of his Canadian-born wife who, he assured audiences, was from Milton, Ontario, northwest of Toronto.

By the mid-1920s, Hawkins and his wife had seven children. At some point, he joined the Klan as part of the explosive growth of Klan memberships in Virginia during these years.[7] Hawkins took on Klan leadership roles in Maryland, serving as a grand dragon in Baltimore, while his wife appears to have stayed home with their growing children. Journalist Chris Higginbotham, who observed the imposing six-foot, three-inch tall, 250-pound Hawkins in action during his time in Saskatchewan, wrote that "he looked like every southern gentleman is supposed to look, but whether he was a gentleman from anywhere is questionable."[8]

His colleague Dr. Charles Lewis Fowler, short, dumpy and unremarkable in appearance, tended to stay in the shadows even though the results of his activities were very much in the public eye. Fowler had held Klan positions in New Jersey, Tennessee, Georgia and elsewhere.[9] By many accounts — including his own — he created the Klan legends that shrouded the organization for decades. Fowler had served in the heart of the Klan bureaucracy in Atlanta, worked closely with Klan founder Colonel William Simmons and was the key player in elaborating the Klan's mystique and mythology. His new Toronto neighbours in the Excelsior Building were almost certainly ignorant of his pivotal role in creating the Ku Klux Klan of the 1920s.

Charles Lewis Fowler was born in Monroe, North Carolina, in 1877. He was educated at various religious institutions before landing in Clinton, South Carolina, where he served as a Baptist minister for four years. In 1911, he took over as president of a small college in Missouri. In 1914, he became "co-president" of Cox College, a women's school in Atlanta. Three years later, he founded and became, as he later put it, "Sometime President" of his own college, Lanier University, also in Atlanta. He promoted the university as the state's first co-educational Baptist institution. He sought investors to help grow the school, but that effort failed when the Georgia Baptist Association refused to recognize the university.

One of the reasons may have been Fowler's devotion to British Israelism, a belief that became popular in Britain, Canada and the United States during the late nineteenth century. Based on fanciful Biblical interpretations, British Israelism held that the peoples of the British Isles were direct descendants of the Ten Lost Tribes of Israel. The British Israel canon would become increasingly significant to white supremacy circles in the twentieth century. Fowler packed British Israelism with his religious baggage as he made his way through educational and religious circles in Georgia.

Rebuffed by the Baptists and with the university on shaky financial ground, Fowler refocused his efforts on promoting Lanier as an "All-Southern" college. The curriculum was recast to emphasize southern history and heritage. A course on the Civil War and Reconstruction was taught by "Colonel W.J. Simmons, A.B., L.L.D. and Ph.D.," the imperial wizard of the Ku Klux Klan. Fowler joined the Ku Klux Klan, the board of trustees was reconstituted to include Klan sympathizers and Fowler pitched the idea that the Klan should take over the university. After the increasingly wealthy Klan agreed to buy Lanier, Simmons was named as its figurehead president and Fowler moved on to work in the Klan's propaganda department.[10]

In this role, Fowler was the author of myths and ideologies that gave Klan members a shared vision of their organization and its purpose. In July 1922, he published a sixty-page book entitled *The Ku Klux Klan: Its Origin, Meaning and Scope of Operations* that served as a doctrinal document for what Fowler called "the most remarkable movement of our times."[11] Fowler also offered for sale two companion works — *Rome — A Menace to Modern Civilization* and *The Jew — A Menace to Modern Civilization.* All three books shared a vision of a forbidding world that threatened the white, Protestant populations of the United States.

*The Ku Klux Klan* was a book of dark warnings. "There are forces at work in America which, if allowed to continue, will undermine the pillars of the temple of our civilization," menaced Fowler. "These forces are led by enemies of popular, free government and Protestant institutions." The Georgia clergyman cum academic cum propagandist was prepared to be helpful in identifying these enemies. "One of the great enemies of America today is the 'Hidden Hand,'" he wrote in reference to an imagined international conspiracy of Jewish leaders. The "Hidden Hand" must be "perilized *[sic]* and destroyed at any cost" before it succeeded in its goal of world domination. Roman Catholics "have but one purpose, the supremacy of the Pope in America, the overthrow and destruction of all free and Protestant institutions . . . Rome is forever opposed to American ideals of government."[12] All Catholic organizations, including the Knights of Columbus, were, Fowler assured his readers, committed to these goals. The book made no mention of Canada, his future home and place of business.

Fowler expounded at length on the Klan's origins in the mythic Old South, ruminated on its mystic origins and rituals (virtually all of which Fowler created out of his imagination), argued for the necessity of separating church and state, promoted the right to organize against the perfidy of the Roman Catholic Church and propounded various conflicting theories of government. It was a combination of recruiting pamphlet, bigotry of imaginative kinds and muddled ideology.

Fowler assumed a leading role in the Klan's propaganda department in the imperial palace in Atlanta. As the Klan grew, Fowler championed direct investments in movie theatres and film companies as part of a robust sales strategy. In 1923, Fowler was named president of a newly incorporated Klan film production company, the Cavalier Motion Picture Co., all of whose officers had Klan connections. The vice-president of Cavalier was Mayor J.E.D. Smith of Buffalo, who also served as the kleagle for the city. Roscoe Carpenter, the company secretary, was a well-known Klan lecturer in Indiana, where he ran with David Stephenson, the state's grand wizard, who boasted of his immense political influence.[13] Stephenson was also the major shareholder in Cavalier.

Cavalier only made one film during its existence — *The Traitor Within*. The plot line reflected the Klan's stated objective of cleaning up political corruption, but the film was never seen again after its initial release. No copies survived, and it made no impact on the motion picture industry.[14] Cavalier went into receivership only to rise from the financial ashes in the form of a new company, the Twentieth Century Motion Picture Company of Indiana. Roscoe Carpenter was the president, Charles Lewis Fowler the vice-president. Edward Younge Clarke, former imperial kleagle in Atlanta, emerged as the creative force behind the new company, announcing plans to invest heavily in Indiana and Florida. The dreams dissolved in the face of financial challenges.[15]

Fowler was intimately involved with these Klan initiatives and the major figures in the Klan's national leadership before moving to New York in 1923. The Klan had established its own newspaper there, the *American Standard*, a publication described as having "a particularly latrine nature."[16] Fowler became editor of this twice-monthly publication, which offered the unique Klan view on current events.

One example involved the rumours that flew when President Warren Harding died in San Francisco in August 1923. "Fowler it was who made the astounding disclosure that the President had not died of pneumonia," reported Reuben Maury, "but had been jollied into the hereafter by hypnotic telepathic thought waves generated in the brains of Jesuit adepts."[17] This early appearance of "fake news" was greeted with journalistic skepticism but had no adverse impact on Fowler's career. He continued to travel around the United States offering the booming number of Klan chapters a philosophy around which they could organize their thoughts and actions.

In New York, Fowler and his nineteen-year-old son, Louis, were arrested in June 1924 for criminal libel. Their target was New York State Governor Alfred (Al) Smith. The complainant, Jacob Alschuler, described as a former soldier, said he was sold a copy of the *American Standard* for ten cents while standing outside Madison Square Garden. Inside the Garden, the Democratic Party's hotly contested 1924 national presidential nomination convention was underway. Supporters of the party's many factions milled in the streets outside.

The convention was a raucous affair that reflected a badly divided Democratic Party. One branch of the party was supported by the Ku Klux Klan, flexing newfound political muscle at the national level after surging at state and local levels. Another faction represented by Smith opposed the Klan, opposed Prohibition and offered an expansive vision of the future.

William McAdoo, a California lawyer, was the Klan's preferred candidate. His supporters chanted "Mac! Mac! McAdoo!" Smith's partisans replied "Ku! Ku! McAdoo!" Dubbed the "Klanbake" due to the Klan's prominent role in the proceedings, the sixteen-day convention went through 103 ballots before a compromise presidential candidate emerged. "When the debris began to fall, somebody looked underneath the pile and dragged out John W. Davis," lamented the *New York Times*.[18] The forgettable Davis went on to lose the 1924 presidential election to Calvin Coolidge.

Meanwhile, Jacob Alschuler continued his legal attack on the offensive article he had found in the *American Standard*. The story called into question Governor Al Smith's fitness to serve as president because he was a member of the Catholic Knights of Columbus, which was "dictated to by the Church of Rome."[19] This was fully consistent with the views Fowler published in his 1922 Klan handbook.

A New York City police captain testified in court later that Fowler had been under police surveillance for some time. Mayor John Hylan had issued orders in early 1923 that the New York Police Department give priority to breaking up klavern meetings and identifying Klan members.[20] The police captain said Fowler had originally been associated with Klan founder William Simmons, but "after the trouble in Georgia" (i.e., the ousting of Simmons), he now reported directly to the new leader Hiram Evans, the Texas dentist who had pushed Simmons, Clarke and others out of the original imperial leadership. Fowler knew Evans well because they had worked together in the Klan propaganda department. The New York magistrate ordered the Fowlers, father and son, held on a one-thousand-dollar bail.[21] The charges eventually went nowhere, but Charles Lewis Fowler did — to Canada.

Police surveillance was making life difficult for the Klan in New York, particularly now that Fowler was known to be under scrutiny. Membership sales suffered as various scandals, including Fowler's attacks on Al Smith, diminished the Klan's recruiting prospects and jeopardized revenues. The national headquarters in Atlanta was unhappy with the negative attention. When Richard Cowan showed up from Toronto with his Canadian proposition in the fall of 1924, Fowler moved quickly. He pulled his colleague Hawkins into the negotiations with Cowan, signed a contract and caught the train north.

Fowler set up shop on the fifth floor of the Excelsior Building in Toronto "accompanied by several 'go-getter' American organizers," according to journalist A.D. Monk.

> *Why a Virginian and a New Yorker should appoint themselves to teach loyalty to Canadians may well be wondered at, and why they should be so particularly concerned in trying to hold the British Empire together is another cause for wonder. That they should set out on their high mission with the most*

> *un-British agreement that ever raped a virgin sheet of paper leaves one gasping . . . it [the Canadian Klan] was founded by three men as a business enterprise having a clear view of the main chance. They saw Canada as an area to be exploited and set to it.*[22]

Members of the Orange Lodge in Toronto began receiving phone calls in the winter of 1925 inviting them to join the Klan, usually described as another "good Protestant organization."[23] Following a series of meetings at the Iroquois Hotel down the street from the Klan's national offices, Richard Cowan, the Toronto businessman, was named the imperial wizard, Hawkins the imperial klaliff and Fowler the imperial kligrapp.

Early in 1925, Fowler crossed paths with Harold Machin of Kenora, Ontario, and convinced him to join the Klan. Machin may have been introduced to Fowler by Richard Cowan, the stock promoter and co-founder of the Canadian Klan. Machin was in many ways an unusual hire for the Klan's purposes; in other ways, he fit a familiar profile. A lawyer and mining promoter from northwest Ontario, he had served as a private in the Canadian contingent to the Boer War in 1898–1900. He stayed on in South Africa as a member of the South African Constabulary before returning to Canada, where he resumed his law practice, combined with prospecting and promoting mining ventures in northern Ontario and Quebec.[24]

Machin was elected as a Conservative member of the Ontario Legislative Assembly, a position he held through three provincial elections from 1908 to 1919. The First World War interrupted his political career. He rejoined the army as colonel of a northern Ontario battalion and served briefly in France. He returned to Canada, and in 1918 he was named director of the Military Services Branch of the Department of Justice in Ottawa. After the war, he returned to politics and his work as a mining promoter. In February 1925, Machin was confirmed as a Ku Klux Klan organizer and dispatched to Winnipeg to advance the Klan's prospects on the Prairies.

Meanwhile, results of the Klan's aggressive recruiting could be seen in Toronto and nearby Hamilton. The front page of the *Hamilton Herald* on March 20, 1925, was graced by a photo of the local executive of the Women's Canadian Ku Klux Klan. The eleven women pictured wore white masks and white robes carrying the maple leaf insignia of the Canadian Klan. Their spokeswoman claimed there were more than one thousand members in Hamilton, with branches in Toronto, Brantford, Kitchener and Windsor.[25] The Klan's Toronto headquarters claimed a few weeks later that as many as seven thousand men were reported enrolled in the Toronto klavern alone, although this number seems exaggerated.

The success of the recruiting drive generated a stream of money that eventually disrupted the unity of the national office. Otho Elliott, the Baptist clergyman who was one of the original supporters of a national Klan, formally accused Hawkins before the Klan's governing council, the kloncilium, of treachery, failure to account for funds and disloyalty.[26] Whatever the precise details, Hawkins had clearly seen an opportunity to carve out a new role for himself. He moved quickly to set up a rival Klan organization called the Ku Klux Klan of the British Empire. He abruptly left the national office, threatening legal action to recover back salary and costs.

With Hawkins's defection, the enigmatic Jim Lord from New Brunswick showed up in Toronto to help Fowler manage the Canadian operation. Lord was said to be in charge of "the initiation ritual for the higher degrees of the order," according to historian Gordon Unger.[27] Lord began making appearances at Klan rallies in Ontario, building on his credibility as a newly elected member of the New Brunswick provincial legislature. Jim Lord was following up on a remarkably successful recruiting drive that saw the Klan flex its political muscle in the 1925 New Brunswick provincial election.

Klan leadership in the United States had offered Lord the Klan franchise in New Brunswick in late 1924 although the new Canadian headquarters in Toronto would certainly have endorsed the move.[28] At midyear of 1925, Charles Lewis Fowler from Toronto visited Lord, who was by now a candidate in the provincial election. "The work is going fine there," reported the Klan's Ontario news bulletin. "Speakers from the United States have taken part at public gatherings in Victoria and Carleton counties in connection with the Ku Klux Klan activities," reported a local New Brunswick Klan publication.[29]

* * *

Indeed, there was much cross-border Klan traffic in general between Maine and New Brunswick with klaverns visiting back and forth. This traffic intensified during the summer of 1925 as campaigning ramped up for the August 10 provincial election. A burning cross at an open-air meeting outside the city of Saint John was reported in July by the *Saint John Globe*. The newspaper said the cross was "ignited by two men who arrived in an automobile which bore a New York licence."[30]

Stories about the influence of the growing New Brunswick Klan became increasingly current during the election campaign as the Conservative Party benefited from Klan support. Jim Lord was running as a Conservative Party candidate for the constituency of Charlotte County, which encompassed his home district of Deer Island. He was one of three Conservatives eventually elected in the multi-member constituency.

Lord made little effort to keep his Klan membership secret from outsiders, but he was also at pains over the years to throw observers off the track. In some cases, he openly and variously described himself as the imperial scribe of the Fredericton Klan, chief of staff for the Fredericton Klan and the imperial klaliff of the Ku Klux Klan of Canada. At other times, he provided journalists with variations on his name or averred that he came from Charlottetown, Prince Edward Island. Or he simply didn't identify himself when he spoke in public, going with his Klan position rather than his name. With a close-trimmed white beard and fixed stare for the cameras, Lord was a key figure in organizing Klan klaverns throughout the St. John River Valley and far into the northwest part of the province.

The Ku Klux Klan established klaverns in Woodstock, Aroostook Junction, McAdam and other communities in Victoria and Carleton counties. These were by and large English-speaking, Protestant and virulently anti-Catholic regions where the Orange Lodge was strongly present. By 1926, the Klan was said to have seventeen klaverns in New Brunswick, including one in Lord's hometown of St. Stephen. Cross burnings were a regular feature of provincial life during 1925 and 1926, far out in the countryside and around the port city of Saint John.[31]

The Klan was crystallizing popular sentiment in a province where Black Loyalists had accompanied white Loyalists in the 1770s, and slavery and indentured labour had been preserved during the period leading up to the abolition of slavery across the British Empire in the 1830s. The province also counted as a significant share of its voting population the staunchly Catholic, French-speaking, Acadian descendants of the original Acadian population, which had flourished until their expulsion by British colonial authorities in the 1770s. By 1925, New Brunswick was second only to Quebec in its proportion of French-speaking Catholics.

The Klan took up the causes of sobriety, clean living and adherence to what the organization saw as the letter of the law. In February 1925, the Saint John *Telegraph-Journal* reported that Klan members in Woodstock had spent the weekend attacking suspected brothels, card rooms and illegal bars.[32] A couple of days later, the Saint John newspaper reported that a threatening letter had been sent to Fredericton lawyer Fred Peters. He was defending a man named Harry Williams, accused of killing two women. The Klan clearly felt justice required a weak defence and a harsh penalty for the crimes. "Stop now, you are trying to defeat justice, and encourage crime by the same old plea of insanity, and if you succeed you will have to answer for Williams' crime. This is your warning. Beware." Signed "KKK." The letter carried a St. Stephen postmark. Peters's client was subsequently found guilty and hanged.[33]

The Conservative Party's victory over Liberal Premier Peter Veniot, an Acadian and a Catholic, led Veniot to charge that the Klan had campaigned openly against him in the election. He alleged that the Klan sent its members from the United States to New Brunswick disguised as tourists to work against "Veniot the Frenchman" during the campaign.[34] Veniot further pointed to a boast by the imperial kleagle at a Klan convention in Ontario: "The Klan took an active part in politics; look what we did in New Brunswick." The whole operation, said Veniot, was financed by the Klan's office in New York. The 1925 Conservative election victory was celebrated in the northern New Brunswick town of Woodstock with a cross burning on a hill overlooking the community.

* * *

The Ku Klux Klan's growing strength in New Brunswick gave Jim Lord significant credibility when he arrived in Toronto to help out after J.H.

Hawkins's defection from the national Klan office. The details of the dispute that saw Hawkins part company from Fowler and Cowan were murky despite a subsequent court case, which revealed the Canadian Klan's commercial origins.[35] Hawkins promptly launched a summertime tour of southern Ontario to sign up members for his new organization, the Ku Klux Klan of the British Empire. It was unclear what distinguished the KKK of the British Empire from the original Klan — apart from the Union Jack being prominently posted on the white robes and the leadership of Hawkins, who cut a much more imposing figure than the rather bland Charles Lewis Fowler.

Hawkins was not alone in his travels around the byways of Ontario, having joined forces with a woman named Jessie Harris. She came to Toronto by way of Winnipeg where she had worked at a golf club. Originally from Yorkton, Saskatchewan, Harris became close with Hawkins, whose wife and family had stayed in the United States when he came north. Hawkins and Harris shared accommodations in Toronto at the Commodore Apartments on Maitland Street, where it would later be alleged that alcohol was consumed — a serious matter for Klansmen who advocated for prohibition in the name of public morals. The couple journeyed across southern Ontario in the summer of 1925 selling Klan memberships and sharing hotel rooms, according to Hawkins's detractors.[36] New klaverns sprang up in places as far apart as Kingston in the east and Goderich on the shores of Lake Huron in the west.[37]

The membership drive began to have an impact on the Loyal Orange Lodge, an ostensible ally of the Klan, and the Masons, another Protestant fraternal order with a strong presence in Ontario. The Orange Lodge and the Masons thrived on the patronage and support of local political leaders; the Klan was a late arrival that promised to allow members to participate in violence and intimidation. Masonic leaders in particular became concerned about being identified with the Ku Klux Klan, especially as klaverns began to fill up with Orangemen and Freemasons.

William J. Drope, a well-known Masonic grand master, faced the issue head on at a gathering of Ontario Masonic lodges in Hamilton in July as Klan recruiting hit a high pitch across the province. He reminded lodge members that they "will do well to consider seriously before associating themselves with an organization which . . . finds it necessary to conceal the identity of its membership behind a hood or mask."[38] The appeal went largely unheeded as Orange Lodge and Masonic Lodge members continued to flock to Klan gatherings.

The spectacle of two competing Ku Klux Klan organizations vigorously recruiting through southwestern Ontario in the summer of 1925 led to a surge in public attention and notoriety. Although it is uncertain whether all such incidents can be tied to Klan organizers or members, countless crosses were burned near a number of communities including Chatham, Dresden, St. Thomas, Ingersoll, Wallaceburg and London during July and August 1925.[39] These communities had significant numbers of Black residents, descendants of African Americans who had settled in the region after their escape from slavery in the United States via the Underground Railroad. The burnings coincided with the passage of Klan organizers in most areas. Police dismissed cross burnings as isolated events inspired by *The Birth of A Nation* and organized by bored thrill seekers.

A major rally in downtown London, Ontario, in early August 1925 saw Hawkins address a crowd of some two hundred people from the back of a truck whose owner's name had been covered.[40] Almond Charles Monteith (last seen entering the Hamilton jail a few months earlier) was a prominent participant in this rally, having apparently completed his sentence and transferred his Klan loyalties to Hawkins and his recruiting efforts to London.

Another participant was John Hothersall, a supporter of Fowler's rival Klan organization, who spent his time heckling Hawkins. Hothersall was a London stock salesman with links to the well-publicized Klan organizer Hignett.

Rev. Otho Elliott, the Baptist minister from Toronto who had helped found the Canadian Klan, was also at the London rally. After Hawkins spoke, Elliott buttonholed a *London Free Press* reporter to make sure he knew that Hawkins was no longer connected with the Ku Klux Klan of Canada, which Hawkins had just attacked a few minutes earlier as "the outlaw branch" of the Klan. There was considerable rancour in the air of Federal Square, the site of the meeting. Immediately after the rally, Hawkins hustled back to Toronto for the next weekend's events, where there were better prospects and fewer disruptions.

The weekend events began on Friday, August 7, in the west-central part of Toronto at the Parkdale Assembly Hall. Late in the evening, a dozen or more cars packed with Klan members in full regalia left the hall and headed downtown. "The occupants of the car included both men and women. They had removed their hoods, and the glow of the dome lights on their faces added to the 'strange sight' as the sedans drove eastward along Queen Street."[41] When the caravan reached the heart of the Jewish garment district, the cars turned north and then east along Bloor Street, one of the city's main thoroughfares. The route was no accident. The cavalcade was intended to intimidate the Jewish community clustered around Queen Street and Spadina Avenue. The parade caught pedestrians out for a walk to escape the heat by surprise, and many — Jews and Gentiles alike — were left uneasy.

Hawkins sought to reassure the citizenry that no violence was intended. This was just a warm-up parade for bigger rallies to come in the future, he said. Hawkins pointed to a major Klan gathering being held in Washington, D.C., the same week that featured hundreds of thousands of participants. Canada could expect to see Klan gatherings of this magnitude in the future. The Toronto police dismissed the Bloor Street procession as a "youth stunt" or masquerade. A second Klan event followed at the Parkdale Assembly Hall two days later.

More than 150 people attended the gathering in the withering humidity of a Toronto summer. The scene was a classic of mass theatre. As reported by the *Toronto Star*, there were six white-robed, hooded figures on the platform, along with a traditional fiery cross in background, an open bible lying upon a cushion with the Union Jack sewn upon the top of it, two great Union Jacks backstage, and another fluttering in the breeze created by an electric fan on the front left of the platform.[42]

Plainclothes police were said to be mingling in the crowd; a few dozen people signed membership cards.

Generally, the targets of Klan invective — Black people, Jews, Catholics and other minorities — chose not to react to public acts of intimidation and hatred like the Bloor Street parade. "The Jews are gradually taking possession of all the industries of the continent," an unnamed Klan organizer was quoted in the *Toronto Star*. The newspaper tried to elicit some kind of community reaction. Rabbi Barnett Bricker of Holy Blossom Temple, one of the city's leading synagogues, was circumspect. The group, he said, would almost certainly be stopped by the non-Jewish community. "There is no place for the K.K.K. in any country where the British flag waves," offered Edmund Scheuer, another Jewish leader.[43] Other groups chose to respond to the Klan in a similar manner. Keep a low profile, trust in the authorities and hope the Klan goes away.

Within a few weeks, Hawkins's attempts to build the Ku Klux Klan of the British Empire began to fall apart. A meeting of about one thousand people in Woodstock in early September ended "more or less in disorder" after Hawkins could not satisfy public questions about his relations with Fowler's group or the Orange Lodge.[44] Hawkins was soon forced out of his own "organization," which had the same financial motives as the "official" Klan. He made a tactical retreat to the United States after his "banishment" from Fowler's Klan and was not seen publicly in Ontario again. The Ku Klux Klan of the British Empire stumbled along for a while before being folded quietly back into the wider Klan family.

The recruiting season for the "official" Klan (as opposed to Hawkins's "British Empire" group) ended with a major rally at the Dorchester fairgrounds on October 14, 1925. Fowler left the anonymity of his Toronto office to attend. The rally saw 200 men sworn in as new members at a ceremony that attracted more than a thousand onlookers.[45] This event was the prelude to the high tide of Klan activity in the province the following year.

Meanwhile, Klan activities were drawing the attention of Ontario law enforcement officials. The term of Attorney General William Nickle, a lawyer from Kingston, Ontario, ran from July 1923 to October 1926, almost exactly the most intense period of Klan activity in the province. His long-serving deputy attorney general, Edward Bayly, came to view the Klan as a disruptive factor in the province's public life. As a result, there was little official comfort offered to the so-called "Knights of the Knightshirt," to quote journalist A.D. Monk, particularly when the province's newspapers persisted in seeking official statements about the government's response to Klan activities.

The Ku Klux Klan was assigned to the caseload of Inspector John Miller, a veteran Ontario Provincial Police (OPP) investigator with a history of arrests in major cases across the province. The OPP was a small organization with an even smaller Criminal Investigation Division (CID) — Miller and one or two other detectives, depending on available resources. A significant portion of the OPP's manpower was devoted to enforcing the *Ontario Temperance Act*, the 1916 statute that made it difficult to buy a legal drink in the province and that had resulted in a boom in illegal stills, a flourishing population of bootleggers, speakeasies and associated criminality. The OPP had a large unit of liquor licensing inspectors. The miniscule CID was left to look into serious criminal offences, which led to the Ku Klux Klan.

A bulky, dour-looking officer with an affinity for bowler hats, his success against the Klan consolidated Miller's reputation as a copper's cop.[46] He had begun his law enforcement career in Hamilton, where the OPP had made its first Klan arrest — Almond Charles Monteith in November 1924. Miller's operations against the Klan eventually produced rich archival files dealing with the expenses he incurred to buy information from informants in the Klan.[47] The investments would prove their worth in time.

* * *

In British Columbia, the impact of the Klan, its ideas and its violent and illegal methods of targeting individuals from racial minorities was evident in the startling illegal activities of a group of local officials including provincial cabinet ministers and police.

These events arose after the death of a young Scottish woman. On the morning of July 26, 1924, police received a call saying a young woman named Janet Smith had killed herself at 3851 Osler Street in the upscale Shaughnessy Heights neighbourhood, part of the separate municipality of Point Grey, which was embedded inside the Vancouver city boundaries.

Janet Smith was a Scottish-born nanny who looked after the child of Doreen and Frederick Lefevre Baker, a wealthy Vancouver couple who had originally hired her in London before returning to the west coast. In May 1924, Smith moved with the Baker family into the Osler Street home. Smith's personal life was the object of much speculation, with several boyfriends and a close relationship with Wong Foon Sing, a twenty-seven-year-old Chinese houseboy who also worked in the Bakers' home.

When Constable James Green answered the phone at the Point Grey Police station on the morning of July 26, a man told him that Smith was lying dead beside her ironing board in the basement of the Osler Street house. She had a bullet wound over her right eye, and a .45-calibre revolver was on the floor. The only person in the house at the time of her death was apparently Wong Foon Sing, who told police he was peeling potatoes when he heard what he thought was a car backfiring. When he went to the basement, he found the nanny lying dead. The Point Grey Police ruled the death a suicide, a finding that was confirmed by a coroner's inquest soon after: death by self-inflicted gunshot.

Janet Smith was a member of one of the Lower Mainland's most enduring clans — the expatriate Scottish community. The Scots found their collective voice through an organization called the United Council of Scottish Societies. The other pillar of the local Scottish world was a cluster of Presbyterian churches led by a vocal set of clergymen. Smith's friends refused to believe the nanny had killed herself; it just didn't fit with their perception of the twenty-two-year-old, who had planned to return home to Britain.

The United Council of Scottish Societies sent telegrams to provincial Attorney General Alexander Manson in Victoria calling for the case to be re-opened. Local newspapers began printing stories about the casual nature of the police investigation and the haste of the coroner's verdict. Wong Foon Sing was seen by newspapers as the obvious culprit in the whole business. Public opinion needed to be satisfied. Janet Smith's body was exhumed in August and a second inquest held in September. After a week of colourful testimony, the coroner's jury brought back a verdict of death by murder.

Political pressure mounted as the Scottish Societies pushed for answers about the fate of the young woman, who was increasingly seen as a symbol of oppressed Scottish immigrants. That her possible killer was a Chinese man fueled the racial animosities that thrived across the region. Inflammatory media reporting on the case accelerated the popular rhetoric against the Chinese community. Attorney General Manson responded by appointing a special prosecutor to mount a full investigation into the case. The Scottish Societies pressured local MLAs to sponsor legislation "to prohibit employers from hiring white women and Orientals as servants in the same household."[48] A bill to that effect was introduced in the provincial legislature in the fall of 1924.

The Janet Smith case jumped back into the headlines in late March 1925 after several months of relative quiet in the Vancouver newspapers. A gang of men dressed in white Klan-style robes showed up on March 20 at Frederick Baker's house in Point Grey where Janet Smith had died the previous summer. Wong Foon Sing was still working for the Bakers. He greeted the supposed Klansmen at the front door. They grabbed him, pulled him to a waiting car and drove away. He was not seen for the next six weeks. When he reappeared on nearby Marine Drive on May 1, disoriented and obviously in rough shape, the Point Grey police promptly arrested him for the murder of Janet Smith.

As it turned out, the "Klansmen" who took Sing away were actually off-duty Point Grey police officers and private detectives hired by the Scottish Societies. The whole thing had been organized by the Point Grey police commission led by the chair — and mayor — James Paton. The commission paid private investigator Oscar Robinson of the Canadian Detective Bureau some $1,250 for "secret service" work. Robinson recruited his son William (a.k.a. Willie) and colleague Verity Norton to help with the kidnapping along with K.W. Wrightson, the wheelman in the getaway car.

Sing was held in the attic of a house in the western reaches of Point Grey for six weeks, beaten, tortured and interrogated about the Smith killing.[49] Sing later repeatedly testified in preliminary hearings and subsequent trials that his captors interrogated him while wearing white robes — robes that officials considered evidence of Klan involvement. Sing maintained his innocence in the Smith killing. His kidnappers finally decided to release him on Marine Drive, drove around the block and then arrested him for murder in their official capacity as peace officers.

Rumours circulated — fanned by the Vancouver newspapers — that a citizen vigilante group had kidnapped Sing. Attorney General Manson, who had been born in Missouri but kept the fact secret, expressed outrage about the use of American "Ku Klux Klan" methods to administer justice in Canada.[50] The Vancouver Bar Association passed a unanimous resolution that condemned "lynch law, secret society rule, Ku Klux Klan or third-degree methods in assisting law enforcement."[51]

There was no proof the kidnappers were Klan members, but they clearly drew inspiration from the Klan's reputation for administering vigilante justice when the justice system, in their minds, failed in its duty. In the fall of 1925, as the Klan took up official residence in Shaughnessy Heights, Sing's dramatic murder trial came to an abrupt end with the case thrown out for lack of evidence. Private detectives Oscar Robinson and Verity Norton (who had been arrested in Washington State and brought back to Vancouver) and three Point Grey police officers (including Chief John Murdock) were subsequently charged with kidnapping, forcible confinement or conspiracy. Oscar Robinson, his son Willie and Verity Norton went to jail for their roles in the affair.

It was seventeen-year-old Willie who admitted under oath that his involvement in the case started on March 16, 1925, when he went with his father to an address "to pick up the white-robed costumes that had been made for them."[52] He had stayed at the house on West 25th Avenue while Sing was held captive in the attic.

Police commissioners James Paton and H.P. McCraney, along with special prosecutor Malcolm Jackson and three past or current officers of the Scottish Society, were charged with organizing the kidnapping. Then it came to light that Attorney General Alexander Manson himself had known about the kidnapping from the beginning but went along with it in the hope it would lead to a confession from Sing. As Paton, McCraney and the rest were about to go to trial in December 1925, the deputy attorney general, William Carter, stayed the charges on the grounds that "the matter has been fully ventilated, as far as is possible, and no public good can come from further proceedings that are, in my opinion, a useless waste of public money and should be stayed."[53]

The Klan was dismissed as a factor in the case, but Klan leaders used it for their own purposes. James Paton, who published rants against the Asian community for decades, eventually became a Conservative member of the Legislative Assembly. Wong Foon Sing went back to China. Janet Smith's death remained an unexplained mystery. There were strong suspicions her killing was linked to her employer's involvement in narcotics trafficking.

* * *

In the midst of these proceedings, the Ku Klux Klan formally arrived in Vancouver. The leaders — Luther Powell, Keith Allen, R.G. Wallace — acquired a prestige address for their imperial palace. The stately Glen Brae Manor at 1690 Matthews Avenue in the upscale Shaughnessy Heights neighbourhood was a highly visible coup for the Klan.

The mansion had been built by retired lumber baron William Tait, a man wealthy enough to import an enormous wrought iron fence from Scotland to shield the property from the traffic on Matthews Avenue. The Ontario-born Tait had made his fortune operating a lumber mill on False Creek. Tait died in 1919, then his wife died in 1920 and the property began a slow decline until the Klan took out a lease on the eighteen-room mansion. Major Powell, "Dr." Allen and other American organizers delighted in posing for photographs wearing their robes in the gardens surrounding the mansion. It was good advertising.

Glen Brae served as the grandiose backdrop for the recruiting efforts that began on Friday, October 29, 1925. "An informal reception will be held at the IMPERIAL PALACE, 1690 Matthews Avenue West, at 8 p.m.," blared an announcement circulated widely to Vancouver newspapers. "ALL GENII, DRAGONS, HYDRAS, GREAT TITANS, and FURIES, GIANTS, EXALTED CYCLOPS, and TERRORS, will be present to meet under the kindly light of the FIERY CROSS which will illuminate the KLAVERN."

The invitation was issued "By His Excellency, L.L. Powell, Imperial Klazik, Invisible Empire, Kanadian Knights of the Ku Klux Klan." The unique spelling clearly distinguished Powell's group from the "official" Ku Klux Klan based in the Toronto office, or the "British Empire" Klan launched back in Ontario by J.H. Hawkins. The title of "klazik" was Powell's innovation that was not used elsewhere in the invisible empire.

On the night of the gathering, a crowd of several hundred hooded Klan members paraded with torches down nearby Granville Avenue. The object of the parade, as always, was intimidation. The message was clear: the Klan was a force to be reckoned with, woe to those who opposed it. And the message to those targeted by the Klan: be fearful. The robed Klansmen and women crowded through the gates and into the mansion with its dazzling ballroom and the gardens behind.

The editor of the *Point Grey Gazette* attended the evening as a journalist and took note of the goings on.[54] The ceremonial tableau was familiar. There was a flag pole with a Union Jack. A table at the foot of the cross carried "a drawn sword and an open Bible." The doors of the ceremonial chamber (the ballroom in ordinary times) were guarded by two hooded Klansmen. The crowd was predominantly male with a few women attendees. Luther Powell and Keith Allen made presentations on the aims and ideals of the organization. The Klan was "strongly anti-Oriental" and opposed to drug traffickers.

Several cars arrived during the evening, pulling into the driveway at Glen Brae to deliver Klansmen from Bellingham, Washington, just across the border. The new arrivals "gave the American salute to the flag, and then the Fascist, or old Roman salute, with extended arm, to the Klazik," Luther Powell. It was a night of Klan glitter and glory that left the residents of Point Grey, a separate municipality from the rest of the Lower Mainland, uneasy. The Point Grey police chief was consulted on legal options to oust the Klan from the neighbourhood. He responded that "he would not interfere without specific instructions from civic authorities." The nature of unfolding events made that an unlikely proposition. The Ku Klux Klan of Canada was just hitting its stride.

# Chapter 4
# YEAR OF THE KLAN (1926)

The spring of 1926 saw Ku Klux Klan organizers in full public recruiting mode across Canada. Newspapers and public officials saw Klansmen everywhere. When they looked south, they saw electoral battles featuring Klan candidates, Klan rallies, Klan fairs. These Klan gatherings attracted thousands, tens of thousands in some places. The Canadian scene was similar — but not the same.

"Today it is probably the most active and fast-growing organization that this country contains," journalist Patrick Richards reported in *Saturday Night* magazine in June 1926. "Operating, so far, mainly in the rural districts of Ontario, it is nightly staging public demonstrations, burning fiery crosses and initiating new members by the hundred." Richards, a veteran journalist and future managing editor of *Saturday Night,* was an astute observer of the Klan during the 1920s. He noted that the success of this foreign organization was marked by "queer happenings" in towns and cities across the province.[1]

This observation was sparked by a ceremony in March 1926 by approximately a dozen Ku Klux Klan members laying a wreath at the war memorial on University Avenue in downtown Toronto. The whole affair was labelled "weird rather than impressive" by the *Toronto Star.*[2] The purpose of the ceremony (other than honouring the war dead) was unknown, but it may have been a simple reminder to the public that the Klan was still in town, still recruiting. The Klan thrived on this kind of publicity.

The Ku Klux Klan's organizational success was evident in the rural areas of Ontario, where normally the Orange Lodge dominated social life and associated political activities. The town of Barrie, north of Toronto on Lake Simcoe, was the scene of a major demonstration of Ku Klux Klan strength with a mass meeting held on the night of May 23, 1926, during the long Victoria Day weekend.[3]

The rally had originally been scheduled to be held in a park in Barrie until town officials realized it was a Klan gathering and cancelled permission to use the park. (Civic officials in other municipalities were not always as vigilant.) The venue shifted to a hill on the edge of town, possibly an even better location in the minds of the organizers because it offered better sightlines for a cross burning.

A crowd estimated at two thousand — drawn from across the province — watched as the ritual "fiery cross" was burned to start the proceedings. Major Harry Proctor (the source of his rank was unknown), a Klan officer from Toronto, warmed up the crowd. He was followed by the keynote speaker, the Rev. Dr. Charles Lewis Fowler, now identified in public as the imperial secretary of the invisible empire. Following that, new members were enrolled, including a few destined to bring the Klan the notoriety of its American namesake.

Two weeks later came another of the "queer happenings" noted by Richards. On the evening of June 10, an explosion echoed through the quiet streets of Barrie and across the shores of Lake Simcoe. Although many people heard the detonation, neither police nor members of the public seem to have looked for the cause until the next day. It turned out a stick of dynamite had been placed against a brick wall of St. Mary's Roman Catholic Church on a downtown street. A four-foot square hole blasted through the brickwork.[4] Although the damage wasn't considered serious, rumours of a Klan attack against Roman Catholics ran through the province and rippled across the country.

Attorney General William Nickle was immediately approached by the "respectable elements" of the Ku Klux Klan, who denied any Klan involvement. Nickle issued a press statement to the effect that Jim Lord, the New Brunswick MLA and Klan secretary, accompanied by the Klan's attorney, Homer B. Neeley, had met with him to discuss the bombing. They assured him, and Nickle told the press he believed them, that the Klan "would punish any member engaged in these lawless affairs and would cooperate with the authorities."[5] Deputy Attorney General Edward Bayly's reactions to his minister's acceptance of these assurances is not recorded, but OPP Inspector John Miller already knew the facts of the case. The bombing had been planned and carried out by two Barrie Klan officials, along with a third Klan recruit, a recent Irish Protestant immigrant to Canada with a hatred of Catholicism.

Miller arrested William Skelly, a thirty-year-old shoemaker, on the streets of downtown Toronto a few days after the explosion. Skelly was interrogated by Miller and OPP Deputy Commissioner Alf Cuddy. Skelly had been enrolled as a Klan member at the Barrie cross burning on May 23, having paid $16.50 for his membership and accompanying regalia. (Skelly was also wanted on two charges of fraud, unrelated to his Klan activities.)

Harry Proctor, the Klan spokesman, falsely denied to reporters that Skelly was a Klan member. He claimed, in fact, that the Klan had helped deliver him into the hands of the police. It wasn't explained how that could happen if the Klan didn't know him, or if he was not a member. The Klan's national leadership later acknowledged in an information bulletin that in fact Skelly had been a Klan member but was suspended after the bombing and later expelled.[6] Two more arrests followed — William Butler, reportedly the kleagle for the Barrie district, and Clare Lee, the local Klan secretary.[7] Both were rumoured to be associates of Joseph Ballons, a Klan organizer operating out of Guelph, who was in league with Charles Lewis Fowler.

The motives of the accused were closer to Ontario's traditional (that is, religious) animosities than any imported from the United States. Skelly, a Protestant, was originally from Ireland, an ex-soldier and former member of the Black and Tans, the British force viewed as an occupying army by Irish Republicans fighting for freedom from British control. He claimed his wife had been killed by Republican gunmen in the Northern Ireland city of Belfast, "and as a consequence he cherished resentment and bitterness against all Catholics."[8] Klan membership in and of itself did not appear to be a determining factor in the attack, although Klan literature included Catholics in a long list of enemies of the white race.

Provincial officials followed the case closely.[9] Edward Bayly, the deputy attorney general, took a personal interest in the prosecution of the case, retaining leading Toronto lawyer Peter White to act for the Crown.[10]

Skelly initially wanted to plead guilty to the charges against him (wilful damage, possession of explosives) but was dissuaded from doing so by police magistrate Compton Jeffs "as he [Jeffs] did not wish to have the responsibility of imposing sentence and committed him for trial instead," according to White a few days after his appointment as Crown prosecutor.[11] While Butler and Lee were released on bail, Skelly was sent off to be examined by doctors after local Crown Attorney F.G. Evans noted that "Skelly was peculiar when he came up" in front of the magistrate "and made strange statements."[12]

The doctors concluded Skelly was "absolutely sane," and he was scheduled to stand trial on charges of causing an explosion, attempting to destroy property with explosives and being an accessory after the fact.[13] Despite this early finding of sanity, there were lingering doubts as Skelly continued to act "peculiar." He was examined by a psychiatrist a second time just days before his trial in October 1926. The results were the same — absolutely sane.[14] The trial went ahead.

The jury found the trio guilty.[15] Skelly, Butler and Lee were sentenced to five, four and three years respectively; the sentences were to be served with hard labour at Ontario's notoriously tough Kingston Penitentiary. Mr. Justice Logie recommended in pronouncing the sentence that Skelly be deported to Ireland at the end of his sentence, saying, "We do not want dynamiters in Canada. It is a rare and un-British crime." Harry Proctor, the irrepressible KKK spokesman, continued to maintain in spite of the evidence that the Klan had nothing to do with the affair. The sentences effectively removed the Klan leadership in Barrie and area.

* * *

The summer of 1926 became the Summer of the Klan as organizers racked up membership sales. Over the summer months, crosses were burned in communities across the province, from Sarnia and Erieau in the west to Lanark County in the east. The Klan later estimated that more than 130,000 people had attended Klan rallies across Ontario during "the open air ceremonial season" in the summer of 1926.[16] In London, the Klan's reach extended to the grave when a funeral at Woodlawn Cemetery saw mourners attend a burial dressed in full Ku Klux Klan regalia.[17]

The Ottawa Valley and the St. Lawrence River valley were rich sources of recruits, building on long-standing hostility towards Roman Catholics and francophones. While the Orange Lodge had a long history of inflaming local hatreds, the Klan arrived with its coal-oil soaked fiery crosses to ratchet up conflict and hatred. Memberships were sold and klaverns established in Smiths Falls, Perth, Prescott, Brockville, Belleville, Gananoque, Picton and Ottawa, as well as smaller communities throughout the Ottawa Valley. The *Perth Courier* reported in June that a thirteen-foot cross was burned in the small hamlet of Montague just outside the town of Smiths Falls.

> *When it burst into flames at 10:10, it considerably startled the members of W. A. Bissonnette's family, whose home is about 150 feet from the spot at which the cross was erected, and other farmers in the vicinity were also given a shock on discovering the flaming symbol. The francophone, Roman-Catholic Bissonnettes made a perfect Klan target for hatred and intimidation.*[18]

Centrally located, Smiths Falls became the site of annual regional Klan rallies beginning in September 1926 when local Klan members were said to number at least five hundred. The Klan had been present in the community since the spring of 1925 when the principal of the Smiths Falls Collegiate Institute received a threatening letter signed "KKK."[19]

For the 1926 rally, a cross was erected, then burned to the ground, on the outskirts of town the night before the big rally. Hooded and white-robed horsemen paraded through the streets. Local newspapers reported:

> *At several of the most important street corners the symbolic letters KIGY were painted upon the streets, and a huge arrow directed pedestrians and vehicles to McEwen's Field on the east side of town. The letters KIGY mean "Klan Is Gathering Yonder" . . . Only Protestants were allowed into the grounds and the entrance was guarded by members of the order, attired in full regalia and in some cases carrying swords.*[20]

The yearly spectacles typically attracted as many as fifteen thousand visitors from across Ontario, Quebec and the United States. The usual show included Union Jack displays, multiple platforms and speakers, a local band playing loud and patriotic tunes. Klan leadership figures would address the enthusiastic crowd. Names were not published in local newspapers, but "the Imperial Kaliff *[sic]* of the order who hails from New Brunswick" obviously referred to New Brunswick MLA Jim Lord. The king kleagle said to be from London, Ontario, might have been Almond Charles Monteith, John Hothersall or even Roy Hignett, providing his nerves had recovered from the stresses of a few years before. Regardless, "both showed themselves to be very able speakers."

The speeches were classic Klan. The Klan was Christian, Protestant and British. "The Klan was a legacy passed down from the ancient Protestant Scotch clans," declared the imperial klaliff, parroting the origin myths created by Charles Lewis Fowler during his years in Atlanta. The Klan "had no ill-feeling towards the Black, yellow or brown races and was not out to fight them." It was a law-abiding organization, and every member "must swear to uphold national law and order." The klaliff went on to note how the Roman Catholics, Jews, Chinese and "the Japs" had all organized to impose their will on the world. Now, according to Jim Lord, it was time for white men "to come together and stand shoulder to shoulder so that every White man and every White woman is helping in the uplift of the White race."

The festive atmosphere continued into the evening, when more than a hundred men and women were sworn in to the Klan. Five crosses were set alight, providing illumination for the gathering. "The ladies of the Kingston Klan then demonstrated Klan drill," reported the local newspapers. "Light was provided by automobile headlights and by the burning crosses. In the semi-darkness scores of white cloaked and masked figures presented a rather impressive sight." The account describes a typical Klan rally in the Ottawa Valley as the summer of 1926 drifted into autumn.

Local newspapers viewed the Klan phenomenon with bemusement mixed with disdain and occasional hostility. From the national capital, the *Ottawa Citizen* regularly argued that the establishment of the Ku Klux Klan should be discouraged, saying, "Nightshirts should be for sleeping in, not for cloaks to hide crimes by anonymous malcontents."[21] The *Arnprior*

*Chronicle* cast a particularly harsh eye at the goings-on down the Ottawa Valley in Smiths Falls. A June 1926 editorial included the following:

> *The people of Ontario usually have looked upon Ku Klux Klan activities as something not very creditable to any country but nevertheless as something far removed from our peaceful country and not affecting us at all. But now we wake up to find the Ku Kluxers at our very doors. They have been burning crosses at Smiths Falls and in other places in this particular section of the country.*

The paper noted the Klan's intent to get involved in the next provincial election, and noted sarcastically, "Everyone knows what constructive policies these Klansmen seek to carry out, how suited they are in our country of two languages and different religions." It continued:

> *Why such an organization whose very existence depends upon its success in keeping discord, animosity and hatred alive in any community should find any footing in Ontario at all would be hard to understand if we did not know that there is a certain element in any community which will be attracted to any such thing no matter what it may be, and if we did not know that organizers and imperial wizards of the Klan find Canadian dollars just as comfortable in their pockets as they have found millions of dollars in the United States.*

Having noted the likely motivations of Klan leaders, the editorial built up to its conclusion.

> *There is no room for a Klan organization in any part of Canada. We have our little troubles of race and religion, but we are getting along very well, and the different races and creeds are coming to understand each other better every day. Any decent-minded Canadian with an eye to the unity of his fellow citizens will have nothing but contempt for the Klan and its agents.*

It was a view increasingly shared by journalists across the province.

* * *

The Klan had already made itself known in Belleville, Ontario, in a series of events that ended in an attempt to intimidate the local newspaper. Crosses had been burned in the region around the small city east of Toronto in mid-1925 before culminating in a highly visible ceremony at the Belleville fairgrounds in September.

The largest Klan manifestation ever seen in Belleville came on Sunday, June 27, 1926, when spectators arrived in town to attend a Klan fair and induction ceremony. The day was attended by some 1,100 Klan members in full regalia. There were the usual speeches. "During the afternoon, the imperial commander of the Ladies' Ku Klux Klan of Kanada spoke, and a ladies' group from Kingston performed a splendid drill," according to local historian Gerry Boyce.[22] This was undoubtedly the same troupe of Kingston Klan women who performed at Smiths Falls and other Klan gatherings around eastern Ontario. The festivities climaxed in the evening with the lighting of an eighty-foot-high cross. By the light of the burning cross, sixty new Klan recruits — men and women — were inducted into the Silent Empire.

The local Klan leader was Rev. George Marshall, rector of Belleville's Reformed Episcopal Church. Historian Ed Buckley recalled him as "a tall thin man who lived on Victoria Avenue." Marshall was born in England, arriving in Canada in 1912 at the age of fifty.[23] By the time he joined the Klan, he was in his late sixties and full of righteous bigotry towards Roman Catholics. Buckley was a contemporary observer of the Klan in Belleville and "he knew that the Klan frequently burned crosses on the lawns of homes inhabited by philandering husbands."[24] A similar practice was noted in other communities, particularly Moose Jaw, Saskatchewan. A few months after the initiation ceremony, Marshall and two Klansmen — a certain Canniff and Ruttan, both well-known names in the Belleville area — visited the general manager of the *Belleville Intelligencer*, S.B. Dawson. They wanted Dawson to fire a printer working for the paper who happened to be Catholic. "Although they admitted that the young man was honest, capable, and a good husband and father, they objected to a Roman Catholic being given a position of authority over Protestants," wrote Ed Buckley.

The next day's editorial was scathing. "When the Ku Klux Klan of Kanada first came to Belleville, it was greeted with tolerant amusement," wrote Dawson. "It was good fun to watch the "hooded warriors" manoeuvre on unaccustomed horse-back when they held their field days, and their fiery crosses were entertaining and innocuous."[25] But now, in the wake of the bombing in Barrie, enough was enough. Dawson denounced the Klan in print for its "ugly-headed bigotry and intolerance."

* * *

In Guelph, a factory town eighty kilometres northwest of Toronto, William Templeman, editor of the *Guelph Mercury*, was equally fed up. Ray Lewis, the future Olympic runner from nearby Hamilton, knew the city well. He and his friend Lloyd Johnson, also Black, had been in Guelph for a local event. "A white man shoved us both off the sidewalk," he recalled:

> *We tumbled into the street. "Go back to where you came from, n-----s," he yelled at us. No one in the crowd came to our side. I was angry. Where would we go? I thought to myself. We're from here. We're Canadians! This is our country. Lloyd was mad, too, so mad that he wanted to get into a physical fight with the man. But I pulled Lloyd away telling him that the next stop for us would be a jail cell — white people just didn't care about any injustice done to a Black man.*[26]

Editor William Templeman also knew about race, power and politics. His father had been a newspaper publisher in Victoria, British Columbia, a hotbed of anti-Asian sentiment, before getting into politics. The elder Templeman was defeated in the 1908 federal election after Conservative rivals accused him "of favouring Oriental immigration."[27] He was later acclaimed to Parliament in a byelection and served as a federal cabinet minister.

And now William Templeman, Jr., his fifty-six-year-old son, was facing a personal and professional challenge mounted by the Ku Klux Klan. Two cars full of Klansmen had showed up at his house on Queen Street West on the night of Monday, October 4, 1926, "to attempt the intimidation of *The Mercury*, for what particular reason nobody can discover. The only effect of their visit was to frighten some women and sick persons."[28]

The city had been the scene of robust Klan activity over the previous six months.[29] An active kleagle named Joseph Ballons, a loyal supporter of Fowler, had been selling memberships during the winter. By April, he was openly holding Klan meetings at rented rooms in the city hall, presumably with the knowledge if not the support of Mayor Bev Robson and councillors.

Ballons became increasingly aggressive. In September, a cross was burned on the front yard of a local woman in a downtown neighbourhood. Nobody knew why, other than it served to frighten the woman and intimidate others. Then Ballons confronted Thomas Penfold, a city hardware merchant, in front of the congregation of First Baptist Church on Woolwich Street and threatened him for offending the Klan in some way. Again, nobody knew why. Church members complained to the police. Ballons was arrested and required to post a peace bond. Then the Klan came to Templeman's house while he was away, frightening his wife and family who were home on their own.

Templeman understood instinctively that he needed to push back. He used the front page of the next day's paper to denounce the Ku Klux Klan as a foreign organization "used for the exploiting of the credulous and weak-minded people of a community." He repeated rumours that four local police officers and some city aldermen were connected with the Klan, although he had no concrete evidence to offer. Businessmen who associated with the Klan "are not deserving of the business or trade of decent citizens," wrote Templeman. He reminded readers that another flaming cross had been set up the night before outside a local house. It was not the first time. A cross had been set alight in Guelph almost two years earlier.[30] Templeman described the Klan as "a public nuisance" and formally declared war on the group.

The irate Templeman fired off a telegram to Attorney General Nickle, demanding to know if the Klan was operating with a provincial charter. Edward Bayly replied on behalf of his minister to the effect that the Klan did not have a provincial charter — which would give the group some form of legal status — but stated, "Apart from municipal By-Laws, lighting a flaming cross (or any other symbol) is no more criminal by itself than lighting a bonfire of leaves."[31]

He advised Templeman to contact the local Crown attorney or the Ontario Provincial Police or the Guelph chief of police. Given his charges of local police and political involvement in the Klan, the editor deemed such efforts to be worthless. Templeman decided on yet another editorial broadside of invective aimed at the Klan, the city police, city aldermen and the local police commission. Put on warning by Templeman, and with Joe Ballons subject to a peace bond, the Ku Klux Klan faded from public view in Guelph.

* * *

During this period, Charles Lewis Fowler, the imperial secretary, could not be found by newspaper reporters to comment on developments. The questions that William Templeman was asking in Guelph came at the same time as the trial of Skelly and colleagues in Barrie. Fowler's retreat from the public eye was probably seen as a smart public relations ploy but it left Harry Proctor to take the heat for his boss. As subsequent events developed, there were also reasons to wonder if he was even in Canada.

Some Klan members began to smell a rat with how the organization was being managed. Jim Lord made direct accusations in the Klan's information bulletin to members. "Fowler and Jos[eph] Ballons collected money that was never handed over to the Treasurer," he wrote, pointing to yet another instance of money being the source of internal Klan fighting.[32]

The case of Alexander Wakefield, a kleagle working out of Toronto, illustrated how internal dissent drew the attention of authorities and destroyed members' trust in the Klan leadership. Deputy Attorney General Bayly later recounted how Wakefield went to work recruiting Klan members in southern Ontario in mid-1926. The deal was familiar in its structure: recruiters sold memberships for $10 each, $6 of which went to the Klan central office in Toronto (i.e., Fowler and company) and $4 to Wakefield himself.[33] Bayly told the story:

> *When he discovered gross irregularities in the organization and attempted to expose the Klan officials at a meeting in Paris, Ontario, a group of forty or fifty men rushed in, backed him into a corner, forced him to open his attaché cases, taking*

> *from them all papers relating to the Klan, including some damaging evidence and then took him to a Railway Station and put him on board a train.*[34]

Even allowing for some exaggeration by Wakefield in telling the story to paint himself in a better light, he had clearly been run out of town on a rail.

Wakefield was angry about how the Klan had treated him. He wanted revenge, so he offered himself to the authorities as an informer working against the Klan.[35] Wakefield was sent to see John Miller, the OPP inspector who had been working on Klan investigations, including the Barrie bombing. Miller took Wakefield up on his offer and hired him as a paid informant.[36] In the coming months, Wakefield journeyed across southern Ontario seeking information on the Klan and regularly reporting to police magistrates and Crown attorneys as he went.[37]

Wakefield's credibility with local authorities was not high, and no charges followed his reports to authorities. He eventually dropped out of sight or, as Miller put it, "Wakefield was lost to us, as we have never seen him since." The inspector was left to explain Wakefield's OPP links to the deputy attorney general and vainly try to claim related expenses. The sum involved was only thirty dollars, but the amount of paperwork required to support the claim was impressive. Miller was never reimbursed by the OPP for his informer payments in spite of representations from Acting Commissioner Alf Cuddy to the deputy attorney general on behalf of his inspector.[38]

Wakefield was not the only informant working in the Klan. In the London area, Benjamin Eckardt, a fundamentalist minister, claimed in later years to have worked as an undercover police agent during the 1920s reporting on Klan activities.[39] There is some question about Eckardt's actual role with the Klan, particularly among his contemporaries who identified him as a key KKK organizer in Elgin County.[40] Indeed, Eckardt was publicly identified by a newspaper in June 1925 as a Klan organizer.[41]

This might have been a successful undercover police operation with the informant firmly and anonymously embedded in the group. Or Eckardt might have been supplementing his clergyman's salary by selling Klan memberships, much like Harry Humble in Alberta or others in British

Columbia. Whatever the truth behind Eckardt's activities, in 1927 he participated as a leading member of the Canadian Klan's senior governing body, the kloncilium, a key position if he was indeed a police source.[42]

Another member of the Klan kloncilium during this period was Homer B. Neeley, a London lawyer who had served as a city alderman. It was Neeley who had joined Jim Lord to meet with the attorney general after the Barrie bombing. He also acted as legal counsel to George Wenige, the London mayor who had vowed to fight the Klan at every turn.[43] Neeley was born in nearby Dorchester, a hotbed of Klan activity during the mid-1920s. He had been an Independent Conservative candidate in a 1921 provincial byelection and was defeated by the governing United Farmers of Ontario candidate.

The question remained whether Neeley joined the Klan out of conviction or whether he became involved as a means of collecting information for Mayor Wenige and the local authorities. It would be surprising, given the nature of the Klan's reputation, growth and activities in 1925–26, if the OPP and other police services did not have a range of informants inside the Klan. The easiest way to do so would be to assume a role of some kind in the Klan organization, easily done in the context of large-scale recruiting where every new face was money in the pocket of a kleagle. In any event, a claim in later years to have been a police source was an attractive role for those embarrassed by their earlier associations with the KKK.

The Ku Klux Klan became a growing preoccupation for Ontario's law enforcement community during the group's rapid expansion during 1925 and 1926. General Victor Williams, the commissioner of the OPP, noted as early as February 1925 that the KKK was under surveillance:

> *Men can organize for fraternal purposes and if they keep within the law, they're not likely to be interfered with. The moment, however, that the Ku Klux Klan breaks the law, we will drop on them just as sure as anything.*

The statement came only a few months after the arrest of Almond Charles Monteith in Hamilton the previous fall.

Deputy OPP Commissioner Alf Cuddy, who had preceded David Ritchie as Calgary's police chief, was even more specific about Klan members and organizers. "We know who they are, have their names, and they are an American crowd from across the line who are doing the organizing. We know how long they have been organizing."[44] Cuddy knew his way around the country's police forces. Before going to Alberta to serve for seven years as Calgary's police chief, he had completed thirty years with the Toronto Police Service. Cuddy was best remembered in Calgary for leading a years-long crusade against prostitution and drink that saw regular raids on brothels and speakeasies. He then moved on to head up the Alberta Provincial Police before returning to Toronto as deputy OPP commissioner.

Williams and Cuddy were reflecting publicly what was going on behind the scenes due to questions about the Klan's motives and dubious commercial activities. Cuddy later noted that Inspector Miller of the OPP's Criminal Investigation Division assignment to investigate the Klan came at the express direction of Attorney General Nickle who "was concerned about their movements."[45]

Miller himself later recalled that he was assigned in 1925 or early 1926 to look at the group "because at this time several complaints had come in regarding the Klan work. I secured a large number of cards of the Klan showing who were members in Toronto and in fact throughout Canada."[46] It is probably no coincidence that the OPP's first moves against the Klan in 1924 (the Monteith arrest in November of that year) came in Hamilton, where Miller had started his police career. The Klan membership cards may have come from Monteith's briefcase.

* * *

Meanwhile on the west coast, the Janet Smith affair bubbled to the surface yet again as Ku Klux Klan recruiting ramped up on the Lower Mainland and on Vancouver Island during 1926. The provincial attorney general, Alexander Manson, called for police reports on the Klan because he had heard rumours "that the Kanadian Knights of the Ku Klux Klan had been plotting to abduct several people."[47] He shared the results with his federal counterpart, describing Klan literature as being of a "very flamboyant ultra-patriotic and highly exaggerated type — a type that we in this country have little use for." A Klan application to incorporate in the province would be denied because of members' likely involvement in unlawful behaviour. Further, Manson could not abide the local Klan's practice of writing Kanadian with a "K."[48]

Local clergymen were at the forefront of the Janet Smith controversy, and in time they became the new face of the Klan in British Columbia. Rev. Charles Batzold was pastor of the Zion United Church in Vancouver and a prominent proponent of British Israelism. In his beliefs, Batzold joined Charles Lewis Fowler of the Imperial Knights of the Ku Klux Klan of Canada, late of New York, Atlanta and now active in Toronto.

The Ontario-born Batzold enjoyed considerable public prestige in Vancouver as the combat chaplain of the local Seaforth Highlanders Battalion during the First World War. The reverend was an occasional guest speaker at William Aberhart's Prophetic Bible Institute in Calgary. Aberhart would build his Calgary ministry into a political movement that became the Alberta Social Credit Party, sweeping to power in Alberta in the 1935 provincial election. Batzold was also an associate of Rev. Clem Davies, a British-born fundamentalist minister in Victoria who openly proclaimed his membership in the Ku Klux Klan and lectured widely on his British Israelite beliefs.[49]

Originally from Birmingham, England, Davies was a short, handsome man with blue eyes and a dynamic speaking style that made him a crowd pleaser in Methodist pulpits from Manitoba to North Dakota to Utah and eventually Victoria. He married a Canadian woman from Brandon, Manitoba, before venturing to the west coast and establishing a radio ministry out of the Centennial Methodist Church in Victoria.[50] He forged close friendships with members of Victoria's social elite, including Dr. Ernest Hall, a surgeon and the city's police commissioner. When questions were asked about his divinity qualifications, Davies left Centennial Methodist and set up his own congregation in a local theatre.

Like other public figures on the west coast, Clem Davies attacked the local Chinese community after the death of Janet Smith. The way to rid the community of drugs and crime like the Smith killing was to rid the country of the Chinese. He proposed that the provincial legislature be abolished and replaced with a governing committee of six businessmen and warned that failure to do so would mean that "soon this country will be left to the Chinks, Japs, Hindus, Doukhobors and the Bible Students [Jehovah's Witnesses]." In late 1924, he threatened that a lack of action in this regard meant groups like the Ku Klux Klan would be forced to take action.

Clem Davies became the Klan's most prominent member on Vancouver Island and spoke at the first public Klan meeting in Victoria in January 1926. The meeting was held in the newly opened Crystal Gardens, the avant-garde community recreation centre that boasted the city's first indoor swimming pool, a salt water pool. In addition to his public support for the Klan at the Crystal Gardens meeting, Rev. Davies "performed a Klan wedding replete with fiery crosses," an event that guaranteed coverage in the *Daily Colonist*, which reported, "The bride was completely enveloped in the long white robe of the Order. Her head, as was that of the groom, was hidden in the white hood typical of the Klan."[51]

The marriage of Klan members identified as Leila Newman and Herbert Goode of Vancouver made for a tidy public relations coup engineered by Captain Wallace Laycock, the leading Klan kleagle on Vancouver Island and the father of Sylvia Laycock, flower girl at the wedding, who was "also robed and hooded." Laycock may have come by his military rank legitimately; he presented himself as a British army veteran who had served in the Sudan and the Boer War in the twilight years of the nineteenth century. He immigrated to Canada in 1913, setting up house in Point Grey. By November 1918, Laycock was managing the Red Cross Society's warehouse in Vancouver that supported the Canadian army mission in Siberia fighting against the Bolsheviks.[52] A few years later he was an established stockbroker and Klan recruiter with significant membership sales. He helped organize klaverns in Victoria, Nanaimo, Ladysmith and Duncan.

A number of prominent Victoria residents appeared in the Klan's ranks thanks to Davies's and Laycock's powers of persuasion. They included Alderman James Shanks, an Oak Bay barber, and Dr. Arthur Burton, leader of his own religious cult called the New Thought Temple, who described himself as a "drugless healer." After his dalliance with the Klan, Rev. Davies went on to develop an interest in Italian fascism and Benito Mussolini's "direct action" approach to solving political problems.

Another clergyman linked to the Janet Smith affair was Rev. Duncan McDougall of Vancouver. He was the self-appointed leader of a Presbyterian breakaway group called the Highland Church in East Vancouver, where he became a vocal and insistent spokesman for justice for Janet Smith. Grim, humourless and a killjoy at any gathering, McDougall used his pulpit to express "his dislike of Catholics, Jews, foreigners, and particularly Orientals whose ways he feared and often described as evil."[53] McDougall's congregation included members of the Scottish Societies of Vancouver, defenders of expatriate Scots and exponents of a particularly virulent brand of Presbyterian theology. McDougall was also a British Israel believer who was keen to share his beliefs with his congregation and the world at large.

McDougall presided over Janet Smith's burial in 1924, where he spoke of the need for justice for the dead Scottish woman. He also published a newspaper called the *Beacon* that echoed his calls for justice, attacked the credibility of Wong Foon Sing, the Chinese community generally and proclaimed the nobility of the white race. It was no surprise in 1926 when he came out in public support of the Ku Klux Klan in principle, and announced a plan to establish a Canadian-only Klan, separate and distinct from the Shaughnessy Heights American-led klavern. McDougall's proposal for a Canadian Klan initially appeared to be unaffiliated with the Ku Klux Klan of Canada based in Toronto, but that would change in the coming months.

McDougall was joined in his effort to launch a Canadian-led klavern by Alfred John England, the editor of the *Leader-Advocate,* a suburban Vancouver newspaper ("A Weekly Paper For A Waking Community" according to the masthead). England lived on East Twelfth Street, an easy walk to McDougall's Highland Church on East Eleventh Street. The trio of McDougall, Batzold and England set out — successfully — "to rid the local Ku Klux Klan of its American associations."[54] In the course of doing so, the local Vancouver organization reached out to the "official" Canadian Klan in Toronto.

McDougall and his colleagues were successful in Canadianizing the Vancouver operation due to the problems that Luther Powell brought down on himself. A few weeks after the colourful opening of the imperial palace in Shaughnessy Heights in October 1925, Luther Powell tried to re-enter the country from Seattle at the White Rock border crossing post. He told Canadian border officers he was a salesman. He was refused entry in the absence of proof that he had a legitimate reason to be in the country. The major retreated to Blaine, Washington, and launched an appeal.

The major's reputation was an obstacle to his effort to get back into Canada. "Powell is devoid of common decency and can do nothing but harm in the place of my birth," wrote Dr. Martin G. Dunlevy to the superintendent of the British Columbia Provincial Police in November 1925. Dunlevy was born in Victoria and practiced medicine in Portland, Oregon, where he had seen the Klan in action. Dunlevy was alarmed by Powell's move into British Columbia:

> *This rascal is well known in Oregon. This scheme is to try and get as much money as he can by organizing the Ku Klux Klan. They worked Oregon out, and when the field became too tame for them now seek their work of destruction in BC. Powell and his followers caused trouble in Oregon and injured our State to the extent that it will take years to regain Oregon's good name.*[55]

Powell's followers on the Lower Mainland organized a protest meeting at the Hotel Vancouver to pressure the Canadian authorities. Klan members who attended had to find seats amidst the "small army" of RCMP, Vancouver Police Service, British Columbia Provincial Police and Canadian Pacific Railway Police officers assigned to monitor proceedings. Also in attendance were hecklers who drew attention to the fact that only one of the attending Klan members was Canadian — the rest were Americans.[56] While it is doubtful that the protest meeting had much influence on immigration officials, his appeal resulted in Powell being granted entry to Canada for one month.[57]

During this one-month sojourn in Vancouver in early 1926, Powell ran afoul of the local Klan leaders — Batzold, McDougall, England — who had set out to purge the local klavern of Americans who were clearly more trouble than not. Powell upped the stakes by moving to Victoria, the provincial capital, where he tried to start up a women's branch of the Klan. Again, his personality got in the way of success when he clashed with the local Canadian leadership there, now firmly in the hands of Clem Davies and Wallace Laycock. At this point he disappeared from Victoria, from Vancouver and from Canadian jurisdiction entirely, returning to the United States along with Keith Allen.

With the departure of Powell and his gang, Charles Batzold, Alfred England and Duncan McDougall became the faces of the rebranded Ku Klux Klan in Vancouver. England regularly made public speeches reminding the public of the inequities of the Janet Smith case and expressing indignation over the decline in public morals. However, the trio of McDougall, Batzold and England did not last more than a few months. "McDougall would eventually become estranged from Batzold and England after they scammed him in a false bond exchange, took over *The Beacon* while his wife was ill, and changed its name to *The Bisector*," wrote historian Harry McGrath.[58] The magazine was not widely distributed, but it had a core of followers, many of them McDougall's parishioners.

The *Bisector* featured a relentless series of articles about the supposed Oriental menace, the curse of narcotics, the glories of the white race and the virtues of the Ku Klux Klan. Most of the articles were signed by A.J. England. "White Protestants of Canada" were encouraged to unite with an unnamed aggressive organization "Which is Campaigning Against the Flooding of the Dominion of Canada with Alien Hordes." Those interested were invited to send inquiries to anonymous post office boxes across the country. Applicants were required to sign a statement that "I AM A LOYAL, WHITE, PROTESTANT CANADIAN CITIZEN AND WILL BETRAY NO CONFIDENCE." The average informed reader would understand that he or she was applying to join the Ku Klux Klan.

McDougall eventually managed to regain control of his magazine, at which point his "view of the activities of his erstwhile allies had radically altered. For instance, he reported on a meeting hosted by Batzold and England in which only six people were present."[59] All of which suggests that, notwithstanding Klan claims at the time of thousands of members on the Lower Mainland, the real numbers were modest at best and their influence difficult to assess. Batzold and England, though, were able to use their west coast positions to play a key role in the negotiations that led to a renewed national Ku Klux Klan.

# Chapter 5
# THE CANADIAN KNIGHTS (1926–27)

By the end of the summer of 1926, there were signs that the growth in the membership of the Ku Klux Klan of Canada could not last. *Saturday Night* magazine reported in October 1926 that KKK membership in the United States had dropped sharply in the past year and that Canadian membership was levelling off. According to *Saturday Night*, "This country does not possess so many easy marks as the United States and the supply is now pretty well exhausted. Thus the life of the Klan is more or less definitely limited."[1] This confident prediction of the Klan's early demise was premature.

There was no denying there were challenges for the racist organization. The first crack in Klan unity had come in mid-1925 when James Henry Hawkins headed off on his own, selling memberships across Ontario in the short-lived Knights of the Ku Klux Klan of the British Empire. The Barrie bombing in June 1926 had shaken the Klan's public image as a non-violent defender of Protestant interests in the face of a disciplined and cunning Catholic conspiracy. Then Jim Lord, the New Brunswick legislator and king kleagle, parted company from Charles Lewis Fowler, the American who had come north in 1925 to deliver Canada to the Ku Klux Klan. Local klaverns across Ontario and the Maritimes were left wondering at the spectacle of senior Klan officers engaged in bitter feuding.

James Henry Hawkins, who had gone home to Virginia, was repeatedly denounced in print over the course of 1926 by his former colleague Fowler. "Let us regard those who suggest division anywhere at anytime under any condition as enemies to our great cause," Fowler thundered in the Klan's news bulletin to members.[2] "ESCHEW PETTY JEALOUSIES and DIFFERENCES," he urged in capitals, a clear sign that all was not well in the invisible empire.

"Clannishness and secrecy" were the paths to solidarity and success for the Klan movement, Fowler assured his followers. He issued calls for enhanced security within the local klaverns to protect the names of members. Codes were created; passwords were shared sparingly. Leaders were reminded regularly about "the importance of practicing scrutiny with each other" to better protect the internal security of the secret society of racists.[3]

The aftermath of the Barrie bombing highlighted the problems at the national office. Jim Lord took the lead in dealing with Ontario authorities that summer and fall, meeting with the provincial attorney general and trying to regain public confidence. At that point, Charles Lewis Fowler issued a bizarre statement that he was retiring from the position of imperial kligrapp (or secretary) of the organization.

He pronounced himself proud of his role as "the father of the Ku Klux Klan in Canada." In a flowery statement to the membership, he called the Klan "the child of my heart's love."[4] It sounded like a farewell to Canada, except that he was apparently still living in Toronto. The remaining leadership figures, led by Jim Lord, took this as a sign to move forward without Fowler. An unsigned bulletin sent out on November 2, 1926, to regional Klan officers advised them that, in light of Fowler's message, they must attend to more pressing business in the organization.[5]

Survival was the most pressing issue of all. By early 1927, the Canadian Knights of the Ku Klux Klan had splintered into multiple competing factions across the country, all angling for recruits and associated membership fees. There was an increasingly dysfunctional British Columbia group. There were the remnants of James Henry Hawkins's Knights of the Ku Klux Klan of the British Empire, which still had a few branches in eastern Ontario, albeit loosely aligned with the Toronto office. There was a growing Saskatchewan Ku Klux Klan whose American leadership was intent on getting rich (discussed in the next chapter). And there were an unknown number of Alberta klaverns who had cut their ties with organizers in British Columbia.

In early December 1926, calls for a leadership conference that would choose an imperial wizard "who must be a native-born British subject" went out.[6] This would automatically exclude Fowler, Hawkins and any other Americans with Canadian aspirations. The interim national leadership led by Jim Lord called for a klonvocation — a meeting of the Klan's senior leadership council, the imperial kloncilium — for mid-January 1927.[7] The gathering would resolve outstanding issues; it would dispose of the American leaders, select new national leaders and most important, plan for the future.

The gathering was preceded by revelations about the organization's finances that would help seal the fate of Dr. Charles Lewis Fowler. Auditors reported that Fowler had received $3,670 in salary plus travelling expenses of $1,145.16 during 1926, a tidy sum drawn from the sale of memberships around the country. This followed an even more successful (for Fowler) year in 1925 — $5,785 in salary, $390.03 in travelling expenses and an advance of $368.72. In addition, the Klan's auditors found that Fowler and Joseph Ballons of Guelph were collecting money "that was never handed over to the Treasurer."[8]

The kloncilium met in Toronto on January 17 and 18, 1927. First order of business was to banish Fowler and Ballons from the Ku Klux Klan of Canada. While the kloncilium was meeting on College Street, several blocks away from the Klan offices in the Excelsior Building, Fowler apparently visited the headquarters and took away "supplies," according to a later Klan report. The new leadership promptly ordered the locks changed and a new set of keys for the staff.[9] For his part, Fowler responded to his expulsion by denouncing the kloncilium as having no effect or authority. All Klan correspondence, he instructed, should be sent to him care of a Toronto post office box.[10] At this point, it was unclear if Fowler was even in the country. Seven months later it was reported that Fowler was out of Canada "for good."[11]

With the departure of the troublesome Americans, the field was clear for the next stage of the Ku Klux Klan's development in Canada. Negotiations to unite the disparate Canadian Klan organizations had begun in mid-1926 after Alf England, Charles Batzold and Duncan McDougall ousted Major Luther Powell from British Columbia. However, the talks to unify the Canadian Klan groups apparently included the American national Klan leadership. Alf England was interviewed by Hiram Evans, the imperial wizard who had replaced Klan founder William Simmons a few years earlier.

The Klan leadership in Vancouver had come into the hands of Batzold and England just as criminal charges arising from Harry Humble's Alberta Klan operation were brought forward in 1927. Luther Powell and Keith Allen were long gone from Canada by then, leaving Batzold and England as the only officers remaining in the Vancouver Klan office to answer for the money that had gone missing in Alberta. Although Batzold and England were briefly arrested and charged with obtaining money under false pretences, the charges were dropped in January 1929 for lack of evidence. The following year Rev. McDougall left for Alberta.

As these events were unfolding in Vancouver, a delegation from the American Klan Headquarters met with Jim Lord and Alf England in Toronto on October 22, 1927, to finalize the formal arrangements for the revived Canadian operation. The new Canadian Knights of the Ku Klux Klan would be governed by a new national organizational structure that would emphasize its Canadian nature and provide deniability in the event the sordid nature of its American past was raised.

The national structure, however, was still patchy. Alberta klaverns left over from the days of Harry Humble existed mostly in name only. Saskatchewan klaverns were reeling from the disappearance of leader Pat Emmons and his associates in September 1927. The Ku Klux Klan in Saskatchewan, relaunched later in the fall of 1927, made a point of denying all links with the national organization, a not unexpected position given the leading role James Henry Hawkins would assume in Saskatchewan.

The new leadership of the Canadian Knights was a careful mix of regional players as befitted an organization in the throes of balancing a range of diverse interests — provincial, financial and even theological. George Marshall of Belleville, Ontario, the hitherto obscure clergyman notable for trying to get a Catholic pressman fired from the local newspaper, emerged as the Eastern Canada Director. Charles Batzold, the Vancouver pastor and British Israelite, was the Western Canada Director. Jim Lord of New Brunswick, MLA, was notionally the national secretary (i.e., imperial scribe or kligrapp) and Alfred England was the national vice-president.

Charles Lewis Fowler, the ousted imperial wizard of the Ku Klux Klan of Canada, slipped out of the country sometime in early 1927. He returned to New York City where he turned his hand to radio programming at station

WHAP, an outlet known for its isolationist stance during the 1930s. The station's ownership was ideologically committed to avoiding foreign entanglements and leaving the world to deal with Nazi Germany without American involvement. Fowler launched a religious newspaper called the *Kingdom Messenger* and kept a low profile during the war years. In the late 1940s he shifted his operations to St. Petersburg, Florida.[12]

In his new capacity as imperial klaliff, Alf England published a warning about James Henry Hawkins in a display ad in the *Winnipeg Tribune* in late December 1927. "The public is hereby warned that attempts to organize a Klan movement in Manitoba or elsewhere by J.H. Hawkins, a person banished successively from the Klans of the United States and Canada, or any of his agents, are neither authorized nor recognized," intoned the imperial klaliff.

Hawkins was in full flight in Saskatchewan by this time, boosting membership sales and creating a public profile that would serve him well for the first half of 1928. With this notice, though, Hawkins was publicly warned against trying to launch a recruiting drive in neighbouring Manitoba. Daniel Carlyle Grant, a kleagle from Moose Jaw, Saskatchewan, had tried to move into Winnipeg in the early summer of 1926 and failed. He would try again in October 1928, after Hawkins's deportation, this time with modest results. Winnipeg would remain largely unwelcoming to the Ku Klux Klan for another half century.

Meanwhile, the message to aspiring Ku Klux Klan organizers was clear. A new Canadians-only organization was now in charge with some unique Canadian features. The leadership was resolutely Canadian, as required by the 1927 kloncilium. That said, Klan organizations already established in Saskatchewan and Alberta would operate as independent, non-affiliated organizations with long-term hopes that they would rejoin the pan-Canadian Klan.

For a long time, the identity of the head of the Knights of the Ku Klux Klan of Canada was a secret. But eventually, the name leaked out. Dirty Jim Lord, the New Brunswick MLA, was more than the national secretary; he was the imperial wizard of the Ku Klux Klan, presiding over a reinvigorated organization with bright prospects in defiance of the predictions by *Saturday Night* magazine.

The summer of 1927, with the new national leadership in place, saw increased activity across the country. The formation of five new klaverns in

Nova Scotia was announced in June. This followed earlier cases of cross burnings on the lawn of Mount Saint Vincent convent of the Sisters of Charity on a prominent site overlooking the Bedford Basin and at St. John the Baptist Roman Catholic Church at Melville Cove near Halifax.[13] The overall number of Klan members in New Brunswick and Nova Scotia remained unknown, but rallies and initiation ceremonies attracted hundreds of participants and spectators. In Nova Scotia in particular, the secrecy required by the Klan protected its activities from the surviving historical record.

* * *

That same summer, a large open-air Klan demonstration in June in Brockville, Ontario, was followed by an even bigger gathering of 25,000 people at the end of July in Kingston. "All White Gentile Protestants Are Cordially Invited to be Present," beckoned the advertising in the *Kingston Whig-Standard*.[14] A cross was burned at Bracken's Grove just outside the Kingston city limits and thirty-five new members were initiated.[15] The event attracted visitors from new klaverns across eastern Ontario and upstate New York. A crowd of thousands watched a parade of some two hundred fully robed Klan members in St. Thomas, just south of London, in early September. The chairman of the proceedings was John Hothersall from London, who was identified as the grand kleagle of Western Ontario. The event pulled in Klan members from across southern Ontario and the state of Michigan. The parade was noteworthy because participants left their faces unmasked as they marched to Pinafore Park.[16]

In late October 1927, a cross was burned on a vacant lot in west-central Ottawa, a few weeks after rumours flew of a klavern being organized in the national capital.[17] A klavern was clearly active in the city, but it was rarely seen or heard of over the next year. Eighteen months later though, Mayor Arthur Ellis received a typewritten, unsigned letter on embossed Klan stationary. It warned that a proposal for ward redistribution must give "proper aldermanic representation to the progressive and rapidly growing Protestant wards of Ottawa."[18] The mayor was dismissive. "I really had doubts that any Canadian was foolish enough to belong to an organization such as this," he told reporters.

*Three American Ku Klux Klan organizers, Keith Allen, R.G. Wallace and Luther Powell, hold the Union Jack outside the Vancouver headquarters of the Ku Klux Klan of Canada in November 1925.*

*Luther Powell, leader of the Ku Klux Klan of Kanada, salutes the camera outside the group's Vancouver headquarters in November 1925.*

*The Loyal Orange Lodge dominated politics for decades in Ontario, the Maritimes, the West and particularly the City of Toronto. The annual July 12 parade makes its way through downtown Toronto in 1924.*

*Ku Klux Klan riders from southern Ontario and Michigan parade through St. Thomas, Ontario, in early September 1927.*

*Ku Klux Klan members parade through St. Thomas, Ontario, in early September 1927. Unusually, the Klan members appeared in public with their faces unveiled.*

*A Ku Klux Klan parade in St. Thomas, Ontario, features a senior Klan official dressed in black robes and an American flag in the procession. The event in early September 1927 included Klan members from Michigan state and from across southern Ontario.*

*The district meeting of women members of the Ku Klux Klan circa 1930 near Desoronto, Ontario. Higher ranking members are wearing black.*

**Klansmen and Klanswomen at Provincial Field Day, Saturday**

Above is shown a group picture taken at Barker's Point Saturday afternoon, shortly before opening of Provincial Field Day of Order of Ku Klux Klan. The group was formed largely of male members of order, but a few women also are in the party. The Nashwaak River is at the rear of the party posing.

*A photo of a Ku Klux Klan gathering in Fredericton, New Brunswick, appearing in the* Daily Gleaner *newspaper on August 10, 1931.*

*Isabelle Jones and her mother enter the police court in Oakville, Ontario, on March 10, 1932. Isabelle and her fiancee, Ira Johnson, who the Klan mistakenly believed was Black, were threatened by a Ku Klux Klan mob from neighbouring Hamilton.*

*Klansman William Phillips, a Hamilton chiropractor, served a jail sentence for his role in threatening an Oakville, Ontario couple. Phillips is seen outside the Oakville police court at his trial on March 10, 1932.*

*Klansman Ernest Taylor, a Hamilton Methodist minister, was also charged in connection with the Oakville incident. Taylor is shown leaving the police court on March 10, 1932.*

*Klan members prepare six crosses for a rally at the Edmonton Exhibition Grounds in August 1932.*

BLAIRMORE
MAY 15, 32

MR PETERS

THE K.K.K. JUST
WANTS TO GIVE YOU
FAIR WARNING THAT
YOU ARE A MARKED
MAN. SO JUST WATCH
YOUR STEP. TAKE
OUR ADVICE AND
KEEP OUT OF SIGHT
OR THINGS MIGHT
HAPPEN

K.K.K.

*The KKK delivered this threatening letter in 1932 to a striking coal miner in Blairmore, Alberta. Ku Klux Klan symbols were painted on buildings to intimidate union members.*

*Supporters of Ku Klux Klan leader J.J. Maloney met in Edmonton's Memorial Hall in March 1932. The headline in his newspaper* The Liberator *suggests the meeting came as Maloney was criticizing the creation of a Catholic school district in Wainwright, Alberta. The white-haired man with glasses in the front row may be Dan Knott, who was elected mayor with Klan support later in the year.*

*Hooded Ku Klux Klan members astride hooded horses next to a cross near Belleville, Ontario, circa 1935. Their left hands are raised in salute.*

*Two members of Ku Klux Klan Hastings Club #3 on horseback next to a cross near Belleville, Ontario, circa 1935. Hastings Club #3 was active from about 1925 to 1936.*

*Ray Snelgrove (far right) was a well-known Ku Klux Klan organizer in Saskatchewan and Alberta. He was also an officer with a railway union. He is shown at a banquet of the Brotherhood of Railwaymen in Edmonton in 1949.*

# Chapter 6
# MOOSE JAW MOMENT

The epicentre of Klan activities in Saskatchewan in 1926 was Moose Jaw. Travellers arrived in town via the Canadian Pacific Railway main line from Toronto, Winnipeg and Regina from the east and Calgary and Vancouver from the west. The Soo Line, direct from the Midwest rail hub in Chicago, met the CPR main line at Moose Jaw, making the city a major junction point for Canadian and American continental train travel. From the station, the great and the good and the greedy could fan out across the province and the Prairies.

Stepping off the train, travellers passed through the prairie-modern style Canadian Pacific Railway Station with its new clock tower. All manner of itinerants passed through Moose Jaw during these years — harvest labourers, newly arrived settlers, commercial salesmen, investors, politicians, Canadians, Americans, citizens of the world. When newcomers ventured outside, they faced north towards Main Street where the city's stores, commercial buildings and offices lined the sidewalk. The easy choice was to walk straight up Main Street to see the sights.

The intersection at the corner of Main and River Streets called for choices. Main Street beckoned with more of the same prosperous but boring commercial activity. But to the east on River Street were a series of bars, restaurants and gaming houses with much to sustain the weary traveller. And to the west were similar River Street establishments, with the brothels tending to cluster at the very end of the road, away from public view. Many of the businesses on River Street had Chinese owners, which immediately rendered them both exotic and suspect in the public's mind. Their cafes and restaurants were considered opium dens or gambling houses or worse. Hotels on the disreputable end of River Street were deemed brothels even when they weren't. Moose Jaw's hustle and bustle was an ideal launching point for Ku Klux Klan organizers in 1926 as they stepped into its promising, sleazy streetscape.

The city of Moose Jaw was "part rounder and part evangelist" in the words of historians John Larsen and Maurice Richard Libby.[1] A rounder in the language of the times was a person who frequented bars, brothels and jail cells; evangelists claimed to exemplify the highest moral standards as they travelled the continent bringing Christians closer to their God. The Klan had a proven record of thriving in these conditions. On the one hand, the Klan appealed to religious leaders and upstanding citizens to help lift public morality, smite rum-runners, brothel keepers and crooked politicians all while advancing a robust form of white, Anglo-Saxon Protestantism. On the other hand, Klan leaders indulged in false pretences, larceny, hypocrisy and dubious politics both in the city and around the province. Moose Jaw offered an ideal base for the Ku Klux Klan in Saskatchewan.

The city was well-positioned to take advantage of illicit pursuits. During the Prohibition years of the 1920s, Moose Jaw was close enough to the American border for bootleggers to run fast cars filled with whisky across the border to thirsty American customers in North Dakota. Gambling houses ran twenty-four hours a day along River Street. The brothels were a five-minute walk from the railway station. With fifteen theatres and movie houses, some two dozen places of religious worship and the distractions of River Street, the city offered a wide range of entertainments for all, and the Klan found friends, rivals and potential suckers on every corner.

The point man for the Klan in Saskatchewan was Pat Emmons of South Bend, Indiana.[2] Emmons was the exalted cyclops of the five-thousand-strong local Klan chapter in South Bend, a centre of viral Klan activity in a state known for its virulent and robust Klan membership. Emmons worked the production line at the Singer Sewing Machine factory in South Bend before moving on to the Studebaker car assembly line, the largest such plant in the United States at the time. He appeared in city churches as a sometime evangelist preaching the hot gospel of 1920s America.

The showmanship of evangelism gave him the skills to shine in local Klan circles. A move into the city's Klan leadership saw him exercise significant influence in political contests ranging from local elections up to the United States Senate. A modest salary as klavern leader gave him the financial flexibility to leave the Studebaker plant to work full-time for the local klavern. In this role, he got up to various kinds of mischief.

The klavern's membership began questioning how Emmons was managing Klan funds. There was a major discrepancy — about $6,000 — between what Emmons said was the cost of the Klan's purchase of some property and the real cost. Then a U.S. congressional travelling committee inquiring into the KKK called him as a witness. He spent weeks testifying before the committee, whose primary interest was allegations of corrupt Klan influence on American politics.[3] The Klan exercised enormous influence on state elections in Arkansas, Oregon, Maine and elsewhere, claiming credit for helping to elect candidates to office. There were well-founded allegations of Klan support — and intimidation — in electing senators and members of the House of Representatives in the United States Congress.

Indiana was a state where the Klan held such sway. The U.S. Congress took an interest in the Klan's political activities, and Emmons was persuaded, or pushed, into helping with their inquiries.

Emmons passed through this rough patch with dimming options both for him personally and the Indiana Klan generally. David Stephenson, the charismatic leader of the Indiana Klan, was convicted in 1925 of the rape and murder of a young woman. After that, the organization began a slow decline. For Emmons, the implications were serious. The national Klan organization was unhappy with him, the local membership didn't trust him and he couldn't get his old job back at the Studebaker plant. Lewis Scott, another South Bend Klan leader, had an idea for Emmons.

Scott had somehow wrangled an appointment as king kleagle, or lead recruiter, for far-off Saskatchewan on the Canadian Prairies. The link may well have been Charles Lewis Fowler, who by mid-1926 was well set up in Toronto controlling the Canadian Knights of the Ku Klux Klan. Fowler had lectured widely in Indiana a few years before and likely knew Scott and possibly Emmons. He certainly knew the now-disgraced David Stephenson, who was his fellow officer in the Twentieth Century Motion Picture

Company. Fowler may also have been alert to the new opportunities available in the Canadian west as a result of travels there by his new associates Jim Lord and Otho Elliott.

In the early fall of 1926, Scott suggested Emmons come with him to Saskatchewan to set up a new organization and help sell the Klan on the Prairies. In his mind, this was a chance to create a Klan free of the violent reputation of its American parent. There was also the promise of distance — far from the troubles of South Bend — and the chance to make money in an untapped market. Emmons checked with his family, and then set off to Saskatchewan with Scott and a younger man, Harold, said to be Scott's son.

Lewis and Harold Scott stayed in the provincial capital of Regina, but Emmons pushed on a further sixty kilometres west to Moose Jaw where, in November, he set up shop in the five-storey Empress Hotel in the heart of River Street West. Along the road from Indiana, Emmons changed his name to Emory, in part to distance himself from the notoriety of the American Ku Klux Klan. It also gave him a convenient alias far from the questions lingering in the air of South Bend.

He was not the first Klan organizer in Saskatchewan. The ubiquitous Jim Lord had already toured the province in May 1926 as part of a western tour that included Winnipeg, Regina, Edmonton and Vancouver.[4] Premier Jimmy Gardiner, the powerful Liberal Party leader of the provincial government, was informed of his passage, although some of the details were muddled.[5] "A friend from his youth had told him to watch out for one J.S. Lord, a Conservative member of the New Brunswick legislature who, travelling west as an organizer for a Bible students' league, was also organizing for the Klan."[6]

A similar tour was undertaken about the same time by Rev. Otho Elliott, the Toronto clergyman taken to court by J.H. Hawkins along with Fowler, Cowan and others who had launched the Klan in Ontario in 1925. Elliott in turn had denounced Hawkins to the Klan's governing body for financial improprieties. In light of the Klan presence in British Columbia and Alberta in 1925–26, these visits to Saskatchewan may have been scouting expeditions to test the climate for recruitment in the province.

The conditions they found suggested Saskatchewan was another market ripe for exploitation by the Klan, which prided itself on taking advantage of local resentments to set up klaverns. Immigration in particular was a sensitive topic in Saskatchewan, where the proportion of people with British origins dropped from 54.7 per cent in 1911 to 47.5 per cent in 1931. During the same period, the proportion of people with European origins increased from 14.8 per cent to 20 per cent.[7] The remaining demographic was French-Canadians, Métis and Indigenous peoples.

An old way of life dominated by British/English Canadian settlers was seen to be slipping away in the face of a wave of immigration. Social historian James Gray put it this way: "To the British of western Canada, as elsewhere, the people of the world were divided into two groups — those who spoke English and those who did not. Which was to say, those with a high order of intelligence and those of demonstrably low levels of intelligence."

The implications went even further. "Not only was inability to speak English proof of downright stupidity, it was also regarded as bordering on sedition."[8] Immigration also put pressures on the schools where English was supposed to be the language of instruction. In districts with French-Canadian or Catholic populations, there was concern that the English language was losing its dominant place in the schools.

The Saskatchewan Liberal Party under Jimmy Gardiner found much of its support among farmers, recent arrivals and francophones. The provincial Conservative Party, which emerged from the political confusion of the Progressive and United Farmers movements after the First World War, claimed the role of defenders of British identity and English-language education rights.

The Conservatives also benefited from the strong presence of the Orange Lodge in the province. As in other provinces, members of the Orange Lodge could be counted on to support measures that promoted "British interests" in opposition to the Catholic Church, the French language and the supposedly negative influences of Quebec. By 1920, Saskatchewan had more than 230 local Orange Lodges across the province. Only the province of Ontario had more. Howard Palmer wrote that the Orange Lodge and the Klan "regarded Catholics not only as members of an idolatrous church, but as citizens who placed devotion to the Vatican above their devotion to the Crown."[9] The scene was set for suspicion and acrimony.

After his arrival in Moose Jaw in November 1926, Pat Emmons launched himself straight into organizing. He primed the recruiting pump with some

800 free Klan memberships (including free memberships for the Moose Jaw clergy) and signed up 1,400 paying members within weeks. It was unclear which Klan organization Emmons was selling for, but later evidence suggested there was some link with the Canadian head office in Toronto — or at least with Dr. Charles Lewis Fowler. It was also clear that any cash that came in from selling memberships stayed with Emmons himself. He had previously used the tactic of handing out free memberships in South Bend to bring in new Klan members. It was a clever strategy. The Klan could present itself as an ally of the established churches, who were opposed to the goings-on of River Street; in turn, the clergy could point to the arrival in town of a new moral force whose goals and objectives coincided with those of right-thinking Protestants.

One of Emmons's early recruits was optometrist Fred Ivay, who in due course became the exalted cyclops of the Moose Jaw Klan. Another was Sam Hamilton, a city alderman who had served as mayor in 1919 and would be mayor again over the course of his career. Hamilton's first time as mayor ended abruptly with his resignation over a jurisdictional dispute with the city commissioner. In 1920, again sitting as mayor after winning re-election, he punched an alderman during a heated argument over gambling. Hamilton pleaded guilty to assault and was fined five dollars.

Chris Higginbotham, a veteran Saskatchewan journalist working in Moose Jaw at the time of the Klan invasion, watched with interest as the recruiting campaign barrelled ahead. "Emmons was a first-rate salesman," he wrote. "Round-faced, with double chins, he exuded sincerity and good will and rarely stopped talking."[10] Emmons was good at what he did, even if the ideological commitment of new recruits remained a question mark.

> *A prosperous and broad-minded Moose Jaw businessman told me how he was hooked by Emmons: "He came into my office and told me he was organizing a Christian foundation which would get rid of River Street and help business. I don't remember whether he once mentioned the Klan, but he talked and talked. I told him I was busy. He beamed and went right on. Finally, I offered five dollars. He told me the membership was thirteen dollars. I gave him ten dollars and showed him to the door."*

With sales booming, Emmons hired a full-time employee, twenty-three-year-old Charles Puckering, the son of a local businessman. Puckering in due course became a featured Klan lecturer at rallies in Saskatchewan, Alberta and Manitoba, collecting fees and a salary for his presentations. After his career with the Klan, Puckering served as secretary of the Regina Board of Trade, a Moose Jaw city alderman and manager of a local milling company. In the late 1930s, he was talked of as a potential Conservative Party candidate for the provincial legislature, but nothing came of it.[11]

The two-room suite at the Empress (one of the rooms served as Emmons's sleeping quarters) became too small for the volume of business. Emmons, Puckering and two more employees moved over to the nearby Hammond Building from where the Klan really seized a hold on the life of the province. One of the new staffers was John Van Dyk, a former Moose Jaw police officer, who was initially hired to be a secretary. He had no talent for the work. He was kept on as a general factotum cum security guard.[12]

The financial basis on which Emmons and the Scotts had been drawn to Saskatchewan became increasingly untenable. A Klan membership cost $10 plus $3 for the first three months with a quarterly payment of $3 to stay in good standing. Under his initial deal with Lewis Scott, Emmons kept $8 and sent the balance to Scott, who was organizing in Regina. Of the $8 he retained, Emmons had to pay for his office and hotel costs plus the salaries of his employees. As winter turned to spring in 1927, Emmons became discouraged with his prospects. He wanted a better financial deal from Scott. Then Emmons disappeared from town as part of a pressure play.

As Chris Higginbotham recalled, "A friendly railway conductor working on the Soo Line dashed into our newspaper office full of news. 'What do you think?' he said. 'That son-of-a-bitch Emmons has done a bunk.' The conductor had picked up his one-way ticket to Grand Forks, North Dakota."[13] But the bargaining tactic worked. Negotiating from Grand Forks, Emmons struck a new deal with Scott and returned to Moose Jaw.

Emmons could keep the full $13 he received from a new Klansman until sales improved. In addition, he could have $2 for each new member he signed up outside of Moose Jaw. With these incentives in play, Emmons launched himself on a series of tours around the province. Moose Jaw remained his greatest triumph, where he claimed to have signed up some 2,200 members out of a population of about 20,000.

Elsewhere in the province, Emmons and the Scotts claimed to have sold almost 42,000 memberships to both men and women (the women paid a reduced fee of $6 each.) Over the course of his recruiting period in the province, Emmons took in almost $22,000, a serious amount of money at the time. Emmons himself claimed in 1927 that there were 46,500 Klan members in the province out of a population of about 900,000. The Klan was an unreliable source for membership numbers however; the more realistic figure was probably closer to 20–25,000. Still, this represented a significant bloc of voters in any provincial election. Premier Jimmy Gardiner took note of the Klan's growth.

The snowball that was Klan recruiting kept growing. On the late afternoon of June 7, 1927, the biggest Klan rally ever held in western Canada convened on the outskirts of Moose Jaw. An estimated 8,000 people were on site, drawn from across the province, as well as neighbouring Manitoba and Alberta. There were also visitors from the United States. A brass band accompanied some four hundred Klan members who came in by special train from Regina. An influx of more than a thousand cars created an unprecedented traffic jam in and around the streets of Moose Jaw.

Pat Emmons had put together a program that offered something for everybody in his new role as the king kleagle of Moose Jaw. Emmons led off the rally with an evangelical message exalting the Klan, its works and its closeness to God. Local clergyman Rev. T.J. Hind, soon to be a paid Klan kleagle, followed Emmons to the platform as dusk fell, giving his support and credibility to this great crusade.

The star of the evening then took the stage. American evangelist David Nygren had made the thirty-six-hour train ride up the twelve-hundred kilometre Soo Line from Chicago to be there. Nygren had a formidable reputation and following on the Baptist evangelical circuit. He may, in fact, have been brought in specifically by his fellow evangelist Pat Emmons to draw a crowd for the Klan's first major spectacle in Saskatchewan. Nygren was renowned for preaching in English and fluent Swedish, having been born in a Swedish town in Minnesota. He was dubbed the "Dynamite and Fire" evangelist. He usually made his appearances a two-night affair — the first night his theme was dynamite, the second night fire.[14]

He assured the massed thousands in Moose Jaw that the Klan was doing the lord's work. As it became dark, hooded Klansmen appeared carrying torches on the margins of the crowd. Then, a large cross on a hillside at the top of Caribou Street burst into flames. The blaze could be seen for many kilometres. The evening went off like an old-time gospel revival meeting with a dash of Klan drama to motivate membership sales.

A familiar theme emerged as the number of Klan members grew in the following weeks and months. Moose Jaw Klansmen began asking questions about how the local klavern was managed. Emmons had personal control over the group's finances, including three bank accounts. Under Klan practices, a local klavern did not assume control of its own affairs until a charter was issued by the national organization. Where, asked members, was the charter? Emmons responded that the charter would come when the klavern was so firmly established that it could operate without his presence. There was grumbling but nothing more.

By September, the local klavern members were again asking about the status of the long-promised charter that would give them control over their own affairs — particularly their fees. Emmons pledged the charter would be issued on September 15, but at that point membership would rise to twenty-five dollars. September 15 came and went, and so did Emmons and the Scotts. They abandoned Saskatchewan on September 17, taking as much money from Klan coffers as they could put their hands on. They disappeared across the American border leaving consternation behind.

The province's Klan leadership reeled, then thought about how to salvage a bad situation. The Regina klavern rode to the rescue. The Scotts had enjoyed considerable success in the provincial capital with their recruitment efforts. They had been able to muster more than four hundred followers, the brass band and the special train to bring them all to the great rally in Moose Jaw at the beginning of the summer. A sombre meeting was convened at Regina City Hall on October 4 to assess the damage and plan ahead. The exalted cyclops of the Regina Klan, Rev. William Surman of the Cameron Memorial Baptist Church, addressed the meeting on the subject of the crisis faced by the Saskatchewan Klan.

He was joined by a crowd-pleasing guest speaker, John Joseph Maloney of Ontario, freshly arrived in the province to fight the Liberals, the Catholic Church and popery in general. Maloney, a former Catholic seminarian, called for a revived Klan dedicated to stopping the Catholic menace that he saw standing by to take over the country. He cut a refined figure and his message was well-received by the hundreds of assembled Klansmen. The re-invigorated membership agreed to meet in Moose Jaw two weeks later to set a new course for the future.

The Moose Jaw rally in the familiar Stadium Rink saw more than a thousand Klan members forge a new model for how the Ku Klux Klan would henceforth do business in the province. The Saskatchewan Klan would be a stand-alone operation with no ties to the other Klan organizations operating in Canada or the United States. Recruiters would be paid straight salaries and expenses — no incentives to take the money and run. Robes and hoods would be worn only on ceremonial occasions. Otherwise members would operate in the open like other fraternal groups. And finally, the Saskatchewan Klan would obey the law, observe constitutional practice and, in the words of historian James Pitsula, keep Saskatchewan British. In practice, this meant an adherence to an idealized view of white, Anglo-Saxon superiority in the face of Catholic immigrants arriving from eastern Europe, French-speaking Quebecers teaching in the schools and the Roman Catholic Church in all its manifestations.

By the time J.J. Maloney appeared at the Regina city hall to speak in support of the Klan, the arc of his life had shifted many times. His appearance built on the foundations of an anti-Catholic crusade he had conducted through Ontario since his departure from the seminary. He wholeheartedly embraced the theology of British Israelism, which Maloney interpreted as providing "a common ground for all denominations and sects to unite upon."[15] His view of British Israelism became a theological cornerstone for his lectures. With his slicked-back hair and the formal evening wear he donned for speaking engagements, J.J. Maloney had created a public persona that he now placed at the service of the Ku Klux Klan.

Passionate in his hatred of "the Scarlet Woman" of the Catholic Church, Maloney had sided with the Conservative Party in the 1925 federal election. He preached against the perfidious influence of Catholic Quebec. He noted Liberal Party leader Mackenzie King's attempt to return to

Parliament via a 1926 byelection in the northern Saskatchewan riding of Prince Albert. Determined to play his part in defeating a man he regarded as a pawn of Rome (that is, held in thrall by perfidious Quebec and the Catholic Church), Maloney reported to audiences that he had made his way to Saskatchewan to support Conservative candidate D.L. Burgess in the struggle against King. The Conservative lost the election to Prime Minister King, leaving Maloney without a cause.

By the spring of 1927, Maloney had revived his old speaking career in Saskatchewan. He turned up at churches and Orange Lodge halls across the province, slashing into the Catholic Church and all who failed to see it for what it was in his mind. He toured the province, speaking often and everywhere. The meetings ranged from a few dozen people to hundreds. Some meetings went well, others did not. He later acknowledged he had accepted the help of Ku Klux Klan recruiter Ray Snelgrove to help organize his meetings.

A rally in Mazenod, where Maloney shared the stage with Kleagle Snelgrove, turned particularly rowdy. Luckily for Maloney, he had acquired a bodyguard in the person of Klan organizer Daniel Carlyle Grant, who shielded him from flying rocks as they exited the hall.[16] Maloney would emphatically say later he was not a Klan member during this period of his life in Saskatchewan, notwithstanding he had claimed a Klan membership in Ontario a few years earlier.

Taking his cue from Charles Lewis Fowler and other Klan leaders across North America, he supplemented his in-person speaking tours with an ill-fated radio program out of Saskatoon. And to round off the media onslaught, he launched a "trashy anti-Catholic sheet" called the *Freedman* that called down the wrath of a Protestant God on Catholics, the Roman Church and all their individual and collective works.

J.J. Maloney claimed full responsibility for reviving the Klan's fortunes in Saskatchewan.[17] The reality was that he shared the distinction of saving the Klan with James Henry Hawkins, late of the Ontario Klan, who appeared in the province in the fall of 1927, soon after Emmons and the Scotts absconded with the Klan treasury. Hawkins put on a memorable performance at his first Saskatchewan Klan meeting in the Regina City Hall, quoting poetry, praising his colleague J.J. Maloney and attacking Roman Catholics and the church in general. Hawkins established himself as a leading Klan spokesman in Saskatchewan, and he made a point of publicly calling himself a Klansman.

* * *

The RCMP Security Service took note of the Klan's arrival in Moose Jaw in 1927 but "the local Mountie was instructed not to investigate since it was being covered from Regina."[18] The early Security Service interest quickly waned with no further reporting from the RCMP either in Moose Jaw or in Regina. The real attention of the RCMP Security Service was focused on Communists, Socialists and fellow travellers who the RCMP believed were everywhere in the western provinces and posed the true threat to Canadian society.

Organizations like the Ku Klux Klan were simply not an RCMP priority during the 1920s. "It is also fair to say that right-wing organizations often espoused values similar to the official ideology of the force and ones much closer to those held by members of the Mounted Police," noted historian Steve Hewitt.[19] So policing the Klan was largely left to the Saskatchewan Provincial Police, with its obscure mandate, or local police, Moose Jaw being a good example of scant competence. And there was always the suspicion that police officers might have a set of Klan robes at home in the closet.

Harry Boyce, a corporal with the Saskatchewan Provincial Police, much like John Miller in the Ontario Provincial Police, was assigned to investigate what the Klan was up to in the province. "My task was to see if they were carrying guns, which of course was unlawful according to the *Criminal Code*," he recalled years later.[20] "They claimed they were in danger of violence themselves, and they were carrying concealed weapons for their own protection." It was an argument that Klan members would rely on over the years.

Boyce worked undercover attending Klan rallies and meetings. When J.J. Maloney spoke in Regina, Boyce was in the audience. "I remember him saying that when he died, he provided in his will that the skin be taken from his body and it would be placed on a bass drum so he would still be marching at the head of the parade. He was a real spellbinder."[21] Boyce claimed to know many men who belonged to both the Klan and the Conservative Party.

The skin drum story was a favourite of Klan speakers. Pat Emmons used it at the Moose Jaw rally of June 1927. The South Bend hot gospeller told the gathering he had been threatened by the villains of River Street intent on shutting down his morality campaign. "The River Street gang have threatened to murder me," he shared with the audience. "Let them do it," he cried. "Then I ask you brothers and sisters to skin my body and make it into a drum. Then beat the drum in River Street to the Glory of God and the Ku Klux Klan!"[22] The line ran well in the newspapers and church pulpits and evoked an image that stayed with listeners for decades.

Harry Boyce's work for the Saskatchewan Provincial Police was the exception when it came to police scrutiny of the growing Ku Klux Klan. This was due in large measure to the fractured nature of policing in the province. The RCMP ignored the Klan and its political implications. The Saskatchewan Provincial Police were tasked mainly to enforce the *Temperance Act* and the truancy laws, an odd mix of mandates. As a result, the SPP had few friends in the immigrant farming communities, where children often worked on the farm to the detriment of school attendance.

Local police forces chose to concern themselves with local matters that had immediate implications for public order. In Moose Jaw, the City Police had a reputation for lax enforcement of the law. In 1924, all of the uniformed officers were fired after being suspended, charged and convicted of running a break-and-enter operation looting city stores. By 1927, suspicions against Chief Walter Johnson reached the point where he was fired. Policing in Moose Jaw and around the province was inconsistent at best, and the Klan proved the point. The Moose Jaw police force under Chief Johnson's successor launched a vigorous enforcement campaign that targeted Chinese restaurants and gambling houses on River Street.

* * *

Left largely to their own devices, Klan organizers tended to base themselves in Moose Jaw and then fan out along the extensive railway network in the province. Moose Jaw was the centre of a thriving region that consisted of Swift Current, a city in its own right, 30 towns, 110 villages and 130 hamlets.[23] A kleagle could realistically start his day in "The Jaw," catch a train up or down one of the rail lines, peddle memberships in one of a dozen stops east, west or south of the city and be back on River Street by nightfall to enjoy the nightlife.

One itinerant kleagle was Daniel Carlyle Grant, who was described as "a political nomad."[24] Grant had multiple occupations. For his day job, he drove a Moose Jaw streetcar. But he was also a well-known spiritualist with a reputation for reading tea leaves. He worked off and on as a bodyguard and advance man for J.J Maloney in his speaking tours around the province.[25] Grant ventured into Manitoba to spread the Klan message, tracking down what the *Manitoba Free Press* called "$13 suckers," people who were prepared to pay that amount for a membership.[26] Manitoba was seen to be an untapped market since Colonel Harold Machin's luckless recruiting visit to Manitoba in early 1925.

Machin had quickly retreated back to his hometown of Kenora, perhaps realizing that this was a group with which he did not want to associate. Although Machin ran as a Liberal-Conservative candidate in the 1925 federal election, he was so ill he couldn't campaign and lost. Other recruiters followed with an equal lack of success. A foray into Winnipeg by an Oklahoma kleagle named J.R. Bellamy in the summer of 1924 had been a failure. As had a visit by R.G. Wallace, a kleagle from Oregon who went on to work in the Vancouver market. Grant thought he could do better.

* * *

Manitoba presented a very different picture than either Saskatchewan or Ontario. History weighed heavily on the province. Louis Riel, leader of the French-speaking Métis peoples, had set up a provisional government in Manitoba in late 1869. The government of Canada had recently acquired the Northwest Territories from the Hudson's Bay Company; the Indigenous provisional government was an attempt to defend local autonomy.

Political unrest followed as rival factions supported the provisional government or called for greater integration with the rest of Canada. A supporter of the so-called Canada faction, an Ontario Orangeman named Thomas Scott, was executed by firing squad after threatening to kill Riel. The resulting furor led by the Orange Lodge in Ontario saw a military expedition arrive in 1870 to occupy the land around what became the city of Winnipeg. Riel fled to the United States, only to return fifteen years later to lead another Métis government in Saskatchewan.

The legacy of 1870 was initially a strong French-language presence in the life and government of the new province of Manitoba. Within a couple of decades, however, the growing English-speaking population exerted increasing pressure on the French-speaking and Catholic communities. In 1890, a law was approved abolishing French as an official language of the province. Other measures followed to remove financial support for French-language public schools, culminating in 1916 with a ban on teaching French in public schools or on French being used as a language of instruction. Throughout this era, the Orange Lodge grew in the province, particularly in the area southwest of Winnipeg, and consistently supported anti-French and anti-Catholic measures.

But the city of Winnipeg was the key to the province. By the mid-1920s, more than a quarter of Manitoba's 700,000 residents lived in or near Winnipeg. The city's population had grown exponentially before and after the First World War. In addition to large French-speaking communities in Winnipeg and nearby St. Boniface, the city had developed dynamic and growing Ukrainian, German, Galician and Jewish immigrant populations. There was a powerful labour movement that played a key role in the 1919 General Strike, when the city divided along class lines. Finally, there was a dramatic difference between the richer and poorer neighbourhoods of Winnipeg.

Daniel Carlyle Grant's early efforts to introduce the Ku Klux Klan to Manitoba were as unsuccessful as those of his Klan predecessors. He set up shop in the southern Manitoba town of Brandon before reaching out to Winnipeg in the early summer of 1926. He called a public meeting on June 1, where he informed the assembly that the Roman Catholic Church controlled the country, Jews crucified Jesus and offered other remarkable if not credible insights about the state of the world. Grant believed the Klan had good prospects in Winnipeg but soon retreated to Saskatchewan to join the rapidly moving bandwagon driven by Emmons and the Scotts. If nothing else, the Klan in Saskatchewan provided him a steady salary while waiting for a better time to realize his Manitoba ambitions. Two years later, he returned to Brandon *en route* to Winnipeg.

During a ten-day period in mid-October of 1928, Grant stirred up a storm of publicity and pushback that ultimately led nowhere. With his headquarters at the Marlborough Hotel on Portage Avenue, Grant advertised a Klan meeting for October 16 at the Norman Dance Hall on Sherbrooke Street. Backed by fellow Klansmen Charles Puckering (Pat Emmons's former assistant in Moose Jaw) and Andrew Wright, Grant promised the audience of one hundred and fifty people that the Klan was ready to work in Winnipeg the miracle it had brought to Moose Jaw — eliminating vice, wantonness, graft and corruption. "We'll clean up Winnipeg," he pledged. As a bonus, he assured the crowd that the Klan was solidly opposed to Negroes, Jews and the eastern European Catholics, "the scum of Papist Europe" in his words, that the federal government was allowing to flood the country.[27] He was presumably referring to the large local immigrant population. In follow-up newspaper interviews, he attacked the Winnipeg police for slack enforcement of the law and the insidious influence of the Catholic Church. He promised to hold a meeting in the neighbouring Catholic, French-speaking community of St. Boniface.

The Winnipeg and St. Boniface police chiefs rejected Grant's allegations and warned against any meetings in St. Boniface. Monseigneur Wilfred Jubenville of the St. Boniface Cathedral warned him not to come to town. He did anyway, holding two meetings there in the following days. Grant assured the forty-five audience members at one meeting that the Klan was not "anti-kikes, coons, or Catholics," not a very reassuring message for any of these groups. As his meetings continued, the opposition against the Klan mounted in Winnipeg. Newspapers rejected his calls to divisiveness. Labour leaders wrote public letters where Grant's words were described "as of such a nature as to fill every decent citizen with disgust."[28]

While many white, Anglo-Saxon Manitobans may have privately sympathized with Grant's opinions, most weren't prepared to be publicly affiliated with the Klan's unsavoury reputation. With his meetings drawing smaller and smaller crowds, Grant quietly left Winnipeg later in the month. He travelled through the province's small towns to sign up new members before returning to Saskatchewan and the political struggle underway there. He left behind at least five klaverns in the province who sent delegates to a Saskatchewan Klan convention in Saskatoon in January 1929.

Grant also left an unexpected legacy in Winnipeg in the person of William Whittaker, an English immigrant who was identified in the mid-1930s by local Jewish leaders as a former Klan member.[29] By then, Whittaker had established the Canadian Nationalist Party, an authoritarian anti-Semitic organization that took its inspiration — as well as direction and probably money — from the German Nazi Party. The Canadian Nationalist Party was variously described as being "built along Ku Klux Klan lines" or, equally ominous, the brown-shirts of the German Nazi Party.[30] The Canadian Nationalist Party was moribund by the start of the Second World War, its ranks absorbed into Quebec fascist Adrien Arcand's movement.

# Chapter 7
# GETTING OUT THE VOTE (1928)

The Ku Klux Klan dominated the political life of Saskatchewan as January 1928 arrived. Premier Jimmy Gardiner recognized in the Klan and its organizers a significant threat to social peace and, even worse from his perspective, a threat to his government. The twenty months that followed were marked by events that eventually saw Gardiner's government thrown out of office and the Ku Klux Klan arguably achieve the high point of its political influence in Canada.

The year opened with two radio broadcasts by J.J. Maloney destined to give the Klan and Maloney the kind of publicity they craved. In early January 1928, he contracted with Saskatoon radio station CHUC to present two religious lectures on successive Sunday evenings. It's not clear who paid for the airtime, but it's clear that J.J. Maloney was the star performer.

The radio station was owned and managed by the so-called International Bible Students Association, the name at the time for the Jehovah's Witnesses religious sect. At this early stage in the development of Canadian broadcasting, religious groups could hold broadcasting licences under the licensing regulations of the federal Marine and Fisheries Department.

The Maloney broadcasts did not go well. He managed in the course of his lectures to "slander the Roman Catholic Church," according to station manager Walter Salter. This had been a feature of Maloney's public utterances for several months, but apparently it was the first time it happened during a radio broadcast. A member of the public complained to the RCMP, and they in turn referred the matter to Charles "C.P." Edwards, the formidable director of the radio branch of the marine department.

Charles Edwards was a pioneer of radio broadcasting in Canada who exercised considerable authority over who could and could not have a licence to operate a transmitter. Neither he nor his deputy minister, Alexander Johnstone, was a fan of religious groups having licences as they tended to create all kinds of problems with their religious followers and religious rivals. Edwards reported to his deputy minister in January 1928 on the Saskatoon imbroglio and the Bible Students' involvement with the Ku Klux Klan programming. "Apparently they cater to this kind of broadcast," he sniffed in his memo to the DM.[1]

The minister of marine, Arthur Cardin, refused to renew CHUC and three other Bible Students' broadcasting licences in the spring when they came up for extension "because of complaints made by the listening public against the matter broadcast by these stations." The result was a political firestorm in Parliament, in which the Conservative opposition thundered that the government was threatening freedom of speech.

Thousands of people wrote to Minister Cardin, mostly from the west. J.J. Maloney seized on the cancelled licence controversy as evidence of the malevolent influence of the Catholic Church in Ottawa. The fact that Johnstone, Edwards and Cardin were all Catholics confirmed his views. He sent off a telegram to Prime Minister Mackenzie King on March 25, 1928, reporting that petitions with 200,000 names were circulating in Saskatchewan in support of CHUC. But the licences were not restored.

Another high-profile moment also came in January through a lurid and well-publicized criminal trial in Saskatoon where Maloney appeared as the victim. After his appearances at Klan events in September 1927, J.J. Maloney's speaking career had flourished with meetings across the province. On October 18, 1927, as his star rose in the Klan world, Maloney spoke at the Old Knox Church in Saskatoon, a building illuminated by an electric cross blazing red at the entrance. This was a recent feature at Klan rallies in American cities, now come to Saskatoon.[2]

The slurs flew as Maloney charged that Catholics owed their allegiance to the pope and not Canada. The Liberal Party, acting as an agent of the Roman Catholic Church, was flooding the Prairies with eastern European immigrants (who were also Catholics) intent on overwhelming Canada's British character. On and on went the invective against the Roman Catholic Church.

Enter Gerald Dealtry, film projectionist, labour agitator and editor/ publisher of the *Reporter*, a muckraking Saskatoon newspaper of uncertain journalistic standards. A few days after Maloney's meeting at the Old Knox Church in October, Gerald Dealtry had published an article in the *Reporter* about the event, describing the star of the show. Dealtry's characterizations of J.J. Maloney prompted the Crown attorney to file a charge of criminal libel, a legally obscure section of the *Criminal Code* with a potential penalty of jail time. The legal action may have had more to do with provincial politics and suspicions about Dealtry rather than any actual harm done to Maloney's reputation. The *Reporter* described the ex-seminarian in print as a "liar" and "a well-known hate breeder" who was "doing his best to enrich his empty pockets in this city by spreading his particular kind of putrid propaganda."[3] The article concluded: "The church of Rome probably did its best to make an educated gentleman out of the little beggar, but not even the Pope can be expected to make a silk purse out of a cow's ear." The Crown argued in court that a criminal charge was required because the alleged libels could lead to public unrest and violence.

Dealtry at the time was forty years old, working as a movie projectionist and an active member of the Saskatoon Trades and Labour Council. As a projectionist, he would have been familiar with the film *The Birth of A Nation* from its repeated showings in Saskatoon theatres during the 1920s. As a result, Dealtry probably already had a dim view of the Ku Klux Klan. Maloney's anti-Catholic rants merely confirmed that he was fronting for an organization that was up to no good.

The RCMP Security Service had monitored Dealtry's progress through the ranks of local social activists for some time.[4] Although he was a member of the local branch of the Communist Party of Canada, the party's leadership also viewed him with suspicion. He was described at a secret party meeting in August 1926 as "a reactionary trickster" who couldn't be trusted. The Communist Party was riddled with police informants, so suspicion and paranoia of one kind or another were common. The apparent absence of police sources in the Saskatchewan Ku Klux Klan points to how differently the police saw the nature of the security threat in the province.

The English-born Dealtry and another party member, Heff Bartholomew, co-edited a publication at the time called the *Furrow*. The paper was popular with farmers, particularly those in the Farmers Union, a group associated with the Communist Party. The party's problem with Dealtry was that it couldn't control either him or the editorial content printed in the *Furrow*. A plan was mounted to take over ownership of the *Furrow* and replace Dealtry with a man named Bartholomew, who was described by the RCMP as "the most effective Communist agitator now at work."

Dealtry ended up being editor and publisher of the *Reporter* and facing a criminal charge for allegedly libelling Maloney. The jury trial began in the Court of King's Bench in Saskatoon in January 1928. Crowds lined up at 6 a.m. to get a seat in the spectators' gallery. Dealtry was represented by local defence attorneys Harvey Hearn and Emmett Hall, the latter a rising young lawyer, member of the Catholic Knights of Columbus and future justice of the Supreme Court of Canada.[5]

The Crown was represented by James Bryant, a prominent Regina lawyer and vice-president of the Conservative Party, who had also represented many Klan members in and out of courts around the province. During jury selection, the Crown maintained that Maloney was not connected with the Klan and had never been an organizer, so there were no grounds to exclude Klan members from the jury. Despite challenges from the defence, Klan members were eventually admitted to the jury. The trial began.

The thirty-two-year-old Maloney was described by a reporter from the *Saskatoon Phoenix* as "a comparatively young man, with claims to good looks, and of neat attire."[6] Maloney testified he came to Saskatchewan on a lecture tour to earn money to study to become a Presbyterian minister, a claim that wasn't obvious in his activities. Why come to Saskatchewan? "As the result of overstrain and persecution, his physician had advised him to go west," reported the *Phoenix*. He was in the province, he testified, "on a pure motive and on the experience of my own heart." It was determined early on that Gerald Dealtry was an Anglican.

Maloney was asked about his experiences with the Catholic Church.[7] He shouted, he pointed accusing fingers, he denied all Dealtry's allegations of wrongdoing. He had never been a Klan member in Saskatchewan, he maintained. Harvey Hearn came at him in cross-examination. Had he ever tried to cash a bad cheque? Maloney replied he had an account with the Canadian Bank of Commerce. Hearn persisted. "Yes," yelled Maloney, "and I don't want any of your Jesuit tricks with me." Mr. Justice Donald Maclean called him to order. Maloney maintained he was and had been a victim of persecution. The judge told him to contain himself.

In summing up, James Bryant contended that the allegations made by Dealtry were false and intended to bring Maloney into public hatred, contempt and ridicule. Dealtry was, he said, "a person of an evil and wicked mind."[8] Harvey Hearn responded that the case was a trial of Canada's reputation for tolerance, citizenship, fairness and justice. The jury was challenged to find in Maloney's published works about the Catholic Church a single truthful sentence. Hearn was later lauded for "his slashing cross-examination and masterful speech to the jury."[9] The defence called no evidence. Mr. Justice Maclean's charge to the jury emphasized the nature of the Klan. If the Klan was as Dealtry described it, then Dealtry was right to warn the public about Maloney and his views: if the Klan was a respectable and law-abiding organization, then Maloney was in the right and Dealtry wrong.

The jury deliberated for ten and a half hours. Witnesses, counsel and court officials mingled while waiting for a verdict. "Maloney and Dealtry met several times in the afternoon and evening and greeted each other courteously," noted the reporter for the *Saskatoon Phoenix* newspaper. Finally, at 9:50 p.m., the jury sent word it was ready to come back to the courtroom. Dealtry entered the prisoner's box. "Few, if any, of the jurors looked to where Dealtry stood, an ill omen for the prisoner," reported the *Phoenix*. The jury found Dealtry guilty. The judge said he had been inclined to a prison sentence. Maloney, through his lawyer, asked that Dealtry not be punished harshly. Mr. Justice Maclean settled on a fine of two hundred dollars or three months in jail.

Maloney walked out of the Saskatoon courthouse a Klan hero while still maintaining that he was not a member of the Klan, a key point in his trial testimony and the Crown's case. Notably, the Klan advanced Maloney $916.26 to help cover his legal costs.[10]

In many ways, the Dealtry case showed the mood of the times and the state of politics in Saskatchewan. The prosecutor was closely connected to Klan members, a leading member of the provincial Conservative Party and an effective defender of Klan interests. The defence attorneys were both well-known members of the Catholic Church. The jury was riddled with self-acknowledged Klan members. The defendant Dealtry was a Communist Party member with a police intelligence file. The judge was a former leader of the Saskatchewan Conservative Party. Given all that, the outcome was hardly a surprise.

* * *

Jimmy Gardiner, the premier of Saskatchewan from 1926 to 1929, was everything Pat Emmons, J.J. Maloney and J.H. Hawkins were not. Gardiner was both a Liberal and a liberal, by the standards of the day. Born into a hard-scrabble family in rural southwestern Ontario, the future premier worked his way up and across the country from farm hand to teacher's college to an elected member of the Saskatchewan Legislative Assembly in 1912.

His teaching experience at a series of rural schools in Saskatchewan brought him into close contact with immigrants — Jews, Ukrainians, Poles, Germans, English. His most formative experience was as principal of the school at Lemberg, just east of Regina near Qu'Appelle. The community in turn supported him by sending him to the legislature as their local MLA. By the early 1920s, he had been appointed to cabinet as minister of highways and put in charge of the Liberal Party organization in the province. With the resignation of the sitting premier, Gardiner was elected Liberal leader in 1926, just as the Klan was beginning to organize in the province.

His formal political rival was James Anderson, the leader of the Saskatchewan Conservative Party, former director of education in the provincial government and a firm believer in the power of public schools to integrate newcomers into Canadian society. Like Conservatives in other provinces, Anderson was struggling to bring his party back from the damage inflicted on traditional party loyalties in the early 1920s by the Progressive Party. But Gardiner's political instincts told him that the Ku Klux Klan — probably in league with the Orange Lodge — was potentially a bigger threat to the Liberal Party than either the Conservatives or the Progressives.

Sensitive to the growing influence of the Klan with its anti-immigrant and anti-Catholic rhetoric, Premier Gardiner began building a file on the organization by the spring of 1927 as its membership swelled. As a biography about him recounted,

> *Gardiner, with his usual thoroughness, collected all the information on the Klan he could get, and actually sent a detective to Ontario, Michigan, and Indiana to gather data, including transcripts of court cases where Klan leaders who later showed up in Saskatchewan had been tried. He had copies of letters between Klansmen as well as dozens of typed pages listing the names of Klan members, and clippings from a variety of journals and newspapers.*[11]

By the following year, he was well versed in the organization and its activities and ready to take action.

The outcome of Gerald Dealtry's criminal libel trial added impetus to Jimmy Gardiner's campaign against the Ku Klux Klan, which could pose a potentially serious challenge in the upcoming election expected in the next year or so. Gardiner spoke to the provincial legislature in January 1928 to highlight the Klan's violent and lawless history in the United States. The speech drew support from minorities and the Catholic Church, but many citizens felt the premier might be ignoring what they saw as the problems associated with foreign immigration, even if they didn't agree with the Klan's methods, either historical or actual.

The premier launched an anti-Klan speaking tour that gave him a platform to espouse his views on the organization. Gardiner spared no effort to link the Ku Klux Klan to the Conservative Party, which he saw as his main rival in the next general election. James Henry Hawkins tracked the premier from meeting to meeting, occasionally heckling from the audience. The Klan organized its own series of meetings to denounce the premier and pledge the loyalty of the membership to peaceful political dissent. The Empire Day long weekend in May 1928 saw crosses burned in communities across Saskatchewan. At Melfort, as many as eight thousand people attended the local Klan gathering that weekend, with some twelve hundred cars parked in a field around the speakers' platform.

The premier's speaking tour and J.H. Hawkins's disruptive counter-tour took place against a backdrop of legal tactics targeting the Klan. These efforts had political fingerprints all over them. First, Pat Emmons was tracked down in Indiana in February 1928 and charged with stealing $1,313 from the Saskatchewan Klan. He was in court in Regina in early May 1928, brought back to Canada to face a range of charges based on information from a former employee in Moose Jaw.

During his testimony, Emmons told a tale of how the Klan organization had been snatched out of his hands by Conservative Party leader James Anderson, former Regina mayor Walter Cowan (who would be elected as a Conservative MP in 1930) and Dr. Robert Smith, a Moose Jaw physician who had replaced Sam Hamilton as mayor in 1921. Smith was subsequently elected as a Conservative to the Legislative Assembly in 1929. These men, said Emmons, were intent on using the Klan to start a religious war. Rather than stand by and see his Klan abused, he had left the province for a second time. Anderson denied in the press that he was a Klan member and refuted Emmons's allegations. Cowan, who was the treasurer of the provincial Ku Klux Klan, stayed silent.

The courtroom audience was packed with provincial Liberal Party officials as Judge J.H. Heffernan acquitted Emmons on the grounds that in removing Klan money from Saskatchewan in 1927 he had acted with the approval and authority of Charles Lewis Fowler from the Klan's national headquarters in Toronto. By then, Fowler had been ejected from his leadership role in the national Klan for misappropriating funds, so it's not clear on what basis Heffernan could have accepted Fowler's written evidence. Despite the acquittal, the magistrate took the opportunity to deliver a lecture condemning an American organization that had come to Canada "to pick the pockets of innocent men."

Barely out of court, Emmons was arrested again and charged with selling a Klan membership by means of fraud and false pretences. The case was heard in Moose Jaw in mid-May. Margaret Wilkinson of Moose Jaw accused him of accepting her $6.50 membership fee and promptly leaving the province with it. She had gone to a meeting where James Henry Hawkins spoke. She didn't agree with what he said, the fact that he was an American and that he would not swear allegiance to Canada. Magistrate L.S. Sifton found that while it was clear that many people had been cheated in the course of joining the Klan, it could not be held that Emmons had sold

Margaret Wilkinson a membership under false pretences. Again, Emmons was acquitted and walked free from the Moose Jaw courthouse.

Emmons was not done with Saskatchewan just yet. At the end of May 1928, as the premier and James Henry Hawkins trailed around the province hurling charges and counter-charges at each other, Emmons called a public meeting in Regina, where he promised to reveal all the Klan's secrets and his role in them.

The gathering was raucous. He had testified during his recent trial that Conservative leader James Anderson regularly met with Klan leaders to coordinate strategy. The Conservatives had denied it all, and the Klan's new leadership had attacked Emmons as a traitor with no credibility. References to events in the United States were shouted down. Klan members in the audience drowned out with howls any attempt to go into detail about the Klan's business. Emmons finally retired to the back of the hall and refused to carry on. But it made for great headlines, contributing to the public debate about the Klan's role and intentions.

The political debate about the Ku Klux Klan came to a head in Rosetown, southwest of Saskatoon, on June 15. J.H. Hawkins was in the audience at one of the premier's meetings. He launched into his usual disruptive tactics and challenged Gardiner to a public debate. The premier pulled out his appointment book and offered June 29 for a face-to-face debate. Hawkins accepted. After some skirmishing about where the event should be held and who would pay for the hall, it was agreed that the debate would be held in the premier's riding, in his own stronghold of Lemberg.

The spectacle promised high drama. Journalist Chris Higginbotham recalled how Hawkins could move an audience, citing one performance at a standing-room-only meeting in the Moose Jaw skating rink.

> *I was writing nothing because at that time we were instructed to write nothing unless all hell broke loose. Dr. Hawkins glanced down at the press table. "Look at him," he roared, "he's not taking down anything. He's in the pay of the Jews and Roman Catholics." The audience growled.*[12]

With such speaking flourishes from Hawkins, the pending face-off with Gardiner was expected to be full of political entertainment.

The night of the event in the Lemberg skating rink, an estimated fifteen hundred partisans of various stripes showed up. Conservatives, Liberals, Progressives, Klan members and agnostics filled the seats to view an epic debate. Hawkins led off, speaking for ninety minutes, refuting the premier's allegations about the Ku Klux Klan. The Saskatchewan Klan was free of American connections, said Hawkins, even if he was himself an American. He had broken with the U.S. Klan to maintain the independence of the Saskatchewan organization. He called for a province free of Roman Catholic influences and argued the Klan was non-partisan and certainly not aligned with the Conservative Party. In any event, a Liberal government that depended on the support of Roman Catholicism was not a government to be trusted.

The premier positioned himself and the government as protectors of Saskatchewan and its citizens from foreign intruders. The Klan had nothing to offer in terms of supporting the province's legal system — British justice worked just fine. The Klan's record of lawlessness in the United States spoke for itself. Further, the Klan in Canada and Saskatchewan comprised primarily a commercial endeavour intended to sell memberships and robes for the benefit of a few men. Then the premier launched into partisan politics. The Klan and the Conservative Party were in an alliance to defeat the Liberals, the protectors of the constitution and the rights of all Saskatchewan residents. The Liberal Party was dedicated to racial harmony — not something the Klan could legitimately claim or offer. The outcome of the debate was generally viewed as a tie.

The Klan continued to have encounters with the courts as the province moved closer to the highly anticipated election. A Klansman in Melville, Thomas Pakenham, was charged with illegal possession of a firearm. He was the town's former police chief, who had gone on to a salaried position as a recruiter for the Klan.[13] Pakenham argued he had a valid permit, was not carrying the gun when arrested, the gun was unloaded and, finally, there was no ammunition for it. Pakenham was initially convicted by a justice of the peace and sentenced to two months in jail and a fifty-dollar fine. The appeal judge dismissed the jail sentence and retained only the fine. His ruling, he instructed, was not to be interpreted as support for the Klan.

Another gun charge recalled the Klan's history of violence. Ray Snelgrove of Regina, a Canadian National Railways brakeman and paid Klan organizer, showed up in Lemberg to attend the Gardiner-Hawkins face off in the local arena. Snelgrove was six feet tall, a big man who had spent two years in the army during the First World War. He was diagnosed in France with the early stages of tuberculosis, was shipped home to Canada and recovered in the military hospital at Queen's University in Kingston, Ontario. He was there when the university expelled all of its Black medical students in 1918 after alleging complaints from military veterans.

Snelgrove was active in the Railway Trainmen's Brotherhood, eventually becoming secretary of the organization in the late 1940s. The union was a keen supporter of segregation in the railway industry, a position that earned it the enmity of Black railway porters, who were relegated to decades of stagnant, low-paying jobs.[14] White workers represented by Snelgrove's union fared well under the segregated system.

Snelgrove had parked his car and was walking towards the Lemberg hockey rink when an RCMP officer stopped him and asked if he was carrying a revolver. The forty-year-old Snelgrove led the officer to his nearby car and showed him a revolver in the trunk with four live rounds and one discharged cartridge in the cylinder. Snelgrove produced a permit for the weapon, but the officer was skeptical. The RCMP seized the gun, and Snelgrove was charged with having a concealed weapon.

Appearing in court a month later, the Crown produced evidence that the gun permit was invalid. The permit had been issued by acting Melville chief of police John Van Dyk before he was officially confirmed in the position. The permit was, as a result, invalid. This was the same John Van Dyk, the former Moose Jaw police officer, who had worked for Pat Emmons and the Klan. When Emmons fled the province in the fall of 1927, Van Dyk cooperated with the Saskatchewan attorney general's department and filed the charges against Emmons that led to his return to Regina to stand trial. Soon after, Van Dyk turned up as acting police chief in the town of Melville, possibly as a reward for his cooperation.

Snelgrove maintained that he had bought the gun for self-defence after being chased and threatened by drunken Roman Catholics. He offered no explanation for how he had acquired the gun permit from an ex-Klan employee. The appeal court reduced his sentence to a month in jail and a fifty-dollar fine. On release from jail, Snelgrove was paraded in celebration through the streets of Regina.

The legal onslaught against the Ku Klux Klan took down James Henry Hawkins, the itinerant Klan kleagle from Newport, Virginia, a few weeks after his confrontation with Jimmy Gardiner in Lemberg. On his previous visit to the United States, after leaving Ontario but before he arrived in Saskatchewan, Hawkins had been outside of Canada for 366 days. Immigration regulations allowed him an absence of only one year from Canada. The extra day away, the immigration department informed him, meant his immigration status was invalid, and he was ordered deported in July 1928. But not without a farewell tour through the heart of Saskatchewan's Klanlands. A rally in Regina gave him an audience of seven hundred, who heard him compare his treatment with that of former enemy aliens who were allowed to live in the province. The message was simple: old enemies were coddled; Hawkins was being persecuted.

Another rally in Moose Jaw the next night drew an audience of a thousand supporters. Hawkins took credit for instilling in Canadians a love of their country. Chris Higginbotham was there to report on Hawkins's last public appearance in Canada.

> *The unctuous voice was tremulous, the fine features were raised toward the rink ceiling. "My friends," he murmured, "they say they are throwing me out of Canada because I am not a Canadian. I love Canada with all my heart. What is more, what they are saying is only a half truth. Some years ago, I married the finest, sweetest woman in the world — a Canadian girl." (Loud applause until the good doctor waved for silence.) When the audience was quiet, he raised his arm once again. "They say I am not a Canadian. But see . . ." Down went his hand to the pocket in his coat-tails, and up came a large-sized Union Jack. The audience went mad.*[15]

The next morning a dozen supporters saw him onto the Soo Line train to Chicago and away to his home in Virginia and his wife Barbara, who was definitely not a "Canadian girl."

Meanwhile, the undeclared war between Jimmy Gardiner and the Liberal Party of Saskatchewan on one side and the Conservative Party and the Klan on the other became real in the Arm River byelection of October 1928. It was a large constituency between Saskatoon and Regina. J.H. Hawkins was gone, but the Klan and J.J. Maloney remained, and the byelection became a close-run affair. The incumbent Liberal had resigned to take a federal job in Ottawa, leaving the riding up for grabs.

The ensuing struggle between the Liberals and the Conservative Party, with strong Klan support, became a classic political battle. Jimmy Gardiner came in to speak on behalf of the Liberal candidate; future prime minister John Diefenbaker, a young lawyer then practising in Prince Albert, came to speak for the Conservative candidate. Religion featured prominently in the debates. Conservatives, with Klan support, said the Catholic Church was bent on taking over schools and the province generally. Gardiner accused the Klan of supporting the Conservatives in their attacks on races and religion. He rejected any endorsement by the Klan as an organization while welcoming the support of individual voters. This was a tacit acknowledgement that many Liberals had joined the Klan in spite of Gardiner's warnings.

Voter turnout on October 25 was near 90 per cent. The Liberal candidate won a mere fifty-nine-vote majority victory in a riding the Liberals had held with big margins since its creation twenty years before. Liberal organizers saw problems ahead in the next provincial election. Critics faulted the premier for coming down hard on the Klan, giving them prominence and a platform and dividing voters along religious lines. Better to have dealt with the Klan quietly, they said, and trust people to make the right choices.

The legal problems continued for the Klan's leadership. Following Pat Emmons's disappearance from Saskatchewan in the fall of 1927, Regina accountant John Rosborough had been selected as the new provincial imperial wizard. In addition to his Klan credentials, Rosborough was also a longtime member of the Orange Lodge. He was not the first choice to become imperial wizard. Walter Cowan, the former Regina mayor and a popular dentist in the city, had been the odds-on favourite until his close links to the Conservative Party were viewed as likely to pose a political problem. So Walter Cowan became the Klan treasurer for Saskatchewan instead.

In November 1928, after the Arm River byelection, Rosborough was charged with embezzling two hundred dollars from the municipality of Mountain View, where he was the accountant responsible for auditing the books. Testifying under oath at his trial, Rosborough said the provincial Attorney General had offered to drop the charge if he would agree to disband the Klan. Rosborough fought and won his case, and he was reelected the following spring to a two-year term as imperial wizard.

All of this was preparation for the provincial general election that was eventually called for June 6, 1929. The unexpected strength of the Klan had persuaded the Liberal Party and the premier to delay the election as long as possible. While the Liberals ran candidates in all ridings, the Conservative and Progressive parties coordinated their candidacies to avoid splitting the vote in ridings with narrow races. With the economy in good shape, the campaign revolved around issues that mattered to the Klan — immigration, education, language, the putative influence of Quebec and the Catholic church.

The Klan, whose name appeared nowhere on election ballots, loomed large in the minds of voters as they considered the issues and who spoke for them. The Klan and its speakers had succeeded in polarizing the election campaign around its issues. The Liberals repeatedly accused the Conservatives of Klan support; the Conservatives in turn accused the Liberals of ignoring the real issues. Platforms across the province rang with charges, accusations, slanders and vituperation.

The town of Biggar in the country southwest of Saskatoon was a regular stop on J.J. Maloney's tours around the province. William W. Miller, owner of Biggar's leading general store and grandmaster of the local Orange Lodge, was an enthusiastic Klan member. J.J. Maloney married William Miller's twenty-year-old daughter, Lenora Miller, in September 1929.[16] As it happened, the Miller family were cousins to Ontario premier Howard Ferguson, the Orangeman who shared some of Maloney's views about the Catholic Church.[17]

J.J. Maloney was not, however, universally welcomed in the Biggar district. A United Church minister, Horace Ranns, was a vocal public opponent. In the manner of James Henry Hawkins, Maloney challenged the clergyman to a public debate; Ranns refused. Maloney ranted and raged, calling Ranns "a yellow dog." Justifiably concerned, Ranns asked Premier

Gardiner for protection, calling Maloney "a menace to public safety" whose statements were offensive to Catholics. Ranns feared they were "boiling over and threatening reprisals." Open violence was a distinct possibility.

The town of Biggar and environs were awash in Orange Lodge rage, Ku Klux Klan recruiting and a tangible sense of threat to the Catholic community. Crosses were burned on the lawns of Catholics across the district that spring and early summer of 1929. The Mother Superior of the Sisters of the Assumption confessed her relief when fire escapes were installed on the new Catholic school outside Biggar. "We will now be less afraid of the local fanatics should they take a notion to set fire to our house," she wrote in her journal.[18]

The campaign for the June 6 provincial election was largely a retelling of the Arm River byelection story, but with mixed results. The Liberals won twenty-eight seats, nineteen of them in ridings where the demographics were largely non-British. The Conservatives took twenty-four seats, independents won six and the enfeebled Progressives were left with five seats. The Conservatives and the Progressives agreed to form a coalition government and called on the lieutenant-governor to convene the legislature so they could take office.

Jimmy Gardiner maintained he should stay in office until his government was defeated in a confidence vote. He managed to delay the return of the legislature until early September, when the Liberals were defeated on a confidence motion. Jimmy Gardiner left office, and Conservative Leader James Anderson, member of the Legislative Assembly for Saskatoon, became premier.

The historical verdict on the influence of the Ku Klux Klan in the 1929 election is firm. According to historian James Pitsula:

> *The Klan was the key to the election turnaround of 1929. The Klan shifted the mindset of the voters. It stirred up the issue of British national identity, especially with respect to the dangers of foreign immigration and sectarian influence on the public schools. The Conservative Party was the beneficiary, and it owed its victory to the Klan."*[19]

The new Conservative government began acting on its political program. Premier Anderson had consistently denied he was a Klansman, although he made up for it by belonging to the Orange Lodge and the Masons. His new government's directions reflected the oft-stated views of the Ku Klux Klan and the Orange Lodge. Religious symbols were banned in the public schools. French-language instruction was drastically curtailed. The importation of French-language teachers from Quebec was effectively ended by refusing to recognize their qualifications.

The political climate began to look and feel like some American states where Klan-supported governments came to office.[20] The Anderson government imposed the same conditions on French-language instruction in Saskatchewan that were imposed in Manitoba schools in the late nineteenth century. The early impact of the Depression, which placed severe demands and restrictions on provincial policies, authorities and actions may have been the reason that the repression of minorities in the province did not hit harder in the years to come. The province had bigger issues to deal with.

Maloney, newly-wed and intensely satisfied with the election outcome, waited for his reward from Anderson's Conservative government. And waited. And waited some more. Even Daniel Carlyle Grant, Maloney's old bodyguard, was given a provincial government job in Weyburn.[21] Maloney began to suspect the Conservatives had forgotten the debt they owed the Klan in general and him in particular. "What thanks did I get?" he demanded years later.[22] "I risked everything at times for a cause I regarded as sacred, yet when the Anderson government got into power, they forgot me. In their pride and conceit, they wanted to believe they did it all." Mostly, the Conservatives just wanted him to go away.

Maloney's father-in-law, William Miller, had been a successful Conservative Party candidate in the June general election. He became, in short order, an MLA and then bankrupt, thanks to Maloney. Local lore had it that Maloney borrowed money from the Royal Bank and William Miller backed his son-in-law's notes. Miller's business was hit hard in 1930 as the Depression bit into his general store revenues. Maloney didn't repay the loans. Miller couldn't make good on them, and the Miller general store was seized by the bank and sold to a competitor. Maloney left Biggar soon after, and his marriage to Lenora eventually collapsed.[23]

The key Klan players in western Canada dispersed. After his deportation from Saskatchewan in 1928, James Henry Hawkins disappeared into the American south and was not heard from again in Canada. He resumed his optometry practice in Virginia where the state's grand dragon, Joel Baskin, presided over a declining but still active membership through the 1930s. Baskin's hold on the Virginia Ku Klux Klan meant there was no place for an itinerant kleagle like Hawkins. He eventually moved to the city of Norfolk where he ran his optometry business out of a small house in the primarily white neighbourhood of Coronado. He died of a cerebral hemorrhage in April 1950.[24] Four years later, county and state police were called to a near-riot of white residents of Coronado when a Black real estate agent, William Love, began showing Hawkins's old house to potential Black buyers.[25]

Back in Canada, Hawkins's old nemesis, Premier Jimmy Gardiner, rebuilt the Saskatchewan Liberal Party during the early 1930s and was re-elected premier in 1934. A year later, he moved to federal politics and was named minister of agriculture in Prime Minister Mackenzie King's cabinet. He held the position for a remarkable twenty-two years, finally going down to defeat in 1957 when the Progressive Conservative Party with John Diefenbaker as national leader swept out the Liberals.

Gerald Dealtry, the gadfly publisher who tormented J.J. Maloney during his days in Saskatoon, met a brutal and mysterious end. By 1949, Dealtry had become secretary of the Saskatoon Trades and Labour Council, a high-profile role in the province's trade union movement. In early September of that year, his battered body was found under a Grand Trunk Railway bridge south of the city. Police speculated he had been the victim of a violent robbery. A few days before he disappeared, Dealtry had been seen carrying a large sum of money, the proceeds of the Labour Council's annual Labour Day picnic. A coroner's jury returned an open verdict on the circumstances of his death.[26] No arrests were ever made. By then, few remembered the spectacle of the criminal libel trial that marked J.J. Maloney's passage through Saskatchewan.

Daniel Carlyle Grant, the Klan worker rewarded by the Conservative Saskatchewan government in 1929 with a job in Weyburn, did not fare well as the Depression hit its depth. The new Liberal government fired him in 1934. Grant wanted revenge, and he sought it by working for Tommy Douglas, the firebrand candidate representing the Cooperative Commonwealth

Federation (CCF), a political formation that found Klan ideals abhorrent.

But Grant was creative, notably in persuading a car dealership to loan the Douglas campaign a silver Hudson Terraplane in return for future payment. The campaign used the car up to election day. Grant organized a raffle and sold tickets at campaign events that helped pay for the car. With Tommy Douglas elected, Grant reinforced his gadfly reputation by reverting right and joining the Saskatchewan Social Credit Party, a move into political oblivion from which he never returned.[27]

There was a footnote to the adversarial relationship between Jimmy Gardiner and J.J. Maloney. They met unexpectedly in the library at the legislature building early on in the term of the Anderson government. Maloney said he was there to see his father-in-law, newly elected MLA William Miller. Gardiner told him bluntly to get out. "An exchange of epithets followed," is how Maloney explained the incident to the *Regina Leader-Post*.[28] The shouting match between the two ended with Maloney leaving the legislature building and William Miller apologizing in the House for him being there at all.

There was nothing to hold J.J. Maloney in Saskatchewan after his marriage disintegrated. Ray Snelgrove, Saskatchewan's premier Klan organizer, offered a solution. Snelgrove had strayed out of the province at the invitation of Loyal Orange Lodge groups in neighbouring Alberta. He started making visits and speeches to groups in northern and central Alberta — Red Deer, Stettler, Vermilion and points between.

The Klan in Alberta had been moribund since the Harry Humble fiasco of a few years earlier. Snelgrove's message was well-received but his brusque public manner was not. The message needed a more compelling messenger. There was an opportunity waiting to be exploited. Who better than J.J. Maloney, out of sorts, out of favour and out of a marriage?

# Chapter 8
# ONTARIO BURNING (1929–30)

The Ku Klux Klan's presence in Ontario in the summer of 1929 was reminiscent of its peak popularity in 1926. In late June, a Klan initiation ceremony for new members was held on the eastern outskirts of Hamilton. A parade by several hundred Klan members in robes through city streets kicked off the proceedings. The familiar figure of Jim Lord was in the vanguard. He told reporters he was from Charlottetown, Prince Edward Island, not Charlotte County, New Brunswick. Four crosses lit up the night skies as a visible demonstration of Klan vitality in the city.[1]

Ray Lewis was a witness to the Klan's presence and prominence in Hamilton. About the time Jim Lord was initiating new Klan members in the city, Lewis's sister came home from her job at a local electrical company. She had been warned by a young white man working there as a janitor that the Klan was going to fire a cross on Hamilton Mountain, the escarpment at the south end of the city. "That Friday night about nine o'clock, a friend and I were walking along Barton Street," Lewis recalled. "As we crossed Ferguson Avenue, we looked to the south, towards Hamilton Mountain. There it was — a tall wooden cross burning in the dusk."[2] The Klan was alive and thriving.

A few months later, Ku Klux Klan members marched across the city in full regalia. "It was a big parade, and the KKK rode through on horses," Lewis remembered years later.

> *Even the horses wore white robes. The police did nothing to break up the event as the Klan members rode through a largely Italian neighbourhood, trying to frighten the locals with their anti-Catholic views. The Ku Klux Klan in Hamilton was active and visible, and operated with no interference from local authorities. Interestingly however, some of the horses, on loan to the Klan, were recognized as belonging to a local bread company (even under their robes). Many people boycotted the bread company in protest and forced it out of business within a year.*[3]

The summer of 1929 ended with large Klan rallies in eastern Ontario on Sunday, September 15. In Belleville, home to the Klan's eastern Canada director George Marshall, a field day attracted a crowd of close to twenty-five thousand.[4] Farther east, in the small town of Richmond, forty kilometres south of Ottawa, a crowd of thousands gathered for a weekend Klan spectacle on the farm of George Lewis.[5] "There was no warning they were coming," recalled Mildred McCoy, a teenager at the time. "At midnight the streets were clear, and at six o'clock in the morning there were crosses painted all along the street going down to where the celebrations were." Signs with KIGY (Klan Is Gathering Yonder) were posted around the town.

The rally was reminiscent of the colourful Ku Klux Klan festival in Smiths Falls three years earlier. Indeed, the *Ottawa Citizen* reported that the event was put together by organizers from Smiths Falls and the Ottawa klavern. It described the scene as follows:

> *At the gateway [to the field] mounted Klansmen, hooded, garbed in the white robes with red trimmings, met the incoming lines of cars and directed the traffic towards the centre of the field. Here other mounted knights patrolled the ground and kept the crowd within bounds. Each rider carried a drawn sword, and there was a glittering sabre stuck in the centre of the field. Five huge crosses, wrapped in oil-soaked rags, were piled on the ground.*

As at Smiths Falls, Jim Lord addressed the gathering on the ills of Catholicism and the modern age, and according to the *Ottawa Citizen*, was particularly effective "as in vivid words he scored the fast pace of this modern age and what he termed its "low standards of morality." He was accompanied by two Americans from New York state — Rev. Thurston Gibbs of Jordan and an S. Loomis of Watertown — who made a lesser impression. After the speeches, when it was dark, the crosses were lit, one at each corner of the field and one in the centre. Garry Vaughan, a young local farmer, came to town to see the Klansmen and "ran into a friend of mine . . . He was outside getting some air; he had his hood off. I surprised him.'Hello, Bruce,' I said. He put that hood on real quick."

* * *

January 1930 saw one of the Klan's more memorable actions in Ontario, cementing the view that the group instigated racist intimidation and violence in Canada. Four months after Jim Lord presided over the initiation of new Klan members in Hamilton, about seventy-five Hamilton Klan members showed up in the prosperous nearby Lake Ontario town of Oakville. Wearing hoods, robes and assorted Klan regalia, the group marched into the town of four thousand and towards the home of Isabelle Jones, a young white woman allegedly living with a Black man, Ira Johnson. They set up an impressively big cross on the main street of Oakville, and then burned it down. They proceeded to Jones's home and took her out, put her in a car and drove her to her parents' house. Johnson was brought out, and he was driven to his parents' house. The parents were warned that if Ira was ever seen again in the company of a white girl, the Klan would deal with him. Their business concluded, the Klan cavalcade headed back to Hamilton.

David Kerr, the Oakville chief of police, later testified in court that a Black resident of Oakville had come to tell him about the Klan invasion.[6] Accompanied by Constable Jack Barnes, Kerr intercepted the caravan of Klan cars at the Sixteen Mile Creek Bridge as they were *en route* back to Hamilton. He recognized some participants as prominent businessmen from Hamilton, including chiropractor William A. Phillips. "He was sitting in the car," testified

Chief Kerr. "He was dressed in his robes with the hood over his head. Later he removed the hood, and we shook hands. I knew him quite well."

Another of the Klansmen was Ernest Taylor, a figure well-known in the Hamilton courts and police stations because of his fluency in Italian. He had been designated a Justice of the Peace and worked closely with the police.[7] Taylor was the leader of a Methodist outreach mission to the Italian community in Hamilton, and regularly featured in newspaper stories because of his involvement in high-profile cases. "He came from the motor cars and shook hands," said Kerr.

Kerr decided to give the Klan cavalcade a police escort back to Hamilton. "There was no semblance of disorder, and the visitors' behaviour was all that could be desired," he told a newspaper later. The Ontario attorney general was clearly suspicious about how the Oakville events had played out, suspicions likely fuelled by his deputy minister, the well-informed Edward Bayly. The attorney general called for a police report on the incident. Three Klansmen were charged under the *Criminal Code* with wearing masks or disguises after dark without a lawful purpose. A fourth man, William Mahoney, was never found and was not charged.

The case went to trial in March 1930 in Oakville in a courtroom packed with supporters applauding the three accused Klansmen. They were Phillips, the Hamilton chiropractor, Taylor, the activist pastor, and Harold Orme, a chiropractic assistant, whose presence in Oakville had been determined by tracing the licence plate of his car. The trial drew an eclectic crowd, including twenty-year-old Ray Lewis, the young Black man making a reputation for himself as a runner.

Orme and Taylor were acquitted on the grounds that they wore only their white robes to terrorize Johnson, not the hoods. The third accused, Phillips, was found guilty and fined fifty dollars. Phillips found himself the focus of head-turning public support. He launched an appeal of his fifty-dollar fine. The case went to the Supreme Court of Ontario. Deputy Attorney General Edward Bayly, by now well acquainted with the Ku Klux Klan thanks to John Miller and the work of the OPP, appeared for the Crown and argued that Phillips's sentence should be increased "having regard to the nature of the offense — namely that the law was taken into Phillips's own hands and that there was a great show of potential force."[8]

Chief Justice William Mulock found the lower court had engaged in "a travesty of justice." After describing Klan lawlessness and the violation of the rights of Isabelle Jones, Chief Justice Mulock sentenced Phillips to three months in jail. Phillips announced a hunger strike. For thirteen days, he sat in the Halton County Jail in Milton sipping water and denying himself breakfast, lunch and dinner.

A few weeks after Phillips's trial, Ira Johnson's house was burned down. Johnson supporters — lawyers and clergymen — received threatening calls and letters. The perpetrators were never found, but there is no doubt about Klan responsibility.

The Phillips hunger strike was reported widely across the country. The Orange Lodge rose to the Klan's defence. The Knights of the Ku Klux Klan in turn sought to justify the Hamilton klavern's actions by arguing that Jones herself had approached a Klansman and asked for help. When that argument fell flat, they said the girl's mother, a fervent Salvation Army member, had asked for help in returning Isabelle to her home.

In the end, it turned out that Ira Johnson, the "Black" man in question, had Indigenous ancestry, and was a wounded veteran of the First World War. Ira and Isabelle Jones eventually married, had three children and lived quietly in Oakville for decades. Phillips served his jail time. The same day he exited the jail in Milton, the council in nearby Oakville refused an application by his co-accused Harold Orme to hold a Ku Klux Klan parade in the town.[9] By then, public support for the Klan was diminishing.

The Oakville incident also demonstrated to both participants and observers just how impractical the Ku Klux Klan's distinctive ceremonial robes were for undertaking violent activities. First and foremost, wrote Katherine Lennard in her analysis of Klan regalia, white hoods and robes drew a lot of attention to the people wearing them, as had happened in Oakville.[10] White robes also showed blood stains, another drawback to keeping regalia in pristine condition. Further, the hoods were a problem because they "accumulated yellow-brown rings of sweat around the wearer's forehead; robes gathered similar stains around the armpits and hems."

The hoods were also hot inside and likely to be removed, again exactly what had happened in Oakville. If that wasn't bad enough, the hems were great collectors of mud stains. All in all, Lennard concluded, and the events in Oakville demonstrated, the long, voluminous white robes of the Ku Klux Klan were ill-suited to inflicting violence. Mostly they just attracted too much attention. They should be saved for ceremonial occasions to enhance the symbolic threat of violence, not when actually committing it.

* * *

The Oakville affair became symbolic of the racism, violence and public disorder that accompanied the Klan wherever it showed itself. The *Canadian Forum* was blunt in its description of the KKK's historical pattern of activity: "It begins with Mumbo Jumbo and ends in bloody murder. There is no place for it in Canada."[11]

The events in Oakville also created unease among others targeted by its hatred. Rabbi Maurice Eisendrath was the recently installed twenty-eight-year-old rabbi of Holy Blossom Temple in Toronto, the city's leading synagogue. He joined the general criticism of the Oakville perpetrators and the Klan more generally. Eisendrath was an American, born in Chicago, who had served in synagogues around the mid-southern United States. He was uniquely placed to understand the conditions that made the Klan possible and the risks of having such an organization active in the community.

In a widely noted sermon on March 23, 1930, he tore apart the Klan's white supremacist philosophy and its focus on repressing Blacks. He also warned that many people publicly opposed Klan lawlessness at the same time that they "silently condone the work which it seeks to achieve. The Klan is saying and doing those very things which myriads of our fellow citizens actually believe."[12] It was an uncomfortable but accurate public denunciation whose truth would become increasingly obvious during the coming decade.

# Chapter 9
# WILD ROSE COUNTRY: THE KLAN IN ALBERTA, 1930s

The revival of the Ku Klux Klan in Alberta in the early 1930s was the singular work of one man — John Joseph Maloney. He was by all accounts a captivating public performer. He was also a confirmed racist and bigot. His public profile in Saskatchewan had been overshadowed by the larger-than-life personalities of Pat Emmons and James Henry Hawkins. With his move to Alberta, J.J. Maloney came into his own as a public figure.

J.J. Maloney came from Hamilton, Ontario, a hub of racism and Ku Klux Klan activity during the 1920s. Maloney's family lived in the north end of Hamilton, "reputed at that time to be the district of the so-called wild Irish living down by the Bay, where men were men, and policemen went in pairs." Maloney's autobiography painted a picture of a childhood in a neighbourhood where the police dared not patrol alone.[1] He was raised in the Catholic Church and attended St. Mary's Separate School, where one of his teachers was Father Charles Coughlin, the rabid isolationist of 1930s radio notoriety. Maloney would later claim he was beaten by the nuns at St. Mary's. Like many of his public declarations, these may have been fabricated for his anti-Catholic audiences.

Maloney went on to St. Jerome's College in Kitchener, Ontario. During the First World War, the college had come under suspicion, along with the Jesuit St. Stanislaus Novitiate in nearby Guelph, of harbouring young men who were evading military conscription. Maloney said he alone amongst seminarians had tried to enlist while at St. Jerome's. He later told a story of travelling to Ottawa, cornering the minister of justice in his office and blackmailing him into issuing an exemption from military service by threatening to expose that his son was hiding out from conscription in the Guelph novitiate.[2]

It was not very subtle blackmail, but he claimed it worked. He also maintained that Colonel Harold Machin, the justice department's lawyer responsible for implementing conscription, personally handed him the certificate exempting him from conscription. This was the same Colonel Machin who was briefly the Ku Klux Klan's representative in Winnipeg in 1925. The story was not true, but it supported Maloney's allegations about the hypocrisy of Catholicism. Also untrue was the claim that the justice minister's son was evading conscription. The story demonstrated Mulroney's penchant for consistently presenting himself as the winner of any confrontation and the wronged martyr in any situation that might make him look bad.

Maloney had a chequered history at St. Jerome's, with accusations of theft from the tuck shop and assault on a prefect. From there he moved on to the Grand Séminaire in Montreal, where he lasted seven months as a candidate for the Catholic priesthood. Maloney fell ill during the Spanish flu pandemic of 1918 and spent time in hospital. He later claimed that one of the nursing sisters took a liking to him and hinted at improprieties that again spoke to the hypocrisy of the Catholic Church.[3]

For wider public consumption, Maloney would say that exposure to the poverty of Irish Montreal opened his eyes to the Church for what it was — an oppressor of the faithful and promoter of the wealthy and powerful. For his special men-only meetings, Maloney talked of the nursing sister who had introduced him to the true nature of the Roman Catholic Church. He returned to Ontario, where he launched an anti-Catholic speaking campaign, first at Cooke's Presbyterian Church in Toronto and later at Orange Lodge Halls and Protestant churches across the province.

Maloney met both Charles Lewis Fowler and J.H. Hawkins in Toronto, which must have happened after the pair arrived in the city in January 1925. Maloney would later testify in court that he had joined and then left the Ontario Klan because he came to believe that it was "un-British."[4] He attributed the failure of the Klan to catch on in Canada as it had in the United States as being due to "newspaper propaganda."[5] His supposed departure from the Ontario Klan would later allow him to say in Saskatchewan that he was not a Klan member.

In August 1924, Maloney was convicted of reckless driving and fined thirty dollars.[6] He was also convicted (with a twenty-dollar fine) of using abusive language against Dr. A.C. Caldwell, mayor of the town of Dundas, near Hamilton. Maloney had been stopped by police on the street in Dundas.[7] While driving past the mayor and town councillors who happened to be standing on the sidewalk, Maloney leaned out the car window and yelled, "Dr. Caldwell, you are a Roman Catholic ________, and I'll get you yet," according to the *Dundas Star*, which declined to print what, exactly, Maloney had called the mayor. The mayor said he didn't know why Maloney would threaten him. The judge found that Maloney must have been "either drunk or under the influence of dope or crazy."[8]

Maloney's star had shone brightly but briefly in Saskatchewan before he moved on to Alberta. His most prominent early visit to Alberta was in July 1929, when he accepted an invitation from the local Orange Lodge in Vermilion. He was to speak at their July Twelfth picnic to celebrate the victory of Protestant King William of Orange over Catholic forces at the Battle of the Boyne in Ireland in 1690. If the Orange Lodge had a holy day, this was it. For an anti-Catholic of Maloney's stature and toxicity, being the guest speaker at a July Twelfth picnic was a high honour and a privilege.

A crowd of some four thousand showed up in Vermilion to hear him. There were two massed bands and a parade with one thousand marchers draped in orange sashes. The appearance in the parade of "King Billy" on a white horse, a longstanding Orange tradition, was greeted with cheers. Orange flashed everywhere, with Union Jacks waving in the sun. Visitors arrived from across northern Alberta. Charles Puckering, Pat Emmons's old employee in Moose Jaw, was also on the program. The twenty-six-year-old Puckering was described as the "Canadian Boy Orator." He was soon to become the secretary of the Regina Board of Trade, but was still active on behalf of the Klan. Orange Grand Master Bert Williams warmed up the crowd and then turned the stage over to Maloney, who delivered his standard anti-Catholic speech.

Other events on the margins of the picnic were equally impressive in scale and even more significant for the Klan's presence in Alberta. The night before the parade, on a hill overlooking Vermilion and visible from far away, a cross burned for two and a half hours until just before dawn. An unknown number of smaller crosses flared in a park and around the town during the night.

The crosses — more so than Maloney's appearance — provoked newspaper attention across the province. They represented a formal declaration of the Klan's active return to Alberta after a dormancy of several years. The mayor of Vermilion told the *Edmonton Journal* he didn't know of any Klan members in town but had been told that organizers had visited recently. It's almost certain that the perpetrators of the flaming crosses were Ray Snelgrove and J.J. Maloney, who shared the platform with the mayor on the "Glorious Twelfth."

Ray Snelgrove's tour of Alberta's Orange Lodge locals in early 1929 provided a particularly useful source of information for Maloney's later efforts to recruit Klan members. As he travelled around the province, Orange Lodge leaders provided Snelgrove "with a list of reliable or sympathetic people in each new area, to which . . . invitations were sent inviting their participation in the organization of a local Klan," reported Alberta historian Howard Palmer.[9] This tactic had served the Klan well in Ontario and Saskatchewan, and continued to be a reliable source of recruits in Alberta.

By the following spring, Maloney and Snelgrove were making regular visits to Alberta, promoting the Klan and selling memberships. Maloney appeared in Red Deer in March 1930 with Snelgrove, who had been there a few months before. The old juices flowed, the rhetoric raged and Catholics were the targets of his vitriol as he spoke to an overflow crowd.

* * *

The reality of Klan activities for Albertans was demonstrated by an incident involving four Red Deer Klansmen. A few weeks after Maloney's speech there, blacksmith Fred Doberstein received a late-night phone call in Lacombe, a smallish farm town mid-way between Edmonton and Red Deer. Could he come into his shop right now to do a job of emergency welding? It was spring planting time; someone needed work done in a hurry. Why not? Doberstein dressed and headed down to his smithy.

"I got down to the shop and saw a car standing just in front of it," Doberstein later told the *Edmonton Journal.*

> *There were two men standing by the car, one had his back to me, and the other had something over his face. I unlocked the shop door, and one of the men motioned towards the car. I believed the casting they wanted welded was in the rear seat and went over to get it. The door was open. I bent over, leaning into the car. The two men outside pushed me in, and two others in the rear seat grabbed my shoulders and pulled me in. I struggled, but they were too strong for me.*[10]

Doberstein was bound with rope literally head to foot, put in the car and driven through the night to nearby Blackfalds. He was beaten, his clothes stripped off and hot tar poured over his legs and abdomen. Feathers were thrown onto the tar. Alberta Provincial Police Sergeant J. Holmes testified later in court that he visited the scene of the beating where he found a can of tar, a pile of feathers and lengths of rope, all consistent with Doberstein's story.

"We are the Ku Klux Klan," Doberstein reported one of the men saying. "We want you to leave Blackfalds on the first southbound train and never show your face in Lacombe again. If you do, we will kill you." Doberstein readily agreed, and the men left him in the bush. He removed the rope and walked to Blackfalds, where he called for help. But he had no intention of leaving town. "They can't scare me out by treating me like that . . . It has hurt my pride." He went to the police instead.

Doberstein said he had broken a window of the car that carried him out of Lacombe. The car was later identified as belonging to Ole Boode, a prosperous businessman with a car dealership on Gaetz Avenue in Red Deer. Following an Alberta Provincial Police investigation, kidnapping charges were filed against four Red Deer men — the businessman Ole Boode, blacksmith Claude Rowe, butcher Walter Butlin and Ralph Mowbray, a farmer from just outside Lacombe. Guilt was not in doubt. Ralph Mowbray admitted his participation to a reporter. "It was a party of public-spirited citizens," he said. What was the point of it all? "What was done was as a hint that Doberstein should leave Lacombe immediately."[11]

Why? Doberstein, a drifter for most of his thirty years, had arrived in Lacombe only a few months before his kidnapping. He was white, had a Jewish-sounding name and uncertain citizenship, maybe American but probably Canadian. He was separated from a wife who had gone home to Swift Current, Saskatchewan. But in Lacombe his social life was robust. He wrote to a young girl — he said she was eighteen, the Crown said sixteen — and promised to marry her. He admitted he had also proposed to another girl. Doberstein said he was a successful businessman who attracted the envy of his competitors, including Claude Rowe. So he had enemies who were capable of threatening him to get out of town.

The circumstances confirmed Klan involvement, but nobody would admit the attack was organized by the Invisible Knights. Even the talkative Ralph Mowbray was silent when reporters asked him the question. Sergeant Holmes from the Alberta Provincial Police wasn't prepared to label this a Klan crime even though the Klan was known to be active in the area. The police chief in Lacombe allowed that Doberstein's assailants might have been Klansmen, but "there is nothing to show that the outrage was organized by the Klan." However, the four accused were known in the community to be Klansmen.

The Red Deer courtroom was full when the case against the four accused was heard at a preliminary hearing on May 31, 1930, by Magistrate H.G. Scott. The judge was renowned for his distaste for foreigners. The week before the hearing, he made a speech praising British heroes and implicitly casting doubts on the loyalty of others. As the case progressed, the charges against Boode were dropped, then Claude Rowe's charge was dropped.

When the case came to trial in December, Mowbray and Butlin were convicted not of kidnapping but of causing grievous bodily harm. They were fined fifty dollars, the same penalty the trial judge had originally handed chiropractor William Phillips in Ontario a few months previous. There was no appeal and the minimal fine stood.

* * *

The general public might have thought this was justice, but Charles Halpin, editor of the *Lacombe Western Globe*, did not. The editor was adamant within days of the attack on Doberstein that this was a Klan job, the work of a "band of unlawful hoodlums." He was just getting started. "That such happenings can take place in the midst of civilization is to be deplored," he wrote. "Such an organization as the KKK should be stamped out of existence in this country."

A few days later, the Klan responded with an anonymous letter that described Halpin's words as "exceedingly displeasing to members of the KKK in this and other districts." They were watching, warned the letter, and if the editor continued to defame the Klan, then Halpin's home and business would be burned to the ground. The police were informed, but no arrests followed. "I don't believe there is any person in Lacombe who would commit such an act as is threatened," offered the Lacombe police chief. Halpin was not deterred. He dismissed the letter but not the Klan's potential for violence. "That bunch is capable of doing almost anything," he said in a statement to fellow journalists.[12] Halpin continued to denounce the Ku Klux Klan and the anti-Catholic statements of J.J. Maloney and Ray Snelgrove.

Maloney's choice of advance man, Ray Snelgrove, was generally disparaged by journalists. Snelgrove was deemed disagreeable by many who met him, particularly reporters. For one thing, Snelgrove was vague when asked if he was a member of the Orange Lodge or the Klan. He said he spoke for Anglo-Saxon Protestantism rather than the lodge or the Klan. "According to Mr. Snelgrove, who announces himself as a sort of a helluva man, Alberta does not need the Klan," wrote *Vegreville Observer* editor A.L. Horton. "The *Observer* knew that long before it sunk into the intelligence of Mr. Snelgrove, who may be what he purports to be — an ex-soldier. We thank God that there are so few ex-soldiers of the Snelgrove kind."

Another journalist, Archie Key of the *Drumheller Mail*, was equally suspicious of Snelgrove and his intentions when he came through that town, dubbing him "Kluck of the Klucks" peddling "a hymn of hate."[13] Key, a pugnacious newsman originally from England, was also a self-declared socialist. He was regularly at odds with his American-born publisher, who was rumoured to be a Klan member.

In the heated politics of a mining town like Drumheller, the presence of a Ku Klux Klan organizer held serious potential for acrimony. Archie

Key reported that the Klan had burned a cross on his front lawn to try and intimidate him into silence. Others questioned the story. But if it didn't happen, it wasn't for lack of Key poking fun at the Klan. In late 1929, Key wrote:

> *We have found that the Klan does add to the gaiety of life. What is more humorous than hearing of a group of full-grown, serious-minded men climbing to the highest spot in town and deliberately setting fire to a miniature telephone pole — or solemnly conclaving in inverted sugar bags and nineteenth century nightgowns — but the most humorous aspect of the Klan to our mind is the fact that they believe they have a God-given right to regulate public morals, influence local politics, and attack any organized faith with which they disagree. It is so funny that the whole world laughs at their antics.*[14]

The absence of a sense of humour in Klan ranks was notorious. Key's articles could well have led to the Klan action he reported. And his writing certainly irritated his publisher, who feared his editor was bad for business.

* * *

J.J. Maloney's speaking appearances in Alberta were full of ominous warnings about threats to the province from Roman Catholics. He perceived the forces of Catholicism to be concentrated in the provincial capital of Edmonton. There were, he said, 165 Catholic properties of one kind or another in the city, untaxed, and shifting the burden of public revenues on to the homes of the "poor struggling workingmen." If Edmonton was the "Rome of the West", then Maloney decided he was needed there in person to fight the unholy influences of Catholicism.

Meanwhile, aided and abetted by Orange Lodge leaders and members, Maloney launched a lecture tour across Alberta. In July 1930, Maloney and "Calgary Dave" Taylor, field secretary of the Alberta Grand Orange Lodge, travelled by train and car through the fertile lands of the Peace River Country far northwest of Edmonton. Maloney called it a Klan tour; Taylor described it as an "Orange Trail" to boost lodge recruiting. The timing suggests the lodge got more out of it than the Klan. Maloney and Taylor were feted at "Glorious Twelfth" celebrations across the region. Catholics were the targets of the speeches everywhere they appeared.

Charles Halpin, editor of the *Lacombe Western Globe,* had loathed J.J. Maloney at first sight. When Maloney and Snelgrove had appeared in Red Deer speaking to large and enthusiastic crowds, Halpin joined with other local Klan opponents to sponsor counter-rallies. He became a well-known opponent of the Klan, a role he had assumed in denouncing the Klan for its involvement in the tar-and-feathering of Paul Doberstein. For Halpin there was no doubt that the Klan was behind this singular act of "citizen justice." And Maloney was the public face of the Klan as the membership grew across Alberta.

By the spring of 1932, Halpin could no longer contain himself. J.J. Maloney was by then publishing a newspaper of his own in Edmonton, the *Liberator,* that splashed anti-Catholic venom across the province every two weeks. Halpin was enraged by the *Liberator's* outlandish anti-Catholic claims. He responded in the *Lacombe Western Globe* with a characterization of Maloney's writings as "the ravings of an apparently deranged brain." He denounced Maloney as a liar, a slanderer, an unscrupulous degenerate and more. "He is a demagogue of the first water, whose only object in life is to separate the gullible from their coin, and he is growing rich at their expense." Maloney, of course, sued for defamatory libel.

It was a standing-room-only affair at the Lacombe courthouse on April 26, 1932, when the preliminary inquiry opened. Maloney suffered one of his "patented breakdowns" in the courtroom, claiming weakness, a sore throat and a gasping need for a glass of water that suspended the proceedings while a glass of water was found for him. The magistrate put the case forward for trial but managed to cast doubt on the proceedings by describing the affair as "scurrilously trivial on both sides."[15] As it turned out, the case went nowhere while Maloney squeezed it for all possible publicity.

* * *

Klan membership surged during early 1932 as Maloney's prominence spread, and he threw himself into the political life of his new province. The number of Klan members probably peaked at around eight thousand in 1931, according to Howard Palmer, who cited the presence of klaverns in approximately fifty towns and villages across the province.[16]

The population of Alberta at the time was about 700,000. In the public's mind, there was growing political unrest as the Depression bit deeper into people's lives. Mass unemployment, farmers in crisis, thousands and thousands living in distress as they tried to pull together the needs of everyday life — food, shelter, money. "They were caught in a steel web from which there seemed no escape," wrote John Irving, who studied the rise of the Social Credit movement in the province during the 1930s. "Their social environment, their feeling for the process of life, their hope for the future, all became meaningless."[17]

The Klan purported to offer both political remedies and social outlets for a population in distress. J.J. Maloney joined the groups and aspiring leaders who sought believers and followers as the misery of the Depression deepened. His main tools were his personal attacks on the Catholic Church and the French-speaking minorities across the Prairies, all amplified through the pages of the *Liberator*. At the same time, new religions and cults had greater appeal as people sought guidance and direction. One of the newly prominent faiths was British Israelism, which initially had few adherents in Alberta but began to attract hundreds of followers to meetings in Calgary and Edmonton during the 1930s.[18]

The proposed creation of a Catholic school board in Wainwright, southeast of Edmonton, prompted Maloney to mobilize a Protestant protest in early 1932. Under a banner proclaiming free speech, Maloney and his supporters boarded a special train in Edmonton in mid-March bound for Wainwright. When they arrived, Maloney was met by hundreds of angry locals who refused to let the passengers debark. The result was a near-riot. Maloney retreated to Edmonton, returning a few weeks later on another special train accompanied by some seven hundred supporters. This time he was able to hold two public meetings without problems to oppose the proposal. The province created the school district anyway.

* * *

The Klan also inserted itself into a bitter miners' strike in the Crowsnest Pass in the spring of 1932, probably through the efforts of local organizers rather than at Maloney's direction. Edmonton was far from the Crowsnest Pass, and without a religious angle Maloney appeared to have no interest. Four collieries in the towns of Blairmore and Coleman, 250 kilometres southwest of Calgary, were shut down by the Mine Workers Union of Canada with the support of the Communist Party. The miners' grievances were many, but low wages were the basic cause of the strike.

Klan organizers, true to the group's American origins, were sworn enemies of communism and socialism, friends to capitalists and supporters of the status quo. With 1,300 miners locking down local industry in a protest against abysmal wages and working conditions, the local RCMP was focused on foreign agitators and Communist organizers in the area. But they also took note of the presence of aggressive Ku Klux Klan organizers.

The strike erupted in the first weeks of May. The RCMP's network of undercover officers and informants soon reported that the Klan was represented locally by two kleagles, who were agitating against the union. They were identified by the Mounties as well-known Klansmen J.C. Gailbraith and A.P. Van Buren of Calgary, the nearest city of any size.

Based on contemporary Calgary city records, they were almost certainly Alfred Clark Galbraith, a forty-seven-year-old investment manager and war veteran, and Abram (Abe) Van Buren, fifty, manager of the Sunshine Auto Camp on Calgary's Bow River. Both men fit the profile of supposedly upstanding citizens attracted to the Klan for its positions on issues of public morality (i.e., opposition to bars, brothels, gambling and the negative social consequences thereof), political rectitude among officeholders and the potential for fraternal contacts that were also good for business.

A cross was fired on the mountain overlooking Blairmore on the night of May 17. Local Klan members were judged by the RCMP to be "respectable citizens" set in opposition against strike leaders and Communists. The letters "KKK" and "Reds Beware" were painted in red on the sides of buildings, including the union hall.[19] Unsigned letters were sent to strike leaders. "The KKK just wants to give you fair warning that you are a marked man," read a letter to striking miner William Peters. "Just watch your step. Take our advice and keep out of sight or things might happen."[20] A few days later, shots were fired at a car carrying one of the strike leaders, John Stokaluk. He accused the Klan of trying to kill him. The strike eventually failed, and whether the Klan's involvement was a factor was unclear.

* * *

The Edmonton city elections of 1932 saw Maloney and Klan supporters pushing hard to replace incumbent mayor James Douglas, who had close links to the Liberal Party. "By Klan reasoning, this was enough reason to brand Douglas a papist sympathizer," observed Howard Palmer.[21] The city had hundreds of Klan members who, under Maloney's influence, mobilized in opposition to Mayor Douglas. All-candidates meetings in particular featured women asking Douglas planted questions about the nature of the support he received from Catholic institutions and organizations.

Douglas was ill-equipped to respond, and he came off looking inept and uninformed. The tactics developed by Maloney and his followers worked. Douglas was defeated by Daniel Knott, and Klan supporters celebrated by burning a cross on the bluffs overlooking the North Saskatchewan River. Maloney claimed the victory as a Klan victory and a personal triumph.

The new mayor, Dan Knott, was a former typographer and printers' union leader. He was also a Mason, a background that gave him some familiarity with secret societies and how they worked. As mayor, he became notorious for sanctioning Klan gatherings and cross burnings in city parks and the city's Exhibition Grounds in the north end.

By June 1933, Edmonton Fire Chief A. Dutton had had enough. "I wish to point out that on the last occasion this organization held a picnic in the same premises fiery crosses were burned," he wrote to the city council in response to a Klan application to have a picnic at the Edmonton Exhibition Grounds and Grand Stand in early July. "While not interested in the Klan or its doings, yet, as Fire Chief, I think it right to call attention to the danger of any fire being lit on the Exhibition grounds."

City bylaws expressly prohibited open fires, but Dutton was the only city official to point out that the Klan was in breach of the law. "I wish to go on record as being opposed to this permission being granted on this occasion except on the distinct understanding that no fires of any kind will be lit during the picnic," he wrote.[22] Police Chief Anthony Shuter advised the deputy mayor that he was "taking this matter up with the Fire Chief to the end that no Fiery Cross will be burned at the picnic." While the city council failed to snuff out the picnic, the incident showed the Klan's influence in the provincial capital during the early 1930s under Maloney's leadership.

* * *

The Klan's membership in Alberta swelled as recruiting kleagles fanned out from Edmonton. By the spring of 1932, Maloney acknowledged eighteen organizers working for the provincial Klan. Ray Snelgrove had been replaced by a new circle of Alberta leaders. All of this activity was based on Maloney's ability to sustain an organization based solely on his personal credibility. There were no links to the enfeebled Ku Klux Klan of Canada in Toronto, or even the American parent organization.

Maloney's officers and kleagles were men with local credibility and roots in the province. J.E. McInnes was the imperial treasurer. M.M. Burr of Calgary was the grand scribe. Farmer Steele, an undertaker and one-time mayor of Westlock, a smallish town northwest of Edmonton, was an American, born in Kentucky, who had served in the 49th Battalion, Loyal Edmonton Regiment, during the war. He actively recruited for the Klan among ex-servicemen. So did Harold Wright, who had served with the Lord Strathcona Horse in the war. Wright was something of a curiosity in the Klan ranks — a former Roman Catholic like Maloney. After the war, Wright had moved from Winnipeg to Moose Jaw, where he found his way into the Klan, eventually moving to Alberta to help with recruitment.

Steele, Wright, McInnes and Maloney travelled the province overseeing recruitment generally and swearing in new Klansmen and women from Red Deer to Edson to Ponoka to Stettler and back to Calgary and points in between. They were sometimes accompanied by the Rev. Duncan McDougall, formerly of the Vancouver Klan, who resurfaced in Wild Rose Country after leaving his church on the west coast. McDougall also served from time to time as contributing editor of Maloney's newspaper, the *Liberator*.[23]

The Ku Klux Klan of Alberta was legally constituted under a provincial charter in the fall of 1932, putting it on the same legal footing as any service club or fraternal organization. Maloney signed the paperwork on behalf of the Klan, putting the lie to his repeated denials of Klan links. Maloney continued his inflammatory speeches, newspaper publishing and the occasional radio broadcast. Restraint went out the window. His perceived enemies inside and outside the Klan became the targets of his increasingly vitriolic statements.

January 1933 saw the beginning of the end of Maloney and the Ku Klux Klan in Alberta. It started with the imperial wizard's New Year's Eve celebration on December 31, 1932. That night, Maloney's car careened into a snowbank close by the Mayfair Golf Club on the south bluffs of the North Saskatchewan River near the University of Alberta campus. He couldn't get the car out of the ditch. His story was that he broke into a tool shed at the golf club looking for tools to help dig out his car. Once inside, he set a fire using papers and blueprints, presumably for light and heat. His car was damaged in the incident.

Maloney submitted an insurance claim alleging that thieves had stolen his car and damaged it. The insurance company responded with charges that Maloney had filed a false claim. The imperial wizard pleaded guilty with little fanfare. He saved that performance for the sentencing hearing five days later. He wept. His hands trembled. He interrupted the judge with a flurry of questionable justifications. "Please, please give me one more chance, just one more chance. I'll show the world what I can do. I was trapped. My parents are sick in Hamilton. Please give me a chance. I have Bright's disease."

The judge halted the proceedings to investigate the claims. He concluded there was no substance to any of them. The hearing resumed. Maloney was sentenced to two months of jail time, a one-hundred-dollar fine and fifteen dollars in damages. He was led away to the cells, but not before seventeen Klan women were turned away as they tried to shake his hand through the bars. A large contingent of Klansmen visited Maloney in police cells before he was moved to the Fort Saskatchewan Penitentiary.

In the meantime, Edmonton lawyer Henry Mackie sued Maloney for $26,000 for allegedly slandering him during a lecture at Memorial Hall in downtown Edmonton on the evening of January 1, 1933.[24] This was the day after Maloney's car ran into the snowbank near the Mayfield Golf Club. Mackie was a former member of Parliament for Edmonton East with a well-deserved reputation to protect. Specifically, he had been a consistent defender of the Ukrainian Canadian community against prejudice and discrimination. Neither the alleged slanders nor the outcome of the case were reported.

Two weeks later, Maloney and two associates went on trial on charges of conspiracy to steal documents — as well as the actual theft of documents — from a downtown Edmonton lawyer's office, the firm of Grant and Stewart. The nature of the documents was not disclosed in court. The co-accused were Klansman Harry Bassett and Murdock McKenzie, the former assistant janitor in the building that housed the law office. Maloney testified that he was being framed by Liberal Party operatives opposed to the Klan's work and him personally. He waxed on at length about his struggles to keep the Klan politically neutral and virulently Protestant. Bassett and McKenzie were described by the presiding judge as "the worst liars in the witness box I have ever heard." Maloney was found guilty of conspiracy and sentenced to an hour in jail and a one-hundred-dollar fine.

By then Maloney's prospects in the provincial capital were in clear decline. His circle of Klan associates — Harold Wright and others — became uneasy about where the Klan's revenues were going. Who controlled the bank accounts? There were endless conspiracies in the senior leadership that saw Maloney target an ever-widening circle of enemies, starting with the provincial attorney general's office and moving on to include lawyers, merchants, Catholics in general and Protestants who Maloney insisted were catering to Catholics. Wright sued Maloney; Maloney sued everybody.

When he got out of jail after serving his sentence on the insurance fraud charges, Maloney sued the Klan for almost four thousand dollars he claimed was owed him for salary, rent and expenses, a familiar legal scenario for Klan leadership figures. The Klan countered with theft charges, alleging the Klan had given Maloney two bonds of two thousand dollars each. The money was intended to finance the publication of Maloney's autobiography. The book wasn't published, the bonds weren't returned. The Klan claimed it was out the money.

Henry Mackie, the lawyer who had sued Maloney for slander in 1933, served as associate Crown prosecutor on the case when the charges came to trial in October 1934.[25] The key witness was the current imperial wizard of the Ku Klux Klan in Alberta, John P. Henry, the owner of an Edmonton brickyard. He testified about Maloney coming to ask for money to publish his book, accepting the bonds, refusing to pay back the money and then writing bad cheques to reimburse the Klan.

The case went to the Supreme Court of Alberta, but a mistrial was declared when Maloney's lawyer, Morris Baker, told the jury his client had previously been convicted of a crime and sent to jail — a revelation deemed sufficient to potentially prejudice the court against Maloney. This legal misstep was one of several that eventually led to Baker, a one-time mayoralty candidate in Edmonton, being disbarred three years later, this time for stealing two hundred dollars from a client. He was eventually sentenced to eighteen months in Fort Saskatchewan prison for theft and jumping bail.[26] He and Maloney were not in jail at the same time.

A new trial lurched on with the theft charges replaced with a single charge of conversion. Maloney failed to appear twice. A bench warrant was issued. His lawyer, again Morris Baker, produced a note from a Calgary doctor that his client was in hospital recovering from an old wound reopened while cranking his car. The outcome of the case was not reported; it disappeared from the historical record as Maloney turned his attention elsewhere.

The former imperial wizard sought compensation from the federal Conservative Party for expenses incurred helping defeat the Saskatchewan Liberals. He was denied. He organized a petition to ban French from the public radio waves. He implored Ontario manufacturers to join his struggle against the use of the French language in the west. Maloney became an increasingly shrill voice in the political din of a cruel Depression.

Later, Maloney fondly recalled his time in Alberta and the city of Edmonton, writing, "I shall always remember Edmonton, and Edmonton will always remember me." Maloney couldn't leave it there, though. "I hold no ill will toward those who double-crossed me. . . No, I forgive you all."[27] Alberta, however, did not forget him. In February 1940, the RCMP in Calgary issued an arrest warrant for Maloney on a charge of false pretences with the message that "further charges would be preferred in other Alberta cities."[28]

Western Canadian politicians accused one another for decades of having been members of the Ku Klux Klan. An early example was the accusation in 1931 from the floor of the House of Commons by Liberal MP Jean-François Pouliot. He charged that two recently elected Conservative MPs from the

West were Klan members. Pouliot was absolutely correct with respect to Dr. Walter Cowan, by then the member of Parliament for the Saskatchewan riding of Long Lake. Cowan was the Klan's former Saskatchewan treasurer. The other accused MP was Ambrose Bury from Edmonton East, a former mayor of Edmonton, whose election victory had been celebrated with a flaming cross on the cliffs overlooking the North Saskatchewan River. "They were there with their nightshirts," Pouliot said of Klan involvement.[29]

The Klan in fact took full credit in the *Edmonton Journal* for the cross burning. "It was in celebration of the election of Mr. Bury," said M.M. Burr, the Alberta Klan secretary. "It made a pretty sight."[30] Other than the burning cross incident, history has not recorded any association between Bury and the Klan. John Diefenbaker, a future prime minister, also consistently denied rumours over the decades that he had been a Klan member in the late 1920s when he was a lawyer in Prince Albert, Saskatchewan.

Elsewhere, the elusive Harry Humble resurfaced in Calgary in the early 1930s, where he ran for a seat on city council and won. He became a convert to the Labour Party and then the provincial Cooperative Commonwealth Federation.[31] He signed the nomination papers for CCF candidate Amelia Turner in a January 1933 byelection. As a result, he was criticized by voters for running as an independent candidate, when his sympathies were clearly with Labour.[32]

Humble appeared at a Turner rally during the campaign, where he assured the audience that the economic policies of the CCF "were the economics of Jesus Christ."[33] He participated in radio broadcasts, where he criticized William Aberhart and his political ambitions. After a series of murky controversies over more missing money and possible ownership of a brothel, Humble went home to Yorkshire, England, in November 1936 and apparently never returned to Canada.[34]

And J.J. Maloney? Maloney's life spiralled downwards in the years after he abandoned the leadership of the Alberta Ku Klux Klan. He was charged with a range of criminal offences, usually false pretences or fraud involving bad cheques, in cities across the country — Calgary, Winnipeg, Sarnia, Cornwall and others. He drifted in and out of Vancouver peddling his autobiographical book, *Rome in Canada*, occasionally stopping at the Elysium Hotel on West Pender Street.[35]

By the early 1940s, he was back in Ontario and said to be working as an agent for a publishing company. This involved selling magazine subscriptions. He died in the Hamilton General Hospital in April 1944 of general poor health that culminated in a fatal embolism.[36] His mother, Margaret, buried him. Legend had it that on his deathbed he called for a priest and returned to the Catholic Church. The story sounded suspicious.

# Chapter 10
# WAITING FOR HITLER (1930–39)

The outbreak of the Second World War in September 1939 overshadowed the decline and demise of the Ku Klux Klan in Canada. The end came quietly in the midst of a hard Depression and fears about a coming war. Ironically, the Ku Klux Klan in Canada was at the peak of its prominence and influence in Saskatchewan and Alberta just as the organization was on the edge of extinction.

The political clout that the Klan wielded in Saskatchewan, and to a much lesser extent in Ontario, Alberta, British Columbia and New Brunswick, slowly declined after the economic collapse of October 1929. Hard times saw the Ku Klux Klan decay and die as the 1930s descended into gritty poverty and hardship.

There was no money to pay fifty-cent admissions to hear lectures on the evils of Catholicism, or to buy Klan robes or to support J.J. Maloney on his personal ultra-Protestant crusade. In Saskatchewan, the Conservative government's aggressive implementation of anti-Catholic and anti-French measures gave the Klan (and the Orange Lodge) what they sought. The Klan became increasingly irrelevant.

Early signs of disintegration surfaced in British Columbia. Rev. Charles Batzold and Alf England, who had taken on national roles in the revitalized Ku Klux Klan of Canada in the late 1920s, eventually moved on to other political endeavours at the municipal level in the Vancouver area. Batzold campaigned for mayoral candidate William Malkin, a Conservative newspaper owner, who was elected in 1928 on the strength of a campaign promise to restrict the growth of the Chinese community. England was a supporter of Louis Taylor, a seven-time mayor of the city with Liberal Party credentials, who was re-elected in 1931 just as the Depression began to hurt Vancouver badly.

By then, there weren't enough active members remaining in Vancouver and the Lower Mainland to keep the Ku Klux Klan functioning as a meaningful organization, although a few diehards stayed active into the 1930s. At this point, the secrecy that was a hallmark of the Klan became an impediment to the political influence they sought. The local Klan leadership, probably at Alf England's instigation, bombarded Vancouver city council with a series of petitions on issues it considered important — misappropriation of government funds, high freight rates for grain, unfair tax burdens for individuals compared to big companies, Chinese money driving down the price of farmland owned by whites, control of the media by the "big interests." These were often not, strictly speaking, Klan demands but those of citizens seeking to influence local governments.

Vancouver city council ignored the Klan's representations, primarily because of a bylaw that required petitions to be signed with the names of individual citizens. Klan members were sworn to keep their involvement secret, "and their refusal to sign their petitions meant that some of their civic efforts were disregarded by City Council."[1] The Klan in turn condemned the council for ignoring its submissions. Really, the local kligrapp said in a 1929 letter reeking of self-righteous martyrdom, "altruism is our only aim."

This was one of many signs that the Klan in British Columbia was a spent force. "The Klan's influence diminished considerably in Vancouver by the 1930s, because of their extremist position and because most of their agenda had been taken up by other nativist and mainstream organizations," concluded one study.[2] The Klan brought little new to the racist culture of British Columbia, and its novelty soon wore off.

The waning of the Klan in British Columbia was matched elsewhere. Imperial Wizard Jim Lord presided over an increasingly fragile national organization, notwithstanding occasional spasms of activity around the country. The Klan enjoyed a resurgence in Ontario between 1927 and

1930, but thereafter there was little good news for the organization, with the possible exception of New Brunswick. In 1930, Lord spoke to a large Klan rally in Moncton "about the objects and aims of the organization, and held the attention of the audience for one hour and twenty minutes, with his eloquence and earnestness."[3] Lord focused heavily on the issue of mixed-race marriages, saying "The boys and girls should be kept of the pure Anglo-Saxon blood, for if God gave us an inheritance of boys and girls, they should be kept pure."

Jim Lord made one of his last official appearances at a Klan gathering at Barkers Point outside Fredericton on August 8, 1931. "Klansmen and Klanswomen met in the community for a provincial field day complete with a fiery cross of electric lights," reported the local newspaper, commenting favourably on the move to modernity signified by an electric cross.[4]

Jim Lord went home to Deer Island, New Brunswick, to die in the summer of 1932. He had been diagnosed with liver cancer in Toronto a few months earlier. Alone, unmarried, he was buried by his sister.[5] The robes of the imperial wizard passed to George Marshall of Belleville, Ontario, the dyspeptic pastor of a local church. He managed to keep some klaverns operating in a few isolated places in eastern Ontario. Historian Gerry Boyce reported that the Klan was active in the Belleville area as late as 1935.

In the intervening years, national and international events resonated with echoes of the Ku Klux Klan. Adolf Hitler and the Nazi Party came to power in Germany in January 1933. Members of Toronto's Jewish community closely followed the news about the persecution of Jews that ensued. The rise of the Nazis prompted some Ontario legislators to try to address the open racism that had fuelled the rise of the Ku Klux Klan in that province.

In February 1933, Argue Martin, a Conservative member of the Ontario legislature for a Hamilton riding, introduced a private member's bill that would outlaw signs and advertisements that discriminated on the basis of race. Although this initiative was timely in light of events in Germany, where the public persecution of Jews was increasingly common and flagrant, it may also have reflected Martin's four years as a member of Hamilton city council during the years when the Ku Klux Klan was active in the city.

Martin was a thirty-four-year-old lawyer and national competition-level amateur squash player, with a reputation for sportsmanship. He framed his proposed bill to the legislature in relation to the concept of equality. He decried advertising that featured "gratuitous insults heaped on persons of a class, race or colour for no reason at all. Each individual should be judged on his own merits, not because of the race or class to which he belongs," he told the legislature.

Martin was obviously referring to the anti-Semitic signs commonly found in southern Ontario. "Such documentation tends to lead to strife, and it is not in the interests of good government. It might start a riot," said Martin. "If some of this material referred to me, I would be glad to take part in a small-sized riot myself."[6] His words to the legislature would later sound prophetic.

Martin's bill was welcomed by the Jewish community. "The proposed legislation is aimed not only against the Ku Klux Klan in Ontario, but against every form of discrimination which we have recently had in our province," commented a journalist for *Der Yiddisher Zhurnal*, a Yiddish-language newspaper read by thousands of Toronto's Jews. "The whole province suffered and suffers still from the "gowned" defenders of the night who are afraid to show themselves in the light of day without masks."

The bill was smothered by the Conservative government of Premier George Henry, who argued it would place limits on freedom of speech. A similar initiative in the province of Quebec around this time met the same fate, some said as a result of the anti-Jewish climate created there by the Canadian fascist movement of Adrien Arcand. The atmosphere in Canada's Jewish community became increasingly gloomy and foreboding, with a feeling that governments' failure to act was likely to lead to more discrimination.

Toronto's Jewish community closely followed the news about the attacks on German Jews that followed Hitler's accession to power. And they became increasingly aware of a local threat to their own well-being. So-called "Swastika Clubs" began forming in Toronto and Kitchener, using Hitler's party as their model. Members made a point of identifying themselves by wearing the Nazi swastika symbol.

The *Toronto Star* claimed on March 29 that the swastika "was an emblem much in evidence in the Ku Klux lodges and on the parades of the order in days gone by."[7] In Toronto, the "Swazis" were most obvious in the strongly "British" east-end community of Balmy Beach, where regular clashes broke out between Jewish and Gentile youths. A Swastika Club in Orillia, north of Toronto, posted signs that summer threatening Jewish cottage owners on Lake Simcoe. There was a sense that a crisis was coming.

The precipitating event was an evening baseball game at the Christie Pits sports field just off Bloor Street in west Toronto in August 1933. In the midst of raucous name calling between team supporters, a group of young men (white, almost certainly Gentile and drawn from a nearby Orange neighbourhood) raised a large Nazi swastika flag and waved it in the face of Jewish supporters of one of the competing baseball teams. The Jewish crowd surged forward to rip it down. The resulting clash saw more than eight thousand people drawn into a violent struggle that surged across the ball diamond and into the nearby streets. Fists, bats, broomsticks and iron bars were used. Hundreds were injured.

The fighting went on into the early morning hours. Jewish fighters were reinforced by cars full of young Italian men called to the scene by their Jewish friends to help even the odds. The Toronto Police Department intervened to bring the rioters under control, although it was slow off the mark in doing so. The riot was a remarkable response to growing tensions in the city between the Jewish community and an incipient Nazi movement. The riot at Christie Pits generated enormous pride in Toronto's Jewish community. Clearly, the Ku Klux Klan had helped create the conditions for such an incident.

The tension grew in Toronto in the following years. Maurice Eisendrath, the rabbi at Holy Blossom Temple, was increasingly outspoken about intolerance, racism and the rise of Nazi beliefs in Germany and in Canada. He became a target of Toronto's pro-Nazi community. On Hallowe'en 1937, three weeks after the end of a bitter provincial election campaign that featured strong debates on the nature of fascism, he found funeral crepe and a swastika nailed to the door of his Toronto home. "What happened on my doorstep is of little moment," Eisendrath told the *Globe and Mail* newspaper.[8] "But what is happening throughout Canada is vitally significant." A subsequent investigation by the *Globe and Mail* uncovered a network of Nazi sympathizers across Canada.[9]

* * *

The evidence documents many overlaps between fascists, Nazis and the Ku Klux Klan in the years leading up to the Second World War. After Klan leader Luther Powell's hasty departure from British Columbia in 1926, he made his way back to Louisiana. He dabbled in right-wing politics and became the leader of a neo-fascist group called the Khaki Shirts of America. "He has lived by his wits for many years — in fact, I have never known him to do any work," wrote a police officer in Shreveport, Louisiana, during his time there. "He pays no bills, and he is a man utterly without standing in the community . . . I am certain . . . that no organization sponsored by Powell could make any headway here because Powell has neither the respect nor the confidence of anyone who knows him."[10]

He eventually left the Khaki Shirts after allegations of financial abuse, moving on to another fascist organization called the Silver Shirts of America. After clashing with his old Oregon rival Fred Gifford, who had also joined the Silver Shirts, Powell decamped from Louisiana to Texas where he became involved in yet another shadowy organization called the Anti-Communist Legion of the World. He died in Shreveport, Louisiana, in October 1951. His days in Vancouver as imperial klazik reigning over the Kanadian Knights of the Ku Klux Klan were the pinnacle of his Canadian career.

Clem Davies, the charismatic clergyman from Victoria who proclaimed his membership in the Ku Klux Klan, was also intrigued with fascism. As early as 1926, he had praised the tactics of Italian dictator Benito Mussolini and his Fascist blackshirt followers. "They knew no mercy and asked for none," preached Davies after Mussolini seized power. "They exacted an eye for an eye and a blow for a blow. Those who defied them found it necessary to consult an undertaker."[11] This chilling approval was modified after Davies toured Italy in the summer of 1930. He returned to Victoria to report that Italy was now a menace to European peace because of a formal alliance between Mussolini and the Catholic Church.

Within a couple of years, he had added several conspiracy theories to his sermons, including the conclusion that the Depression was the work of a cabal of international bankers who controlled the world's finances and governments. This was a contemporary reworking of the *Protocols of Zion* myth propagated in anti-Semitic circles. Davies became involved with British fascists who were invited to speak to his Victoria colleagues in the local chapter of the British Israelite World Federation, a group whose evolving views were becoming similar to Nazi racial beliefs.

Davies's increasingly cultlike ministry began to link British Israel concepts with those of German Nazis and fascists everywhere. He approved of the Silver Shirts of America, where Luther Powell was active. He described the organization as "the flower of Anglo-Saxon Manhood," which was preparing for a struggle against evil.[12] With his sway over Victoria audiences waning, Davies moved his ministry to Vancouver in 1937.

Within a couple of years, he decamped to Los Angeles where he moved in spiritualist, fascist and British Israel circles for a decade. He died in Los Angeles in 1950 of malaria that he had contracted on a world tour. Clem Davies's greatest achievement during wartime was avoiding internment in spite of his fascist activities and associates. This was due in large measure to wrapping his ideas in religious beliefs that made him immune to the authorities.

John Ross Taylor, a young Toronto man who would become a living link with the Ku Klux Klan in future decades, had no such luck. Born in 1913, Taylor was a child of privilege raised in the heart of Toronto's elite. His father was a successful lawyer, his grandfather a highly regarded soap manufacturer, who had served as a city alderman during the late 1890s and early twentieth century.[13]

Taylor graduated high school, spurned university and become enamoured with the German project of Nazi Party leader Adolf Hitler. He looked around for Canadian examples and fell into the circle of Adrien Arcand, the Quebec-based leader who emulated British and Italian fascist leaders with an anti-Jewish, race-based political program. By 1937, the twenty-four-year-old Taylor had been selected to lead an Ontario division of Arcand's National Social Christian Party.

Taylor and Arcand were close associates of William Whittaker, the former Winnipeg Klansman who had founded the anti-Semitic Canadian Nationalist Party (CNP). Whittaker was likely responsible for letters signed by the Ku Klux Klan that were delivered to Jewish residents of Winnipeg during the 1926 federal election campaign. In an ominous reference to future events in Europe, the letters were noteworthy for "threatening them with physical extinction."[14] Whittaker died in late 1938, and the remnants of the CNP were folded into Arcand's organization.

With a provincial election looming in 1937, Taylor announced he would run in the predominantly Jewish downtown riding of St. Andrews. He took to appearing in the streets wearing a swastika on his lapel and giving the "Heil Hitler" Nazi salute. Perhaps sensing public disenchantment, and bowing to internal party dissension about political priorities, Taylor stepped away from the election. He moved on to join the Canadian Union of Fascists just as war loomed.[15] As a Nazi sympathizer, Taylor spent the war interned. Forty years later, John Ross Taylor would be an inspiration to a new generation of Canadian Klansmen.

The Ku Klux Klan in Canada may have experienced its last days before the Second World War in the St. Lawrence River valley of eastern Ontario. An attempt to burn down St. Francis Xavier's Roman Catholic Church in Brockville in October 1938 was attributed to the Ku Klux Klan.[16] The attack came five days after a cross was set afire in a field in the northeast section of Brockville. Ninety minutes later, a barn near the site of the cross fire was burned to the ground in a clear case of arson. The perpetrators were never found. Newspapers speculated that the series of events were the work of the remnants of the Ku Klux Klan in Ontario.

***

The Ku Klux Klan's impact in Canada in the interwar years was real but difficult to quantify. It played a role in some electoral contests in Saskatchewan, Alberta and New Brunswick, but pre-existing social conditions meant that the Ku Klux Klan served more as an accelerant than a spark. The spectacle of U.S. state governors, senators and members of the House of Representatives owing their election victories to the Klan was not repeated in Canada. Only in Saskatchewan, where James Anderson's Conservatives benefited from their alliance with and support from the Klan, did the American model of Klan electoral influence come close to reality. And even there, the Klan's objectives were shared by the Orange Lodge and its homegrown prejudices.

The Orange Lodge, with its deep roots in Anglo-Canada, was certainly a stronger political influence.

Further, the violent reputation and actions of the Ku Klux Klan in the United States did not travel well into Canada. There were relatively few cases of serious violence — the Barrie bombing, the burning of Ira Johnson's house, the assault on Paul Doberstein, the kidnapping of Wong Foon Sing, isolated fires of unknown origins — were the most egregious. Also, it was often impossible to distinguish violent attacks perpetrated by random racists from violence sponsored and inflicted by the Ku Klux Klan as an organization.

For the most part, the Ku Klux Klan in Canada traded on intimidation, coercion and threats to impose its Protestant white supremacist model of society. And at a certain point it triggered public backlash. "People who were duped by the Klan's high-sounding "creed" were ashamed of themselves when they saw its slimy methods in actual practice," recalled the *Calgary Herald* in 1946. "Good riddance."[17]

A more human reaction to the Ku Klux Klan's hateful messages was printed in the *Wainwright Star* in March 1932 as the misery of the Depression hit Albertans hard. "In times of depression, we need our good neighbours," wrote a local correspondent in a strongly worded letter opposing the Klan. There was no place for hate in this climate. "There appears to have been some feeling that during a period of economic distress, religious bigotry was a luxury," concluded historian Howard Palmer. There were no luxuries in Depression-era Alberta.

The mood of menace was very real for the Klan's victims — Black people, Asians, Jews, Roman Catholics — but history does not record widespread lynchings, arson or violent beatings administered as a matter of course by Canadian Klan members. In many ways, the Ku Klux Klan in Canada benefited from an already stratified society, where minorities were marginalized and excluded from the full benefits of citizenship. Discrimination and institutional racism were embedded in Canadian society of the period and did not rely on vigilante activities.

As the country edged closer to the Second World War, rank-and-file Ku Klux Klan members across the country folded up their robes, hid their Klan literature and hoped the world would forget their actions in the strange decade when the Ku Klux Klan had flourished in Canada. Some, though, recalled the era with fondness, a sign that for many the Klan was a social outlet as well as a racist and political organization. "We had a good run and lots of fun for a little over ten dollars," recalled one former Klan member in Saskatchewan in the 1970s.[18] But most Canadians failed to see the fun, and the Klan was erased from public memory during the decades that followed.

# PART II

# Chapter 11
# KLAN REDUX

The centre of the new Ku Klux Klan in Canada in the early 1980s was — as it had been for much of the 1920s — Toronto. But this was a city and a country with a much different character and complexion than fifty years earlier. Toronto had come through the 1930s Depression, the Second World War and finally the 1950s and 1960s with energy and wealth, notwithstanding its reputation as a staid and conservative provincial capital. Through the postwar years, immigrants and refugees from around the world flocked to Toronto. Displaced Europeans, anti-Communist Hungarians, Black people, Chinese, Indians, Pakistanis and more — they all came to Toronto, making it one of the most diverse cities in the world.

At the same time, Canada generally was a desirable destination for immigrants and refugees fleeing murderous dictatorships like the brutal Augusto Pinochet regime in Chile, or for Americans leaving the United States to avoid military conscription. The highly unpopular war in Vietnam divided Americans and repelled Canadians. The American draft-dodgers joined the stream of newcomers to Canada. The racial and political diversity that flowed from this influx became a magnet and a target for a range of right-wing and racist organizations — some domestic in origin, some foreign — but all providing the backdrop for a revived Ku Klux Klan.

The Orange Lodge was a stale memory in most parts of Canada by the 1970s. William Dennison, the last Orange mayor of Toronto, retired in 1972, marking the end of a long tradition of political dominance for the order that saw the city labelled "the Belfast of Canada."[1] The Orange pledges of loyalty to Britain, the Crown and Protestantism withered and went silent after the Second World War as the country changed direction.

A diverse range of new immigrants felt no particular need to support these archaic values. The rural societies that gave growth to the Orange Lodge were in decline. Many of the social services, social opportunities and community meeting points provided by the Orange Lodge were replaced by other organizations and governments. The Orange Lodge as a rallying point for bigotry and racism was effectively moribund by the time the modern Ku Klux Klan reappeared in Canada. In the years between the 1930s and the 1970s, the historical record shows no evidence of organized Klan activity in Canada, only a few isolated cases where racism and bigotry hid behind the KKK acronym scrawled on walls. Yet, in the 1980s, the Klan reappeared in Canadian life.

The country in general viewed race, religion and national origins differently than in the past, in part because of the experiences and aftermath of the Second World War. Canadian soldiers had fought across Europe against Adolf Hitler's Nazi forces. They liberated death camps, where they were sickened and repulsed by the results of Nazi and Fascist movements. The barbarism of race and religious hatred seared the collective memory of Canadian soldiers, journalists and politicians. The consequences carried through to how Canadian society evolved in the postwar years.

Alphonse Ouimet, a correspondent for Radio-Canada during the war, personally wrote a letter to the still-active and unrepentant Canadian fascist leader Adrien Arcand in 1961 to chastise him for continuing to deny the reality of the Holocaust death camps.

> *That you can, after so many years and despite the accumulation of evidence and testimony from those who were its victims — and they are legion — deny or try to diminish the horror of mass murder is beyond my comprehension. All the more so as in my capacity as a war correspondent I had the opportunity to go to Belsen and Buchenwald, among other extermination factories. There I saw firsthand how it was done to eliminate human beings against whom the most common complaint was simply their religion.*[2]

While Arcand continued to have his supporters, the general public view was that the sacrifices of the war called for a profoundly different and aggressive approach in Canada to civil and human rights.

This was a widely held national sentiment. Canadians helped create, and the country supported, the 1948 United Nations *Declaration of Human Rights,* with its principles of equality and fairness. The war brought home the horrific depths to which unchecked racial and religious and political hate could descend. The political and legal system at the national, provincial and local levels responded to the reality of this social awareness and the need for legal fairness and protections in the midst of social change.

An increasingly long list of laws across the country enforced the concepts of racial and legal equality.[3] Ontario's legislature passed the *Racial Discrimination Act* in 1944 that prohibited the public display of signage representing discrimination based on race, ethnic origin or religion. Fifteen years earlier, Argue Martin's private member's bill with the same objective had been sidelined and smothered in the legislature. In 1951, the *Conveyance and Law of Property Act* prohibited conditions on the sale or transfer of property based on race, ethnic origin or religion. The *Fair Accommodation Practices Act* of 1954 barred discrimination in providing "the accommodations, services or facilities usually available to members of the public."

Other provinces approved similar kinds of legislation over the two decades following the war. Saskatchewan, political home of the Ku Klux Klan during the 1920s, was the exception to a piecemeal approach to rights. The province approved a broad-based comprehensive bill of civil rights in 1947 under the leadership of Premier Tommy Douglas, the spiritual heir of Jimmy Gardiner, the Klan's nemesis in the 1920s. The federal government, led by Prime Minister John Diefenbaker, the Prince Albert lawyer whose relationship with the Klan was a sometime topic of speculation, passed the *Canadian Bill of Rights* in 1960. The bill should have removed any residual taint on Diefenbaker's reputation.

The culmination of these initiatives was the passage of the *Canadian Charter of Rights and Freedoms* as part of the *Constitution Act* of 1982, along with amendments to the *Criminal Code* prohibiting hate propaganda and promotion of genocide. These measures, along with the creation of the

Canadian Human Rights Commission in the 1970s, provided robust legal tools that went a long way to blunting racist messages and hate groups in the late twentieth century.

Over these years, individuals nevertheless continued to suffer from racially motivated injustices. Viola Desmond was one such victim. She was a Halifax businesswoman with a rapidly expanding beauty salon. In November 1946, her car broke down in New Glasgow, Nova Scotia. It wouldn't be repaired until the next day. She decided to pass the evening attending a movie at the Roseland Theatre. She may not have known that the Roseland, where *The Birth of A Nation* had been an annual feature only a couple of decades before, had officially segregated its seating in 1941 under pressure from white customers. It was the kind of practice that persisted for decades in communities across the country.

So when Viola Desmond bought her ticket to see *The Dark Mirror* starring Olivia de Havilland, she was told she had to sit upstairs in the balcony reserved for Black patrons. She tried to pay the extra ten cents for a ticket to sit downstairs, something she did in Halifax so she could be close to the screen because of her poor eyesight. The cashier refused to sell her the more expensive ticket. She went and sat in the downstairs section anyway. The theatre manager and a local police officer forcibly removed her. She was taken to the local jail and held there overnight.

Viola Desmond was brought to court the next morning. She was convicted of defrauding the Government of Nova Scotia of one cent, the difference in the amusement tax between sitting in the upstairs balcony versus the downstairs seats. When she got home to Halifax, she appealed her conviction to the Nova Scotia Supreme Court. And lost.[4] It was a graphic demonstration of the Canadian legal system endorsing racial segregation.

Segregation was still a living practice in many parts of the country during those years. The southwest Ontario town of Dresden, the scene of cross burnings during the Klan's growth years in the 1920s, was a case in point. Historically, the Dresden-Chatham region saw many escaped American former slaves settle there in the mid-nineteenth century. It was one of the destinations on the Underground Railroad to freedom. Josiah Henson, the inspiration for novelist Harriet Beecher Stowe's fictional escaped slave Uncle Tom, settled near Dresden and was buried there. The Black community prospered and grew in and around the town, but it wasn't always a happy coexistence.

The local *de facto* segregation was exposed in a famous 1949 article in *Maclean's* magazine by journalist Sidney Katz. He described a community where white and Black residents lived parallel but separate lives in the same town. Black residents were effectively barred from certain barber shops, beauty parlours, churches, pool rooms and service clubs. The rules in force at Kay's Grill illustrated how community racism worked. Owner Morley McKay had the largest of the three restaurants in town. He barred Black individuals at the door, and the other restaurant owners followed his lead. The ensuing furor from Katz's article fuelled Ontario's move to pass antidiscrimination laws. In 1956, after a series of convictions under antidiscrimination laws, Kay's Cafe capitulated and began serving Black customers.[5]

The quirky but relatively benign beliefs of British Israel adherents during the early twentieth century would come back to haunt both Canada and the United States. Vancouver had been a world stronghold of British Israelism during the Klan's incursion in the 1920s.[6] Scholar Michael Barkun concluded that British Israelism's adherents in Vancouver "nurtured ideas that were more clearly conspiratorial and anti-Semitic" than more conventional followers elsewhere. Their beliefs would have a long historical reach.

By the late 1920s, the community of British Israel followers was reinforced by British clergymen like Duncan McDougall and Clem Davies, who used their pulpits in Vancouver and Victoria to promote British Israelism and the Ku Klux Klan. When Davies moved on to California, he carried his British Israel ideas with him. He was a key Canadian delegate to a 1937 Seattle conference that firmed up the cultlike status of British Israelite thinkers in the northwest United States. J.J. Maloney, the grand wizard of the Alberta Ku Klux Klan during the 1930s, made British Israel beliefs a keystone element of his teachings in Saskatchewan and Alberta.

During the 1940s, the British Israel movement generally took on a distinctly anti-Jewish tone in response to Zionist calls for the independence of Palestine from British occupation, which was finally achieved with the creation of the state of Israel in 1948. The resulting antipathy to the existence of Israel may have been due to resentment among British adherents to the loss of the British mandate in Palestine. In the western United States, the views of British Israelites were filtered through the extreme right-wing views of figures like Clem Davies. What emerged from these religious brews was a set of beliefs that became known in North American circles as Christian Identity. They in turn formed the basis of extremist political and racist movements labelled as "Aryan" that closely aligned with contemporary versions of Nazi and Fascist ideologies.

Christian Identity proponents argued that white "Aryans" were descended from the biblical tribes of Israel, an old British Israel theme.[7] Unlike the traditional interpretation that reinforced the inherent superiority of the British as the natural successors to God's chosen people, Christian Identity theology held that Jews were different, not connected to the Israelites and in fact "the children of the Devil." This had significant and wide-ranging implications. The world was seen to be on the verge of an apocalyptic struggle between good and evil, where white Aryans "must do battle with the Jewish conspiracy and its allies so that the world can be redeemed."

The consequences of this line of thinking were seen in white supremacist circles during the 1970s and 1980s. The Ku Klux Klan seemed to some relatively quaint with its cross burnings, funny titles and racist mumbo jumbo. The real action during these decades was with groups calling themselves Aryan Nations or the Aryan Resistance Movement or the Brotherhood, collecting arms for the purported final struggle against the Jewish conspiracy, robbing banks and assassinating rivals, critics and opponents.

The government of the United States became known to these true believers as the Zionist Occupied Government — ZOG. It was the enemy, and its agents were to be resisted by violent force of arms. By the 1980s, the more organized members of these groups retreated to strongholds in the Pacific Northwest of the United States, particularly the Aryan Nations compound at Hayden Lake in Idaho presided over by "Pastor" Richard Butler. A number of Canadians were regular visitors to these strongholds of racism and incubators of armed struggle.

The religious musings of right-wing extremists intersected in the decade from 1954 to 1964 with social and political upheaval in the United States as civil rights activists sought to address the discrimination faced by Black citizens. The 1954 United States Supreme Court decision in *Brown v. Board of Education* sparked the beginning of mandatory integration of schools across the country. The ensuing turmoil revived racial animosities to a level not seen in many parts of the United States since the 1920s. Under the guise of protecting states' rights — one of the rallying cries of the Civil War a hundred years earlier — politicians and civic leaders resisted the mingling of Black and white students in local school systems.

The civil rights struggles were a gift to the likes of Charles Lewis Fowler, the American founder of the Ku Klux Klan of Canada in 1925. Fowler arrived in Florida in the late 1940s and was well known in the state for his Klan links. He operated the Kingdom Bible Seminary in St. Petersburg, offering Bible correspondence courses well into the 1960s. The 1954 United States Supreme Court ruling provoked the creation of segregationist groups across the U.S. south called Citizens' Councils. Their stated goal was to reinstate racial segregation. Fowler became a leading figure by helping to establish one of the earliest Citizens' Councils in St. Petersburg in the summer of 1955.[8]

Specifically, the council was organized to prevent Black residents from using a local beach at St. Petersburg. Fowler led a delegation to city hall to warn that "integration would destroy the Anglo-Saxon race." Fowler had not mellowed with time, his words echoing his calls to racist action in Canada thirty years earlier. The former imperial wizard described integration as a fiasco engineered by the United States Supreme Court. He assured his audience that U.S. Chief Justice Earl Warren "was chosen by agitation of an international cabal," and he promised to return with documentary evidence to prove his case. He did not. Racial integration of the beach became a reality after a long legal and political battle. Fowler lived out his final years in obscurity.[9] He died in Pinellas, Florida, in 1974 at age ninety-five, the last Canadian Klan leader of his generation.[10]

In the midst of the 1970s racial unrest, a young Louisiana racist named David Duke led the creation of the modern American Ku Klux Klan. The group had survived over the years in pockets across the south. As the Civil Rights era saw a revival of the nightriders with white hoods and brutal attacks on minorities, state and regional leaders created their own new Klan organizations. Duke believed there was a way to make racism respectable. A native of Tulsa, Oklahoma, Duke attended Louisiana State University in Baton Rouge wearing a brown shirt and swastika armband. He acquired the dubious label of "the campus Nazi" for his rabble-rousing as leader of an organization called the White Youth Alliance (WYA).[11] He hired a security guard to protect him from fellow students.

Duke became a modern Klansman with modern good looks. He abandoned the white robes of the traditional Klan for trim, well-cut business suits. Rather than call down hellfire and damnation on Black people, Duke converted the rhetoric to a defence of white rights on behalf of what he claimed was an increasingly embattled white minority facing waves of advancing Black, brown and Hispanic assimilation. David Duke worked hard to make racism respectable. In his new role, Duke made his first visit to Canada in March 1971 as head of the WYA.[12] It was the first of multiple visits Duke made to Canada in the following decade, before he was eventually deported.

The Canadians he met were a varied lot drawn from the range of characters in Toronto who inhabited the domestic right wing — reading the *Toronto Sun* and raging against perceived liberal bias in Canadian society. First and foremost was a group called the Western Guard, the creation of Vilim Zlomislic, better known as Don Andrews. Born in 1942 in what was then Yugoslavia, Zlomislic's Croatian father was a partisan fighter killed by German occupation forces. His mother was sent to Germany as a slave labourer. Vilim ended up in an orphanage. At war's end, his mother married a Canadian serviceman, returned with him to Canada and began searching for Vilim. She found him with the help of the Red Cross. In March 1952, the ten-year-old Vilim arrived at the Toronto Airport to be met and hugged by a woman he did not know. "Are you my Mum?" he asked.[13]

Renamed Donald Andrews by his mother, Don/Vilim had a hard time adjusting to his new country. It wasn't the language. He learned English quickly and easily. It was his sense of being different in a new society where he didn't quite fit. This was compounded by long hospital stays to treat a bone disease, his Yugoslav background and a lack of money to attend university. Instead, Andrews attended a technical institute and became a public health inspector. He became a fierce anti-Communist, then a socialist and eventually ended up declaring himself opposed to all forms of totalitarianism.

Political engagement initially took the form of involvement in the anti-Communist Edmund Burke Society, named for an eighteenth-century

British conservative free speech advocate. Andrews associated with Paul Fromm, a long-time 1960s right-wing agitator, who became a teacher, and John Ross Taylor, an enduring Nazi fixture in Toronto's extreme right-wing political scene. Andrews became increasingly immersed in racist literature and thought, reflecting in part the evolution of the fairly conventional Edmund Burke Society and its defence of free speech. (The Edmund Burke Society was regularly confused with the virulently anti-Communist but U.S.-based John Birch Society.)

The *Toronto Sun* reported in early May 1972 that the Ku Klux Klan had announced its presence in Canada at a secret banquet hosted by the Western Guard. This insight may have been simply an acknowledgement that specific individuals like John Ross Taylor and Dutch immigrant Jacob Prins had joined American Klan affiliates as individuals. There was no indication that the Klan existed in Toronto at the time as a separate and functioning organization. Regardless, the Klan, the Western Guard, and the Nationalist Socialist Alliance (a small group of neo-Nazis) claimed to be in solidarity against "the threat of the communist left." Overlapping membership between what was described as the Klan and other radical right organizations was an enduring feature of the extreme racist milieu in Canada during the 1970s.

In the spring of 1972, Edmund Burke Society members agreed to change the group's name to the Western Guard. Fromm resigned amid allegations that he had pilfered money from the organization and that the police had in fact set up the Edmund Burke Society to attract and monitor extremists. This was familiar fractious territory for the right wing, which regularly saw groups split over ideology, money or hateful and insupportable personality differences.

Don Andrews and John Ross Taylor took over the Western Guard as leader and deputy leader respectively. Taylor was an old and familiar face in Toronto racist circles. After his foray into Nazi politics in the 1930s, to nobody's surprise, he had spent the Second World War in an internment camp for Canadian Nazi sympathizers at Petawawa, Ontario, in the Ottawa Valley. He was joined by Adrien Arcand and his dwindling band of fascist followers. If William Whittaker had not died before the war, he would certainly have been behind barbed wire too. The postwar years saw Taylor continue to advocate — quietly — Nazi beliefs, a difficult path in a nation that had endured loss and suffering in the struggle against Hitler. In a perverse historical development, the glorification of Adolf Hitler and the anti-Jewish credo of the Nazi Party overtook British Israelism in racist circles. The advent of Christian Identity as a belief system was a handy adjunct to the Nazi-inspired philosophies of the postwar right wing.

John Ross Taylor emerged from obscurity in the early 1960s after years of working as a salesman in Saskatchewan and raising a family. He relocated to Haliburton in rural Ontario and launched a mail-order business selling pro-Nazi, anti-Semitic publications. Politics beckoned as Canadian society became more open, more diverse and hopefully, Taylor believed, more accepting of an old Nazi. CBC journalist Larry Zolf interviewed Taylor at his country home in the 1960s as he researched a story on the revival of Nazi activities in Canada twenty years after the end of the Second World War. The flamboyant Zolf was not impressed. "Taylor was a meticulous, boring man," he recalled.[14]

For contemporary extremists, John Ross Taylor provided a living link to the fascism of the 1930s and the Ku Klux Klan of the 1920s. He embraced anti-Communism and joined forces with old comrades. He ran in a Toronto riding in the 1963 provincial election and finished last. He ran for Toronto city council in 1972. Last place yet again. But as deputy head of the Western Guard, Taylor had moved into the leadership of a small but pivotal organization that served as the focal point for several emerging right-wing figures. John Ross Taylor became an elder statesman of hate.

As leader of the Western Guard, Don Andrews in 1972 threw himself into the first of multiple political races for the position of Toronto mayor. Journalist Christie Blatchford spent time with Andrews as he and a young follower drove around east Toronto. She recalled that the tour turned into "what I called count-the-turbans, with the candidate periodically crying out with glee, 'There's one!'"[15] Andrews's platform was based on three points — he was white, he was young and he disliked "all things black." Andrews garnered about 2 per cent of the vote, finishing fifth after winner David Crombie. That was the public face of the Western Guard.

The other face was the remarkable level of violence and physical intimidation it brought to politics in the city. The early 1970s in Toronto, partly in response to changing demographics, was marked by a vigorous Western Guard campaign of defacing buildings and construction sites with racist, anti-Semitic slogans. Guard members appeared as security at the meetings of affiliated groups. Or they rode the Toronto subway system ostensibly protecting white commuters from racist attacks.

Western Guard member Geza Matrai went to jail for sixty days in 1972 for spraying noxious gas at a gay rights meeting. Another member, Armand Siksna, became the first person in Canada charged in 1974 under new hate propaganda provisions in the *Criminal Code*. He had allegedly posted "white power" placards on a wall. Siksna was acquitted because of insufficient evidence.[16] Another member was put on probation for possession of a dangerous weapon.

The Western Guard, with its sprinkling of self-proclaimed Klan members and assorted fascists, smashed up a meeting supporting liberation for Mozambique at the University of Toronto in 1974. The same year, the Western Guard attacked a Black musician and a nine-year-old boy on a stage at Citytv. Andrews was arrested after a band member's wife was kicked in the stomach. It was the latest in a long history of incidents where he was invariably acquitted of criminal charges. Then his luck ran out.

In July 1976, Andrews and two other men were charged in connection with a plot to disrupt an Olympic soccer game featuring the Israeli national team. The planning involved possession of weapons and explosives and attacks on synagogues. An RCMP human source named Robert Toope was the star witness against the Western Guard leader. Toope joined the guard in late 1975 under RCMP control and was a keen participant in the vandalism campaign that marked this period of right-wing activity in Toronto. His enthusiastic involvement in criminal acts led a commission of inquiry to question how much control his RCMP handler had over this source.[17]

The RCMP had targeted the Western Guard for investigation well in advance of the 1976 Olympics that were to be held mainly in Montreal with certain events like soccer scheduled in Toronto. In the wake of the 1972 terrorist attack on the Israeli team at the Munich Olympics, this was an understandable precaution given the history of anti-Semitic propaganda and violence associated with the Western Guard.

Toope testified later that Andrews himself was rarely involved in illegal activities but ordered others to do the dirty work. Andrews and an associate were found guilty on the weapons and mischief charges. He was sentenced to two years in jail. The judge who sentenced Andrews described him as the instigator of racist attacks in Toronto; he was ordered to cease his involvement with the Western Guard.

The toxic mix of racism, politics and disorder that characterized the life of the Western Guard attracted scores of young people. They tended to show up at the guard's storefront operation in downtown Toronto, forming friendships, sometimes becoming tenants in one of the many rooming houses that Don Andrews bought and managed as he sought financial stability. He also worked in a hospital kitchen and published newsletters, including one that was essentially a marketplace for mercenaries.[18] Andrews's home in the heart of east Toronto's Greektown was a meeting place for a floating population of young, disenchanted racists or wannabe Nazis. Andrews welcomed the company, the attention, being at the centre of an ever-expanding circle of potential recruits.

Into the circle came James Alexander McQuirter, "Sunshine Boy," soon to become the latter-day grand wizard of the Ku Klux Klan of Canada. He would be the new face of the new Ku Klux Klan in a country much changed since the evaporation of the old Klan in the 1930s. The general view was that the twenty-two-year old was too cute to be a grand wizard, a far cry from the likes of Charles Lewis Fowler, James Henry Hawkins, Dirty Jim Lord and George Marshall, the last leaders of the Canadian Ku Klux Klan.

The Sunshine Boy label came from the *Toronto Sun*, a daily tabloid newspaper that had emerged from the 1971 collapse of the venerable Toronto *Telegram*. The *Sun* catered to a blue-collar market that appreciated its news nuance-free, with large headlines and big pictures. The old *Telegram* had been resolutely Conservative and firmly lodged on the right wing; the *Sun* carried on the tradition, with a populist overlay that allowed for idiosyncratic displays of jingoistic ardour, stick-it-to-the-unions and stick up for the "little guy." It was a sympathetic echo chamber for right-wing messages. the *Sun*'s model was the colourful world of British tabloids. And in the spirit of its British counterparts, the *Sun* regularly published a page-three picture of a so-called "Sunshine Girl" wearing very little. In response to charges of sexism, *Sun* editors launched a Sunshine Boy feature.

James Alexander McQuirter, with his good cheekbones, good hair and toothy smile, was a classic Sunshine Boy. His picture was published in March 1980, with no mention of his political views, although the poster he posed beside spoke volumes. It showed a young Black man with the text "He may be your equal, but he's not mine." The *Sun's* politics veered erratically right, so its choice of model was apt. The cutline said Jim hoped for a seat in Parliament some day.

James McQuirter brought to the grand wizard's role a sure hand in managing the Klan's media profile. Unlike the 1920s when radio was young, the 1980s media landscape included newspapers, radio, television and cable — many of these outlets national in scope and readily accessible. As in the 1920s, the Klan benefited from and exploited the media to tell its story. And few were better at it than McQuirter.

He grew up in a downtown Toronto public housing project, the oldest of five children, his parents separated.[19] He later offered that he entered his early teens reading racist literature as an extension of his concern for threatened wildlife, claiming the white race was a threatened species. This was a media talking point in the 1980s for those right-wing extremists articulate enough to get an interview. Politically, McQuirter said he started as a Marxist, decided left-wing literature was too obscure for ordinary people to understand, ruled out university and began reading right-wing and racist materials.

McQuirter appeared to have few anchors in his early years. He joined the Canadian Forces reserves, served for four years, rose to the rank of lieutenant and was an instructor. He tried working as a security guard in the late 1970s, but it didn't go well. He stole a typewriter and stationery, was convicted of theft and sentenced to a brief time in jail.

According to social scientist Stanley Barrett, James McQuirter was a young man in a hurry. He wanted to have a position, to do well, to have wealth, to enjoy it. He ended up working in a hospital along with several other like-minded right-wing figures. McQuirter focused on getting ahead in life. He had a landscape business, a mail-forwarding business and a stake in several houses where he aspired to become a low-rent landlord. But by all appearances, McQuirter had no set role in his life other than working for right-wing causes — the Western Guard, the Nationalist Party and ultimately the Ku Klux Klan.

Wolfgang Droege was another Toronto youth who drifted into the orbit of Don Andrews, John Ross Taylor and other long-time racists. Wolfgang ("The Wolf") Droege was an unlikely but obvious recruit for the reborn Ku Klux Klan. He was born in 1949 at Forchheim, a small town on the rail line 35 kilometres north of Nuremberg, Bavaria, in what was then West Germany. The city of Nuremberg was the site of Hitler's notorious Nazi rallies during the 1930s that set the scene for his murderous regime. The city was marked by the architecture and memories of the Nazi era.

Droege's family were hoteliers. His grandfather was a staunch Nazi sympathizer closely associated with notorious anti-Semitic propagandist Julius Streicher, whose political power base was Nuremberg.[20] His parents divorced when he was five. Droege lived with his grandparents until he was thirteen and arrived in Toronto in 1963 to rejoin his mother, who had remarried.[21] His background was reminiscent of Don Andrews's except they came from opposite sides of European history. Droege was short and squat and spoke English with a German accent, traits that left him socially isolated in his new country and new city.

He dropped out of high school, returned to West Germany in his mid-teens and tried to join the military. No luck. His interest in history and his time back in Germany exposed him to Nazi and racist ideas. He came back to Canada and worked for a brief time in the nickel mines of Sudbury in northern Ontario, eventually drifting back to Toronto where he became a printer's apprentice. He was a prime recruit for the burgeoning right-wing scene, made up of what writer Stewart Bell described as "self-loathing, psychologically beaten-up misfits."

Don Andrews scooped up Droege for the Western Guard at a pub near his east-end home on Kingsmount Park Road. In the spring of 1975, Droege, Armand Siksna and Leo Jutting, all followers or tenants of Don Andrews, were arrested for spray-painting racist slogans on construction site walls and charged with mischief to private property.[22] Later in the year, Droege accompanied Andrews on a road trip to New Orleans to meet David Duke. It was the first of many visits and meetings between David Duke, Don Andrews, Wolfgang Droege, James McQuirter and other figures in the Canadian right wing.

David Duke put his ideas of creating a modern Ku Klux Klan into force with the establishment in 1975 of the Knights of the Ku Klux Klan, based in New Orleans. Duke's version of the Klan differentiated itself by its leader — educated, articulate and photogenic — and a rhetoric largely free of the race-baiting language of the past. But the new Ku Klux Klan was just as virulent in its hatred of Black people, Jews and Asians and its support for white supremacy.

The backdrop to the resurgence of Ku Klux Klan activity in Canada and the United States during the late 1970s was bound up with geo-strategic politics and Canada's own domestic situation. United States President Jimmy Carter's government was stymied in 1979 when the shah of Iran was toppled from office and replaced by an extremist government under the Ayatollah Khomeini. American oil supplies in the Middle East were threatened. In November, the U.S. embassy in Tehran was seized along with dozens of American officials, who were then held hostage for more than a year. Late in 1979, the Union of Soviet Socialist Republics invaded Afghanistan, further challenging the United States on the global stage. The U.S. government appeared hapless and ill-prepared to deal with these situations. President Carter's re-election hopes in 1980 were dashed when an operation to rescue the hostages in Iran failed. America presented itself to the world as a shambling giant, an image that emboldened right-wing extremist groups who blamed America's woes on traitors within.

The Canadian context was more benign but equally fraught. The separatist government of René Lévesque's Parti Québécois was elected in 1976, pledging a referendum on creating a sovereign country. The political system was on edge for years waiting for a crucial vote. In 1979, the Conservative Party under Joe Clark ousted Pierre Trudeau's Liberal government. Ten months later, Clark's minority government was voted out and Trudeau was returned to office.

In May 1980, the long-threatened referendum vote saw the defeat of a proposal for "sovereignty-association" between Canada and Quebec. After this protracted period of political uncertainty, Trudeau and the Liberals launched an initiative to modernize the Canadian constitution by formally repatriating all residual authority from the British Parliament to Canada. The new constitution would include a *Charter of Rights and Freedoms* that would enshrine concepts of equality, freedom and access to justice that were inimical to the ideas promulgated by the Ku Klux Klan. The rebirth of the Klan in Canada in 1980 was part of the reaction to the social and legal changes proposed to be enshrined in the new constitution.

David Duke later took credit for helping to revive the Klan in Canada, and in many ways that was true. Duke claimed to have affiliate Klan organizations in Canada in the mid-1970s, probably a reference to his contacts with the Western Guard. He visited Toronto in 1977, appearing on radio and TV talk shows and perfecting his newfound role as the leader of American white supremacy.[23] Wolfgang Droege later recalled that Duke's visit to Toronto created "a storm of letters and requests for memberships" in the Ku Klux Klan. At the time, there was no Canadian Klan to join.

"Canada is the last bastion of the white race on this planet, but we're going to lose the battle unless something is done," Duke told media interviewers during his Toronto visit.[24] According to Duke, it was already too late to save the United States, but in Canada the imperial wizard saw both challenge and hope. Looking around, Duke claimed to see a difference from his earlier visits. Canadian cities were now becoming "dirty, overridden by nonwhites." The Klan was the answer. A handful of Canadians seemed to think so too.

# Chapter 12
# GOAT WORSHIPPERS

James Alexander McQuirter and Wolfgang Droege worked in the Western Guard's Yonge Street storefront office in the late 1970s as Don Andrews was solidifying his role in the right-wing scene in Toronto. They were increasingly resentful of Andrews. They were also impressed by the rising tide of requests for information on the Ku Klux Klan, particularly when David Duke's visits to Toronto generated media attention.

An idea formed slowly, then took shape. Why not revive Canada's Ku Klux Klan in the image of David Duke's more modern, more polished and sophisticated version? They saw themselves as the rising new generation of right-wing leaders, not just in Toronto but across Canada. Why shouldn't they be the leaders of a new movement in Canada?

Meanwhile, John Ross Taylor, a leading figure in the Western Guard, was building contacts with American figures and groups. He often travelled to the United States for rallies and gatherings. He had contacts with the Ku Klux Klan that went beyond David Duke and into the more traditional Klan groups of yesteryear.

Journalist Patsy Sims wrote of encountering Taylor ("quiet and gray in complexion and dress") at a Klan rally in West Virginia in the 1970s, accompanied by Jacob Prins. They were on-site representing the Western Guard, although Prins introduced himself as the grand dragon of Canada. This may have been a self-proclaimed title since there was no formal Klan organization in the country at the time. Sims reported both men had been Klan members for four or five years. Prins, a burly truck mechanic who claimed a role in the Dutch Resistance during the Second World War, told Sims he was carrying "a special knife" to protect himself from Communists.[1] Prins had joined the Western Guard in 1972, had run for Toronto alderman twice and by 1980 had become deputy leader of the guard.[2]

James McQuirter had begun his formal association with the American Ku Klux Klan about 1977, probably joining Duke's American organization during or after a visit to Louisiana that summer. Or it may have been the year before, when Tyler Bridges reported that McQuirter, Wolfgang Droege and John Ross Taylor attended a gathering called the International Patriotic Conference in Metairie, Louisiana.

"I felt uplifted," said Wolfgang Droege when recalling the gathering years later. "I will never forget this event."[3] The conference was a formative event for the young Canadians. Surrounded by no-hope white supremacists and old-time Nazis in relatively staid Toronto, David Duke became an inspiration to the ambitious McQuirter and Droege.

"Many times you have right-wing leaders who were misfits or inarticulate misfits that people can't identify with," McQuirter later told an interviewer.[4] "David Duke wasn't like that. He was a good speaker. He discussed issues at the level of the common man. He was young, a college graduate and good looking." Just like McQuirter in many ways, except for the university degree.

The Toronto police knew James Alexander McQuirter for his right-wing politics in addition to stealing office supplies. In March 1978, he and Armand Siksna were charged with conspiracy to distribute hate literature. McQuirter and Droege decamped to Vancouver with a plan to make a living selling used cars. "We were selling cars here and there, but we really didn't do too well at it," Droege said later.

What they did do well was chat up local contacts that David Duke had developed on the Lower Mainland. Soon they were hosting meetings in Vancouver with like-minded racists. Then Don Andrews got out of jail back in Ontario after finishing his sentence for the plot against the Israeli soccer team. McQuirter returned to Toronto to resume working with Andrews, while Droege stayed on the west coast.

In mid-1979, Droege moved to Victoria to take a short-term job managing a business forms company.[5] In addition to his day job, Droege was able to present himself as the west coast face of a renewed Canadian Ku Klux Klan. David Duke came to visit in 1980 after several years of boasting of hundreds of Klan members in the Vancouver area. He made a splash in the city's radio talk show circuit and in local newspapers. Wolfgang Droege appeared with him as the Klan's lead organizer in British Columbia. The visit ended with Duke's deportation from Canada on the grounds of hiding a criminal conviction for inciting a race riot in New Orleans a decade earlier.

Back in Toronto, James McQuirter formally announced the return of the Ku Klux Klan to Canada in June 1980. The first official Klan office was in the living room of his house at 1439 Dundas Street East in the Riverdale district of east Toronto. The building was in a predominantly white neighbourhood bordering on an area with a large East Indian population, an ideal location for building on racial stereotypes.

When the neighbours realized who was in the house, the reaction was immediate. A group called the Riverdale Action Committee Against Racism organized street demonstrations outside the house. There were ugly confrontations. McQuirter then moved the Klan operation to an office in the upscale Davisville neighbourhood on Toronto's Yonge Street, then closed it later in November 1980 when the Jewish owners realized who their new tenants were. McQuirter's story in later years was that the other tenants forced the owners to evict him.[6]

The political reaction to the Ku Klux Klan's presence was predictable. "They're bloody well not welcome in this province," said Ontario Attorney-General Roy McMurtry. "They will be watched, but until they break the law there's nothing we can do." The message echoed what Attorney General William Nickle and his deputy minister Edward Bayly had said sixty-five years earlier. "I can only reiterate that there's no law preventing a citizens' organization calling itself the Ku Klux Klan," said McMurtry. "If they wanted to call themselves goat worshippers, we wouldn't stop them."[7]

McMurtry had prior experience dealing with the Klan. When David Duke passed through Toronto in 1977, the grand wizard had tried unsuccessfully to visit McMurtry in his legislature office. Duke left a letter behind for McMurtry that threatened unnamed reprisals if the attorney general did not stop protecting the rights of minorities. McMurtry framed the letter and displayed it in every office he held over a long legal career.[8]

McMurtry had personal understanding of the plights of minorities. His brother Bill had worked a summer job in the 1950s as a sleeping car porter for the Canadian National Railway, a job that was usually held by Black workers. Roy and Bill had both become friends with the porters who experienced segregation in the railway industry.

McMurtry was clearly miffed by his exposure to Duke and the Klan. "I personally regard [the Klan] as representative of the lunatic fringe of the community," he said in 1980. "But we are concerned about creating unnecessary worry among visible minority groups in our community." Toronto's police chief, Jack Marks, was more stoic. He told the media the Klan had been in Toronto for about three years with only a few members at most.

The attorney general's office paid close attention to the Klan. When the group began recruiting in Toronto schools in the fall of 1980, McMurtry ordered an investigation. Klan business cards and pamphlets circulating in secondary schools were collected by the police and submitted to the Crown attorney's office for potential hate crime charges.[9] McQuirter himself spoke to a senior class at Don Mills Collegiate in central Toronto. Before long, the Klan was barred from schools in the city, but that didn't stop organizers from using the tactic elsewhere. McQuirter began focusing efforts on organizing a branch operation called the KKK Canada-White Youth Corps, charged with distributing racist literature in schools.

In July 1980, McQuirter announced that the Klan would open a branch office in Ottawa. "We're not a lunatic fringe — in many ways we could be the racial minorities' best friend," he told the *Ottawa Citizen* in a publicity splash.[10] How this could be so, he did not explain.

A few months later, Klan member Armand Siksna announced he would run for mayor of Toronto in that fall's municipal elections. His platform was remarkably thin on detail and was largely aimed at garnering publicity for the Klan. "We're not monsters like Hollywood makes us," Siksna told reporters. "We want to spread love — not hatred — love of the white race."[11] McQuirter said the Klan did not officially endorse Siksna, even though the candidate continued to say kind things about the organization as he spread love for the duration of his doomed campaign.

Attorney General McMurtry spoke at Ontario universities and colleges in opposition to the Klan. He was particularly concerned about the appeal to youth, whom he saw as vulnerable to Klan activities. "They think it's a frolic that doesn't represent anything very serious," he told students at Wilfrid Laurier University in Waterloo.[12] During hard times, said McMurtry, "people look for a scapegoat . . . people want someone to hate." And the Klan had a unique talent for shaping hate.

The Klan HQ (and McQuirter personally) finally landed in a modest house on Springhurst Avenue in the west-end Toronto neighbourhood of Parkdale. The Ku Klux Klan had held successful meetings in the area back in the 1920s, but the times had changed and so had the neighbourhood. The Klan presence sparked a community backlash, particularly after Klan members began handing out cards and pamphlets at local schools. Demonstrators arrived on Springhurst Avenue in the middle of August 1981 to protest the Klan's presence.[13]

As some 250 protesters jeered at white-robed Klan members gathered on the porch shouting back at them, McQuirter told the media that the home's residents should be left in peace. The householders were, he claimed, a Klan couple who had lived there for many years. As it turned out, McQuirter lived there too — with the Klan's head of security Gary MacFarlane and his wife Jean MacGarry. It was just a temporary office for the Klan while new quarters were found in the downtown core, McQuirter explained to the media.

A truck that served as the Klan's so-called communications centre was parked outside, sporting a Confederate stars-and-bars battle flag on the windshield.[14] Plywood panels eventually were nailed over the front windows of the house as the protests continued for months. "Toronto Cops are Tops" stickers decorated the plywood.

The Klan's case to be a relatively benign, people-friendly organization was not helped by the company the leadership was keeping. McQuirter travelled to London, Ontario, in early November 1980 at the invitation of Martin Weiche, a wealthy contractor and former German Luftwaffe pilot who was the president of the Canadian National Socialist Party. Weiche and his party were Nazis in the Adolf Hitler mould. There were also rumours, consistently denied, that Weiche invested money in an improbable plan to seize the Caribbean island of Dominica as a base for white nationalists.

At a rally on Weiche's farm near London, a cross was burned in the old Klan tradition and new members were signed up. McQuirter defended the event as just a recruiting rally. His host was "nothing more than a friend," and Weiche "doesn't necessarily agree with our principles."[15] That said, the rally had the feel of events in southwestern Ontario in past decades.

With Wolfgang Droege in Victoria, the Klan was able to present the image of a national organization with significant membership. Droege was able to recruit, or the Klan's notoriety attracted, west coast leaders — Al Hooper, Ann Farmer, Dan Wray, Dave Cook and others. The appearance of a traditional organization with a national reach was enhanced by the image of an elaborate structure that was projected by Klan documents and spokesmen.

The Canadian head office was nominally in Toronto, although some would argue it was truly in New Orleans, where David Duke was now in play with a new organization called the National Association for the Advancement of White People. His leadership role with the U.S. Imperial Knights of the Ku Klux Klan was taken up by his deputy, Don Black.

McQuirter and Droege exercised full control of the Canadian Klan as leader and deputy leader respectively, although each was deeply involved in other endeavours, such as Operation Red Dog, discussed later. In a nod to familiar Canadian federalist principles, each province was designated a "realm" with a provincial leader who was styled a grand dragon, although most provinces appeared to lack either membership, or leadership or both.

The grand dragons were local leaders in their own right.[16] Jacob Prins, seen consorting with John Ross Taylor at KKK events in West Virginia, held the post of grand dragon in Ontario. Dave Cook was the grand dragon in British Columbia, until he displeased national headquarters by pushing back on national policies; he was replaced in 1981 by Al Hooper, who knew some bikers and sold Klan paraphernalia and Nazi regalia to make a living. Tom Zink was said to be the grand dragon for the Maritimes, but his profile was so low as to be subterranean. No other grand dragons appeared in the public eye.

The national Ku Klux Klan organization featured other players and other entities, at least on paper. Security was handled by a group called the White Security Force. "Preference will be given to those having military or police background," said a Klan handbook, which stipulated who could be a member. The force had three sections: a Defensive Security Branch trained in defence, crowd control and use of attack dogs; the so-called Klan

Intelligence Agency, tasked with spying on left-wing and antiracist groups; and the Klokan, which styled itself a police and enforcement organization but which was so secret that even its existence was in doubt. The Klokan had always existed in Klan mythmaking. "Doctor" Keith Allen had operated as the Klokan (head of inquiries) for Oregon's Fred Gifford back in the 1920s before moving north to Vancouver to work with Luther Powell.

The Klan's security and intelligence arrangements featured truly seamy characters. The White Security Force was led by Gary Eugene MacFarlane, said to have been a member of the United States Marine Corps at some point in his past. More recently, he had just been released from the Penetanguishene Asylum for the Criminally Insane in Ontario, where he had spent seven years for killing a man in Toronto in 1973. He worked as a security guard with a specialty of handling guard dogs.

The Klan Intelligence Agency was under the leadership of William Lau Richardson, an American whose background raised ongoing suspicions that he was a law enforcement source. Richardson apparently landed in Canada about 1970. Court records later stated that, before his appearance in Canada, he had worked in some capacity for the Central Intelligence Agency and United States Army Intelligence.

Richardson's work history in Canada was riddled with legal problems. Daniel McGarry, who had once been a Toronto police officer, operated a security firm called Centurion Investigations Ltd. The company specialized in strikebreaking and union-busting. Richardson worked for Centurion during the late 1970s. In 1979, he put a fake bomb in a car used by union organizers working at the McDonnell Douglas aircraft plant in northwest Toronto. It was a bid to get union organizers fired from the plant. A couple of years later, Richardson turned up as head of the Klan Intelligence Agency and was identified as an RCMP informant. This was no surprise to many, including James McQuirter, who said he knew about Richardson's contact with the RCMP — which the American described as a "professional relationship."

The new Klan followed the old Klan's traditional structure. The local klaverns were now called "dens," but the concept remained the same. Each den could have between five and thirty members. In areas like Toronto and Vancouver with several dens, chapters were created, led by an official known as a giant.

The so-called "den commander" in Etobicoke, a suburb in west Toronto, was Kenneth David Whelan. The twenty-five-year-old Whelan and his partner Carole Ann Miller died under suspicious circumstances in late May 1981 when a fire started in the living room of their house in the middle of the night. Upstairs, the pair died of smoke inhalation. Homicide detectives were called in to investigate. Gary MacFarlane, head of Klan security, acknowledged Whelan's role with the Klan but showed scant sympathy when talking about him to the media.[17]

Sociologist Stanley Barrett studied the right wing in Canada during the 1980s. He described the 1980s Klan as "above all else a propaganda vehicle." The new Klan generated public interest — and reaction — across the country. An organizational presence was harder to achieve. More substantively, though, and to illustrate Barrett's point, the new Ku Klux Klan failed to generate a public policy debate. A fundamental flaw in McQuirter and Droege's search for political relevance was an inability to mount a constructive debate about matters of current concern or attention, such as constitutional change.

Beginning in October 1980, when the Klan was most salient in the media, the country's political discourse was dominated by Prime Minister Pierre Trudeau's constitutional initiative to repatriate the constitution from Britain and create a *Charter of Rights and Freedoms*. The proposed *Charter* was an issue on which the Klan could be expected to have opinions, since its principles would challenge the Klan's core values. Yet no Klan briefs were submitted to the parliamentary committee created to consult the public on the *Charter*. McQuirter, Droege and other Klan figures said nothing that was reportable, or nothing at all, in public on the topic.

The Klan's policies and goals were limited. As McQuirter and Droege travelled the country, they talked of limiting immigration, deporting Black and brown people and bringing Canada to a state of pure white citizenry. McQuirter described Canada's policies of multiculturalism as "just a fancy name for race mixing."[18] When he and Droege landed in Vancouver in the fall of 1980 fresh from the publicity of the Klan's Toronto debut, the region was in the midst of an influx of South Asian immigrants — Indians, Bangladeshis, Pakistanis.[19] The ostensible reason for their visit was to shore up recruiting, but others saw mischief.

They managed easy access to media circles, including the Canadian Broadcasting Corporation (CBC), which provided a platform in interviews for McQuirter to argue for "an all-white Canada — and a return of nonwhite Canadians to their countries of origin." According to their vision, this would occur under the auspices of a democratically elected Klan government, thus providing legitimacy.[20] A CBC interview broadcast on October 23, 1980, prompted a round of complaints under the provincial *Human Rights Code* and the hate propaganda section of the *Criminal Code*, options not available to offended citizens during the Klan's activities a half-century earlier.

The Klan leadership did not have the qualities or instincts that could take them beyond the level of shabby street-level politics. The Klan's stated ultimate goal was control of all three levels of government — municipal, provincial and federal. The route to political power had four stages: conducting propaganda and media publicity; developing organizational rigour; building mass political support leading to electoral success within the existing system; and, finally, seizing power from the "liberal left."

The Klan's literature for members was full of tips for the aspiring racist candidate to public office — publicize rivals' peculiarities, sexual deviations, personal vulnerabilities. Exaggerate incompetence and wasteful spending. Disrupt and divide opposing forces by infiltrating and acting as *agents provocateurs*. It's unclear how much of this advice came from within the Canadian Klan and how much was borrowed from David Duke.

With national media exposure and the appearance of a national organization, the reborn Klan began picking up members — mostly in Ontario and British Columbia, and to a lesser extent on the Prairies where unexpected pockets of Klansmen popped up. The number of Klan members was a favourite topic of speculation. McQuirter, the media and interested observers estimated the national numbers variously: from many thousands to a few hundred to scores concentrated in Toronto.

The reality fluctuated depending on who asked, who answered, who was listening and the consequences of high or low or middling numbers. In Ontario, dens were reported in sleepy places like Hanover, Walkerton and Barrie, through to regional centres like Windsor, Kitchener, Hamilton and Niagara Falls.[21] In B.C., the Klan was primarily a Lower Mainland affair, with members in Surrey, Burnaby and Vancouver proper.

McQuirter and the Toronto leadership — but mainly McQuirter — made themselves widely available to the media, either travelling to events or giving interviews by phone to anybody who asked. McQuirter's knack for grabbing media attention reasserted itself in late November, when he announced the impending expansion of the Klan into the Halifax area.[22] The first sign of the Klan's presence would be a phone number with a direct line into the Toronto office where, he pledged, he would be personally standing by to talk to Maritimers. The next step would be to actually buy a building in Halifax for Klan use. The ultimate goal would be to lobby "for white rights and organizing white people to work for their interests just as minorities are today." One of the Klan's Toronto members, Jim Summer, who described himself as the "Titan of Ontario," told the media there was already a secret den in Halifax, "but a larger group would be revealed soon." It never happened.

Then McQuirter told the Fredericton *Daily Gleaner* in December 1980 that "the time is ripe" for a Klan return to New Brunswick, the centre of Jim Lord's invisible empire of the 1920s. "Right now, this country is falling apart . . . The Klan is an organization that wants to do something about that." Anti-French, anti-Catholic bigotry was no longer on the Klan agenda; the focus was on white supremacy. "We want to maintain the white race as the dominating force in this country . . . We should look after our own family."[23] Who was in the family wasn't clear, but there was little doubt about who was out.

The media's fascination with the Klan continued through much of 1980, even if the news value was questionable. In September 1980, Wolfgang Droege had told the *Vancouver Sun* that the Klan would formally merge with Don Andrews's Nationalist Party. This was not much of a stretch given the overlap in membership, but it also never happened. In October, when McQuirter and Droege appeared in Vancouver for media appearances and general rabble rousing, posters featuring a hooded Klansman began circulating around the province. Business cards with Klan slogans were handed out near secondary schools. These publicity efforts gleaned media attention and also yielded membership results.

This was evident at an initiation ceremony for new members that was staged in October on a Vancouver beach south of Marine Drive. A burning cross helped identify the location. The Vancouver Police took an uncharitable view of the thirty or so Klan members milling about in the light of the flickering flames. Six police cruisers, two paddy wagons and uncounted police motorcycles descended on the scene to calm the celebrants. There were no arrests, but two rifles and a shotgun were seized. Also, a Klansman was bitten by a police dog.

McQuirter was using a media plan designed to drum up attention. The Klan was organizing, he said, because of white resentment over Pakistani and East Indian immigration. "I'm not a hate-monger, I'm not out to belittle people," he said. "I just want to improve the quality of life for the people that built this country — the white people."[24]

The Ku Klux Klan's presence on the Lower Mainland began to take on a familiar shape. Klan literature was handed out on the campus of the British Columbia Institute of Technology, one of the region's major colleges.[25] Nigerian students at the BCIT were targeted for violence in late November 1980. Their homes in Burnaby and New Westminster were spray-painted with racist slogans including the letters "KKK." Garbage was dumped on their property. Obscene and threatening phone calls punctuated their days and nights. One of them was beaten badly by unknown assailants. The campaign, which went on for almost four months, began roughly about the time McQuirter and Droege arrived in Vancouver.

The new year brought a series of attacks on South Asian targets. On January 3, 1981, the home of Gurdev Singh Sidhu in Delta was firebombed. A flaming five-gallon gasoline can was thrown through a window. The attack provoked demonstrations in front of the burned-out structure by hundreds of protestors with origins in India, Pakistan and Bangladesh. "Self Defence Is the Only Way Out," read placards brandished by the crowd. Race relations in the region were tense.

Three weeks later, on January 22, 1981, a young East Indian man, Avtar (Terry) Dhami, was sitting in a car with a friend outside Windermere Secondary School in east-side Vancouver. A group of about twenty white youths approached, one carrying a baseball bat and another an iron bar. The car windows were smashed and the two were roughed up. "There were a lot of white people on the street they could have attacked. Why did they pick on me? Because of my colour," Dhami told a protest meeting a few days later. "The police didn't do anything about it."[26]

The violence continued. On February 11, 1981, four Molotov cocktails were thrown at the home of Kuldip Gill, a sawmill worker, in Ladner. On April 10, 1981, Hillel House, a Jewish student facility at the University of British Columbia, was spray-painted: "KKK forever," "Death to Jews" and "Death to Hillel House and all Jews." The same night, the bus of the Jewish Community Centre and Chabad Centre was broken into and set on fire.[27] Targeted violence, arson, intimidation — it all had a familiar Klan feel.

Dave Cook, the former grand dragon for British Columbia, told an interviewer in April 1981 that the Klan had four dens in the Greater Vancouver area with others in Cranbrook, Victoria and Sidney on Vancouver Island, Captain Wallace Laycock's old recruiting ground for the Ku Klux Klan of the 1920s. Cook allowed that there might be dens elsewhere in the province. One of the reasons he was vague, apparently, was that his role as recruiter ended when a den reached four to ten members. After that, he had no further contact, and the den went about its business unsupervised.

There were signs that the Ku Klux Klan of Canada was suffering from organizational disintegration, a familiar condition in KKK circles. Dave Cook had been dumped by the Klan's Toronto head office. Now, he claimed his mandate directly from the Klan organization in Tuscumbia, Alabama, which was headed by Don Black, David Duke's successor as leader of the U.S. Knights of the Ku Klux Klan. Cook and his colleague, David Harris, a twenty-nine-year-old Vancouver bus driver who claimed five years' service in the Canadian army, denied that their activities were in the violent tradition of the Klan.

Yet Cook was quoted as saying the Klan was preparing for a race war by recommending its members arm themselves with rifles and sidearms and stock up on survivalist supplies.[28] Harris, an ex-member of the Princess Patricia's Canadian Light Infantry regiment, was even more explicit about preparing for a race war. "We don't have stockpiles of arms or anything," he said, but then acknowledged he had been giving weapons training to Klan members. "We're not ready, but that time will come if we don't get the political situation turned around in this country." He sounded ominous. "The time will come soon."[29]

The implied threats in these pronouncements led to questions for the RCMP, which provided policing services across the Lower Mainland. Staff Sergeant Paul Starek of the Burnaby detachment fielded inquiries about guns and the Klan. Starek was a long-serving officer on the Lower Mainland, who began his police career with the old Surrey Police Department in 1950 before joining the RCMP. He had seen it all — strikes, student protests, Doukhobors stripping naked in public.

Starek dismissed a lot of the Klan's activities as incidents designed to provoke media attention. "But if they are dealing in arms, that's something we would be interested in," said Starek, who then said something truly interesting. "Our intelligence in that area is pretty good, and if the Klan were up to anything illegal, I think we would find out about it sooner than they think."[30] The RCMP was clearly running intelligence operations against the Klan.

The Klan's rebirth and spread across the country in 1980–81 saw the rise of regional groups and leaders, some talented and organized, others bizarre, crude or simply inept. Almost all had some criminal tendencies. The Vancouver klavern — or den in the modern terminology — was disturbingly competent. The same couldn't be said of other groups. McQuirter's leadership from Toronto was increasingly contested during the early months of 1981, particularly with Wolfgang Droege absent in the United States and focused on what became known as Operation Red Dog. Further, as McQuirter would later acknowledge, he was leading a frenetic lifestyle that probably would have killed him if it had continued much longer.

The reborn Klan encountered a bizarre situation in Alberta. A full-fledged Klan leader in the person of Ivan Ross Macpherson had assumed the mantle of J.J. Maloney, the imperial wizard who had led the Alberta Ku Klux Klan during the 1930s. Macpherson was a transplanted Maritimer, born in Prince Edward Island. Adopted and renamed Barry Dunsford, he arrived in Calgary in 1965 at age seventeen. At some point, Macpherson/Dunsford took on the Gaelic form of his name and became Tearlach Mac a' Phearsoin. In 1974, he was convicted of criminal negligence in the shooting death of Mexican national Elias Acuilar Ramirez, a twenty-one-year-old boarder who lived in the basement of Macpherson/Dunsford's parents' downtown Calgary house. Macpherson/Dunsford, whose mother testified he was on medication at the time of the shooting, was fined fifteen hundred dollars for criminal negligence and five hundred dollars for dangerous use of a firearm.[31]

By 1980, he was flourishing as the self-styled head of his own Alberta Ku Klux Klan, complete with a genuine legal provincial charter and a claim of nearly three hundred members. To add to his credibility, Macpherson/Dunsford had struck up a relationship with Robert Scoggin, grand dragon of a South Carolina Klan group, with an eye to future shared initiatives. He welcomed a Black man into his local klavern, playing the move for its publicity value. In the summer of 1980, after crosses were burned on the lawns of Japanese and Pakistani families in Red Deer, Macpherson/Dunsford proposed to initiate twenty-five new members into the local klavern with an even larger public cross burning. The City of Red Deer said no.

Macpherson/Dunsford described McQuirter's Klan as a Nazi organization; McQuirter and company described Macpherson/Dunsford as "a nut who shot his male Mexican lover, accepted a Black man into the Klan, and even was in favour of Jewish members."[32] Fraternal solidarity did not follow. Macpherson/Dunsford gave credibility to McQuirter's allegations about his mental condition in the early 1980s when he started claiming healing powers channelled through the spirit of his dead Mexican shooting victim. There was no discernible link between the revived national Klan and Macpherson/Dunsford's activities.

The absence of affiliation did not mean the absence of activity, however. Several years later, in June 1988, two of Macpherson/Dunsford's Klan members were arrested — and subsequently convicted — of conspiracy to blow up the Calgary Jewish Centre and kill local real estate businessman Harold Milavsky. At trial, it turned out that Macpherson/Dunsford had dreamed up the plot himself to generate publicity and sell Klan memberships. In two of his followers he found willing co-conspirators. "He was the author, initiator and mastermind of the whole plan," contended John James, defence lawyer for one of the accused Klansmen. "He was a manipulative predator with respect to my client."

In fact, Macpherson/Dunsford tipped off the police about what was planned as a way to win favour with the Jewish community and thereby make money.[33] The Calgary police assigned an undercover officer to the case. The officer convinced the two would-be bombers that he could build the bombs to carry out the plot. The officer arranged to meet them to deliver the bombs that turned out to be harmless collections of lights, batteries and switches. They were arrested and charged. MacPherson/Dunsford had already gone to local Jewish leaders claiming credit for breaking the case and promising similar results in future cases of threats against the Jewish community, for a price. There were suggestions in court that he had been a paid police source for years. MacPherson/Dunsford retreated to Edmonton in later years, reverted to the English form of his name and immersed himself in spirituality, Indigenous medicine and self-promotion.

* * *

The revival of the Ku Klux Klan in the 1980s was accompanied by a remarkable community response wherever the group appeared. When the Klan tried to distribute leaflets on "morality issues" in Toronto's Parkdale neighbourhood in 1981, a multicultural community coalition formed to oppose the group's activities.[34] "We wanted to make it clear that the opposition was going to follow the Klan wherever they went and that communities were not going to tolerate the KKK," recalled John Meyers, one of the organizers. A similar pushback occurred when the Klan appeared in the Riverdale neighbourhood on Dundas Street East. The same thing happened in Montreal, in Halifax and most decidedly in Vancouver. This phenomenon of community opposition hadn't happened when the Klan organized during the 1920s. It was in many ways a reflection of how much Canada had changed in the intervening years.

In response, the Klan tried to infiltrate the opposition groups, sending operatives like William Lau Richardson to join in the planning activities of the Riverdale Action Committee Against Racism. "It is disturbing that such a person should be around," said Rev. John Robson of the Queen Street East Presbyterian Church, who helped organize a rally outside Klan HQ on Dundas Street East in 1980. Richardson's notoriety preceded him. By then, Richardson's infiltration of unions and local organizations opposed to the U.S. military draft and his spying on Chilean exiles in Toronto had been widely reported in the media. When Riverdale organizers realized his real identity, he was told to leave and not come back.[35]

Community resistance to the Klan took a similar turn in Halifax, where organizers sought to counter the Klan's recruiting initiatives. Four local women led by community worker Jackie Barkley went one step further.[36] They formed an *a cappella* singing group and performed at an anti-Klan rally in 1981. The quartet called itself Four the Moment. Over the years, the membership of the group changed, but their message did not. They appeared at rallies, women's events and Black culture celebrations across the province and then across the country. Their repertoire was resolutely political, with an antiracist message that reflected the opposition the Klan sparked.

For the Ku Klux Klan, the police, media and community opposition was all part of the struggle and the notoriety. With economic and racial ferment in Canada and the United States, the times were ripe for movements like the Ku Klux Klan, which offered simple solutions to complicated problems. For James McQuirter, Wolfgang Droege and local Klan leaders, this was their heyday. They had profile, they had influence and they had aspirations for more.

# Chapter 13
# ISLAND IN THE SUN

The dream was the creation of a Caribbean nation-base where white supremacists could safely make a lot of money to pursue their racist dreams. It was a dream that drew in a clutch of characters with diverse motives, objectives and degrees of commitment to the Ku Klux Klan. For James McQuirter and Wolfgang Droege, the dream took their focus off Canada and into the United States and the Caribbean. The dream was preposterous, but the spirit of the times made it seem plausible. The scheme was given the name "Operation Red Dog."

The dream originated with Mike Perdue, an aspiring con man leading a fantasy life as a successful international mercenary. He claimed a record of fighting Communism in league with the United States Central Intelligence Agency, foreign despots and anybody else who would pay him. It was a fantasy he cultivated assiduously in his contacts with a shady netherworld of racists, con men, rich men and white supremacists.

A mustachioed bodybuilder with a prematurely receding hairline, the thirty-year-old Perdue was living in early 1979 in a tidy suburban house in Houston, Texas. He shared the antique-filled house with his long-time partner, Ron Cox, who owned a design drapery business.[1] Perdue boasted of his military career in the United States Marine Corps. The reality was a seven-week stint that ended with his discharge after the corps learned he was a house burglar in his off-duty hours.[2] After his release from prison, he moved to Houston, where he worked in a psychiatric hospital. Perdue was in a gay relationship with Cox, a fact he sought to hide from his mercenary comrades.

Perdue told his gun-toting anti-Communist stories to anybody who would listen. He sought out a new listener in 1979 in the person of David Duke, former imperial wizard of the Invisible Empire of the Knights of the Ku Klux Klan. Perdue told Duke about reading a *U.S. News and World Report* magazine story about leftist rebels seizing power on the eastern Caribbean island nation of Grenada in March 1979. Perdue somehow conceived the idea that Grenada would benefit from a mercenary force retaking power and returning the country to its ousted leaders.

The United States government labelled the new Grenadian government Communist, yet another domino in the relentless Soviet campaign to take over the world. First Cuba, now Grenada, went the message. Perdue instinctively thought this was his chance to make his mercenary dream a reality. He flew to San Diego to meet deposed Grenadian Prime Minister Eric Gairy. He spun a tale of how a small group of armed men — his mercenaries — could seize power and return Grenada to Gairy. The ex-prime minister was noncommittal, maybe yes, maybe no. So Perdue looked up David Duke.

The imperial wizard would later take a step back from any affiliation with Perdue. "He came to one of my public meetings, that's how I met him," said Duke. "I didn't know anything about him."[3] But he wasn't unhelpful. Duke provided Perdue with names and phone numbers of people he thought might be interested, among them the name of Don Andrews in Toronto, leader of the Nationalist Party of Canada.

Don Andrews, David Duke, Wolfgang Droege and James McQuirter all knew each other, shared a similar white supremacist worldview, aspired to positions of power and leadership and hoped to remake the world to fit their views. Why wouldn't Don Andrews take Mike Perdue's call in May 1979 on the basis of a referral from David Duke? Andrews was intrigued when Perdue spun his tale of mercenaries, a coup and an island in the sun. Andrews went away and did some research and concluded that a proper coup couldn't be mounted from Canada or the United States. It needed an offshore base far from police, intelligence agencies and prying eyes.

One of his political pals proposed a solution. Aarne Polli ran in Andrews's anti-Communist circles, but he was no hanger-on. He was a businessman — someone with a contract here, a contract there, someone who followed up leads with potential for profit. The eastern Caribbean nation of Dominica offered such a lead. Polli persuaded Andrews to invest in a Dominican company to roast, grind and package Colombian coffee on the island.[4] It was a good cover story.

The island of seventy-five thousand residents also had undeveloped timber tracts. Polli was working with an Ottawa businessman to get access to Dominica's timber and sell the product into North America. Don Andrews thought this suggested an interesting opportunity, too. A timber company operating on Dominica would also provide good cover to launch an invasion of Grenada, just four hundred kilometres away across the sea.

Andrews threw himself into the Dominica project. He contacted a Belgian mercenary and dispatched him to the island to gather information on local conditions. He financed a reconnaissance trip there for Aarne Polli too. By October 1979, Polli was back from the Caribbean island and ready to move ahead.

Polli's report described Dominica as an island nation in crisis. A series of violent confrontations between mobs and the ruling government had led to a change in leadership in June 1979. A new government with a decidedly leftish tinge assumed power. Then on August 29, Hurricane David struck. Much of the population was left homeless, thirty-seven people died and the banana crop was destroyed. Nobody in Dominica cared much about the idea of setting up a timber company; they were too busy trying to survive.

This was all good news to Mike Perdue. Why take on the well-armed "Communists" in Grenada when the next-door neighbour, Dominica, was practically prostrate and ripe for conquest? Why not shift the target? Instead of Grenada, Perdue proposed that the project work towards the takeover of the island of Dominica. The government had all the marks of heading down the same roads as Cuba and Grenada. A strike against Dominica would still meet the criteria of fighting Communism while enriching Perdue and his mercenary associates.

Mike Perdue's fixation on fighting Communism in the Caribbean came during a period when the United States appeared ready to confront the Soviet Union. The 1980 U.S. elections saw Ronald Reagan elected to the White House. He took office in January 1981 on a wave of anti-Communist rhetoric and assertions that the United States would no longer shy away from conflict with the USSR. The appearance of Cubans building a runway on Grenada that the Reagan administration said could be used by Russian and Cuban aircraft raised tensions. Before long, the United States was supporting forces in Nicaragua and elsewhere in Central America that claimed to be fighting against incipient Communist or Socialist governments. The mood of the times suggested that an assault on Grenada would be welcomed by the United States government. Dominica was an afterthought.

Perdue tapped a lawyer from Memphis for ten thousand dollars in operational funds, to be repaid as soon as Dominica was seized. Perdue and Aarne Polli flew off to Dominica for more reconnaissance. A quick survey of the steamy capital Roseau pointed to the obvious target of any takeover attempt. The Dominica Police Headquarters on the outskirts of Roseau was a compound of several buildings that sheltered the island's emergency communications system, investigative service and barracks. Whoever controlled the police compound, controlled Dominica. It would be the primary objective for any invasion force. Perdue and Polli walked around, took pictures, drank rum and argued about next steps. Polli was beginning to think Perdue was gay, which made him uneasy. There was a big quarrel over expense money. After he got home to Toronto, Polli made a quick exit from the plot.

During this period, in the autumn of 1979, Wolfgang Droege was bouncing between his work with the Klan, his legitimate print shop job in Victoria, working in Louisiana on David Duke's campaign to win a seat in the state senate and regular trips to Toronto to meet up with James McQuirter. The pair were chafing under Don Andrews's imperious leadership style as head of the Nationalist Party and preparing to launch a revived Ku Klux Klan of Canada.

Droege and McQuirter still recognized Andrews's position as a senior leader in extreme right-wing Canadian political circles. So did Mike Perdue, who had more pressing reasons to cozy up to Andrews. Until that fall of 1979, they had only ever talked on the phone. Perdue felt his operational thinking needed a face-to-face discussion with Andrews. The Texan flew into Toronto for a meeting.

Wolfgang Droege was also in town. Accounts would later differ over who introduced who to whom. In one account, Droege was introduced to Mike Perdue by Don Andrews at his house in east-end Toronto.[5] In another, it was David Duke who introduced Droege to Perdue, probably in the midst of Duke's senate campaign in Louisiana.[6] Regardless, they became great pals. The American explained his plans to take over an island in the Caribbean, with Dominica the prime target.

It all sounded good to Droege, who had no long-term career prospects in Victoria, no close family and no role beyond playing second fiddle to James McQuirter in a revived Ku Klux Klan. "He was bored with life," Don Andrews later told journalist Stewart Bell. "He just wanted excitement. He was another guy hanging around, looking for adventure." Perdue wanted Droege to find Patrick John, the recently ousted prime minister of Dominica, and persuade him to hire his crew of mercenaries to restore him to power, all for future considerations. Droege agreed and left for Dominica in December 1979.

Wolfgang Droege wasn't the only chancer scoping out Dominica. As he made his way around the island, he met two Americans from Las Vegas who were assessing the prospects for business opportunities. Carlton Van Gorder was in the gaming industry back home in Nevada, with interests in Puerto Rico and the Caribbean. He wanted to open a casino on the island but couldn't get any traction with locals. Droege suggested a change of government might open the door. Gorder wasn't interested in a coup d'état, but he invited Droege to Las Vegas to talk with others who might be.

Droege began putting together a plan. Casinos, lumber, tourism — all the elements to make a fortune were potentially available in Dominica if the conditions were created to make it happen. The potential was there to make a lot of money for white supremacist causes and get rich in the process. Droege flew off to New Orleans to explain his vision to David Duke, who said he wanted no part of it. He flew on to Houston to tell Mike Perdue about the Americans who wanted to launch a casino. If Perdue and Droege were to carry through on their plans, they needed seed money. This led them to Las Vegas.

Indeed, the odds against the takeover of Dominica as envisaged by Mike Perdue were astronomical. The whole project flew in the face of common sense. How was a gang of white supremacists going to run the government of an overwhelmingly Black population? Answer: they would work behind the scenes propping up a Revolutionary Council led by officers from the Dominica Defence Force.[7] How would profits from the various enterprises proposed by the plotters be moved off the island to support white supremacist activities? Answer: corporations controlled by the conspirators would launder the money and shift it out of the country.

Mike Perdue hinted throughout the planning and search for investors that the U.S. Central Intelligence Agency and State Department were aware of and supported the proposed operation. In fact, the U.S. government was far more concerned about the Cubans and Russians operating in nearby Grenada, a fact demonstrated by the American invasion of the island in October 1983. Why would the American government support the establishment of a regime in Dominica that promised to be more unstable than not while becoming a source of criminality and domestic disturbance for the United States and its allies? Why would the U.S. government want the headaches of Dominica when they saw the real problem elsewhere? Mike Perdue's hints of American government support were a fiction peddled to the unwary.

Don Andrews later said he was in the dark about what was happening. He bought a plane ticket to Dominica in early 1980 to check the situation out for himself. It also gave him a chance to catch up with the coffee company where he had a financial stake. Like Droege, he found the island a destination of interest for other entrepreneurs. Sitting in a hotel bar, he met two California men who were working on a deal to sell Dominican passports to Iranians fleeing from the Ayatollah Khomenei's 1979 Islamic Revolution. The price of a Dominican passport was fifty thousand U.S. dollars. The plan went further — it envisaged setting up a development on the island's north shore to house wealthy Iranians in exile.

Andrews later said he suffered a fit of moral conscience at the duplicity and blatant exploitation of the passport plan. He tipped off the opposition party in the Dominican Parliament about the passport scheme. The Opposition was led by Eugenia Charles, a former student at the University of Toronto and heiress to one of the island's richest families. Charles raised the matter in Parliament to a chorus of public outrage. Safely back in Toronto, Don

Andrews talked about how much he had liked Dominica and Dominicans. He later said he took no further part in Mike Perdue or Wolfgang Droege's bizarre scheme and knew nothing about what happened next.

Droege and Perdue landed in Las Vegas in late December 1979, looking for investors for a scheme to take over Dominica. They painted a picture of future profits underpinned by criminality. Lumber, casinos, brothels, real estate developments for the tourism industry, legitimate passports for a price, money laundering and guns were all on the table. "They were a little on the shady side," recalled Carlton Van Gorder, who showed the pair around town, introducing them to people. "I mean, anyone who talks about toppling a government, they aren't the type of people you go into business with."[8]

Droege and Perdue left Las Vegas empty-handed, only to return in January 1980. A pledge of twenty-five thousand dollars from a guy named "Dick" failed to materialize. They hung around for weeks looking for investors but finally gave up and left. Droege had other interests, and he needed to earn some legitimate money. He returned to his day job in Victoria for a few months, before joining McQuirter in Toronto in June to launch the new Klan office. While James McQuirter busied himself promoting the new Canadian Klan over the summer of 1980, Wolfgang Droege resumed his contact with Perdue on the Dominica project.

In August 1980, Wolfgang Droege travelled to North Carolina to network with other white supremacists, scout for potential recruits for the Dominica mission and shoot guns. "He couldn't shoot worth shit," according to Bob Prichard, a Vietnam veteran suffering from severe post-traumatic stress disorder. "Mad Merc" Prichard, as he was known in mercenary and white supremacist circles, had trained at a paramilitary camp run by a Klan group out of North Carolina.[9] Droege eventually signed him up for what was now being called Operation Red Dog. In Prichard's eyes, Droege gained credibility as he diligently blasted away at targets in the North Carolina countryside. His marksmanship slowly improved.

Mike Perdue came to visit Droege in Toronto in October 1980. Droege took the opportunity to introduce the American to James McQuirter, who had apparently been left out of the scheme until then. Perdue spun his tale of Dominica as a potential headquarters for an international criminal organization. McQuirter was intrigued. He agreed to serve as a communications link between Droege and Perdue as the two operators pursued their plan separately around North America and the Caribbean.

Meanwhile, Mike Perdue scrounged for money, getting much of his funding from L.E. Matthews, a Mississippi electrical contractor and former imperial wizard in the state Klan. He also went to Dominica and finally struck a deal with Patrick John, the former prime minister, to return him to power by force. Then he went back to the States to line up more investors — in Mississippi, Nevada, wherever the leads took him. The plan was coming together.

Droege and Perdue hunkered down in Houston and New Orleans in early winter 1981 to work out the operational details of the attack on Dominica. They needed boats to transport a small group of mercenaries thousands of kilometres by sea from New Orleans to the offshore of the island, and from there onto the beach. They needed weapons suitable for seizing the Dominica Police Headquarters. And they needed about a dozen people with military skills to actually do the job. Perdue began seeking mercenaries through publications with the right readership, publications like *Le Mercenaire* out of Aurora, Illinois, a suburb of Chicago.[10] His advertisement sought persons of "disciplined character" for "security duty for a private employer on a Caribbean island."[11]

Droege knew people across the North American right-wing community thanks to his contacts with Don Andrews, David Duke and Ku Klux Klan organizations in both the United States and Canada. These contacts offered up several recruits all with more or less — mostly less — military experience, but almost all with Klan backgrounds. Among them was Don Black, David Duke's associate and Klan member with former service in the United States Army Reserves and hard anti-Communist views. When Duke left the Klan in the summer of 1979 to found a new organization, the National Association for the Advancement of White People, Black took over his Klan organization. "I was in an adventurous mood, and I also needed the money," he said later.[12] Black was able to interest a couple of his friends in joining the operation.

Perdue finally persuaded James McQuirter, with his four years' experience in the Canadian military, to join the attack team. The grand wizard's role would be to fly to Dominica before the rest of the mercenary team arrived. He would conduct reconnaissance and organize vehicles for the arriving fighters — to carry them from the landing beach to their eventual targets. His reward would be to become minister of information in the new white supremacist-controlled government of Dominica.

Meanwhile, back in Dominica, Eugenia Charles was elected the new prime minister. She began talking publicly in March 1981 about threats to the island's national security, threats reported to her by the national police force. The country's leading newspaper blared out the story that a group led by an American named Mike Perdue from Texas was gathering arms and men to launch a coup against the government. Eugenia Charles went on radio and laid out the plan in startling detail, based on documents the government had seized, showing collaboration between Perdue and senior members of the Dominica Defence Force. Those officers were arrested, removing the leadership figures of Mike Perdue's proposed Revolutionary Council. The Dominica Defence Force was dissolved.

Mike Perdue thought the game was up. Droege not so much. He proposed to send someone he knew to Dominica to check out the situation. Perdue agreed. Droege asked a Toronto acquaintance named Marion McGuire, originally from Northern Ireland, to do the job. McGuire lived in one of Don Andrews's rooming houses and knew James McQuirter, who had already told her of Operation Red Dog. Mike Perdue came to Toronto to brief her, give her money and send her on her way. He also gave McQuirter money to travel to Dominica to organize local transportation for the invading force.

On Droege's recommendation, Perdue also met with Charles Yanover, a Toronto criminal figure with access to explosives. Yanover, originally from Belleville, Ontario, made his name as an enforcer in the mafia-controlled labour rackets of Toronto. He would have what one criminologist called "a varied and eccentric criminal career" that ranged from drugs and guns to precious metals and international assassination plots.[13]

Droege had briefed Yanover on the Dominica plot. Yanover thought the plan should go ahead and, for money and future considerations, he would help. One of the considerations was to be a colonel in a reconstituted Dominica Defence Force. Perdue agreed. Yanover did his own reconnaissance trip to Dominica to check out the situation. The invasion was militarily possible, he concluded, but he had no confidence that these white supremacists were the right people for the job. With the plotters increasingly detached from reality, the planning moved forward.

Mike Perdue chartered a ship to carry his team from New Orleans to Dominica. Mike Howell, the captain, called the United States Bureau of Alcohol, Tobacco and Firearms (ATF) as soon as the Texan left his vessel after making the deal. The result was an extensive law enforcement operation led by the ATF office in New Orleans to verify what was going on. Captain Mike Howell became an ATF confidential source, including wearing microphones for clandestine taping of discussions with Perdue. Mike Perdue was soon under close surveillance. An ATF undercover operative with experience investigating the Ku Klux Klan joined Howell's crew. Law enforcement agencies in Canada and the United States began building a profile of the conspirators during the spring of 1981. The ATF started planning how, when and where to arrest the Red Dog assault team.

It was a wonder the scheme was still in motion, given the number of people who knew what was planned. Prime Minister Eugenia Charles and the population of Dominica were in on the story by early April 1981. Klan circles in Canada and the United States knew something was up. James McQuirter had already told Marion McGuire. He had also briefed Gordon Sivell, a former media contact in Hamilton, who was now a reporter for Toronto radio station CFTR. Sivell in turn had tipped off the Ontario Provincial Police. A biker-turned-police-informant named Cecil Kirby told his RCMP handler that Charles Yanover had offered him a job in a South American coup. It later turned out that Aarne Polli was also a police informant and a stringer for CFTR.[14] Mike Perdue and Wolfgang Droege seemed to be the only people who thought the plan was still secret and viable.

Mike Perdue came to Toronto for the final planning session for Operation Red Dog in mid-April 1981. Wolfgang Droege was there. James McQuirter was there.[15] Gordon Sivell was there to tape interviews and take notes for a future documentary he was planning on the operation. Larry Jacklin from Listowel, Ontario, was there, a recruit brought in by Droege. His major asset was six months in the Canadian Armed Forces reserves. He was a former Western Guard member (or Klan recruiter, depending on the source) active in the Kitchener-Waterloo region under the alias Doug O'Hare.[16] Charles

Yanover was there, marvelling that the group was still planning to go ahead. He left when he learned that the journalist Sivell was in the room. The rest stayed, to their eventual regret.

The Red Dog team began assembling in Louisiana on April 26, 1981. The two Canadians were Wolfgang Droege and Larry Jacklin. James McQuirter had driven Droege and Jacklin to London, Ontario, where they had boarded a bus to the States. They gave him a white power salute in farewell.[17] The Americans included Mike Perdue, Don Black and Bob Prichard, backed up by a collection of past and current Klansmen, military, and law enforcement veterans pledged to fight the good fight against Communism.

Two of Perdue's recruits didn't show up for the rendezvous. Robert Lisenby and Frank Camper were Vietnam veterans, vocal anti-Communists, long-time paramilitary activists and trainers of aspiring mercenaries. They were arrested in Miami two weeks before Red Dog was launched, their car stuffed with illegal guns and explosives. Rumour had it they were planning to bomb the consulate of the Dominican Republic in Miami, having confused that country with the island nation of Dominica. Regardless, they were in jail as the Red Dog team began to gather. Frank Camper, though, was soon released thanks to his status as an FBI human source.[18] This was yet another security leak destined to help sink the Red Dog operation.

Back in New Orleans, Perdue and Droege delivered $9,800 in cash to Mike Howell, who was accompanied by undercover ATF officers posing as his crew. The team was told to show up at nearby Fort Pike State Park at 10 p.m. the following night, Tuesday, April 27. Guns, explosives and equipment would go into one van; the team members would travel in a second van. They would drive to the Harbor Inn Marina in St. Tammany Parish, load the ship and put out to sea.

The next day the ten-man team did as instructed. They collected their equipment at a motel in Baton Rouge, Louisiana — rifles, pistols, ammo, explosives, dinghies, radios — and piled into a van and Mike Perdue's Impala for the two-hour drive to New Orleans. They arrived at Fort Pike after dark, pulling into a near-empty parking lot surrounded by concealed federal agents and local police officers.

Parked in the lot were two vans driven by ATF undercover officers. The gear for the Red Dog team was consolidated in one of the ATF vans. The ten mercenaries were separated from their weapons and climbed into the other van. All settled, the two vans moved slowly out of the parking lot, onto the highway, over a bridge and turned right into the Harbor Inn Marina, where Howell's ship waited.

John Osburg, the ATF agent driving the van with the ten men inside, backed it towards the dock, parked and got out. So did Mike Perdue. Osburg told the Red Dog leader he was under arrest. A spotlight shone brightly on the vehicle. Arrest teams swarmed the would-be mercenaries as they emerged from the van into federal custody. Operation Red Dog was at an end. "You are not going to Dominica!" a federal agent bellowed over a bull horn. "You are going to jail!"

* * *

The end of Operation Red Dog had major implications for the Ku Klux Klan in Canada, even if the enterprise was not a sanctioned Klan initiative. First and foremost, Wolfgang Droege, the deputy leader of the Canadian Klan, went to jail. After Mike Perdue pleaded guilty to a range of offences, Droege followed suit. He was sentenced to three years in a U.S. federal prison. Larry Jacklin, the twenty-year-old from Listowel, was sent to a program for young offenders. Don Black and the other Americans also went to jail for violating U.S. neutrality laws. To add insult to injury, a U.S. State Department official told the trial that the government of Eugenia Charles was deemed to be a strong ally of the United States with no hint of Communist influence. Even that justification for an invasion was a fraud.

Back in Canada, there were several candidates for criminal charges — Charles Yanover, Don Andrews, Aarne Polli, Marion McGuire and Gord Sevill. In the end, only two — James McQuirter and Charles Yanover — were convicted for their involvement in Operation Red Dog. Aarne Polli did not come to public attention again until February 2015, when he perished in a farmhouse fire near Owen Sound, Ontario. Only in Dominica was his death noted in connection with the coup attempt thirty-four years before.[19]

James Alexander McQuirter, grand wizard of the Canadian Knights of the Ku Klux Klan, was clearly a candidate for criminal charges, having talked openly with the media about his involvement in Red Dog. "Dominica needs white order and white government," he had told reporters.[20] He later explained that his absence from the invasion was a result of having been deported from the United States in January 1981 for his Klan activities.[21] McQuirter was confident that he could not — would not — be charged. But he was. The evidence against him was clear, much of it coming out of his own mouth. "If you have control of a country, you can make a lot of money," he had said in a taped interview during the Red Dog planning. "Our purpose was to make a lot of money for white nationalist circles."

McQuirter's decision to plead guilty for his involvement in Operation Red Dog signalled the end of any kind of effective leadership of the Ku Klux Klan of Canada. More legal problems were pending. The grand wizard was out driving his car in the fall of 1981 when he was ostensibly stopped by police for a routine check.

In going through the vehicle, police found two ounces of a white powder, believed to be cocaine, and a restricted weapon. Some reports said police also found five thousand pills of an unknown but probably illegal nature. When the police went to the grand wizard's house on Springhurst Avenue, the scene of demonstrations the year before, they encountered McQuirter's housemate and Klan security director Gary MacFarlane.

The Klansman threatened officers with a loaded shotgun, apparently seeking to prove a boast once made to the *Toronto Star* that "you never argue with a man with a gun."[22] MacFarlane claimed he always carried a pistol and a blackjack. On this occasion, he ended up surrendering the shotgun, two unloaded rifles, a .38-calibre revolver, some cocaine and more pills. Criminal charges ensued.[23] Then it turned out the powder found in McQuirter's car wasn't cocaine, so the drug trafficking charge was dropped.[24] Armand Siksna took the fall for the restricted weapon.

In the months after the drug takedown on Springhurst Avenue, the Ontario Provincial Police began an investigation into the source of forged documents turning up across the province. Certified cheques, birth certificates, Canadian passports. The suspects? James Alexander McQuirter, Gary MacFarlane and Jean MacGarry, all resident at the same house. MacFarlane and his wife worked as licenced security guard dog-handlers (despite Gary having killed a man followed by seven years in a psychiatric institution).[25] Gary also pulled shifts driving a sod delivery truck.

The domestic arrangements on Springhurst Avenue extended to the grand wizard's transportation. McQuirter's car, a black Corvette, was registered in Jean MacGarry's name. The trio's bogus paper enterprise, which McQuirter later admitted earned him more money than the Klan ever did, was based on a business model that required trust. This was a challenge given that Gary physically abused his wife — Jean suffered brain damage at his hands.[26] Then Gary cut the throats of two dogs beloved by Grand Wizard McQuirter and left the bodies to rot in the bathroom.[27] Gary was clearly a threat to the security of the lucrative forging operation, not to mention Klan activities, although his sanity was in question.

Ontario Provincial Police Constable Gary MacDonald was investigating the forgery operation. Working undercover, he became McQuirter's confidant, a man who listened carefully as the grand wizard poured out his problems during a business meeting in a room at a downtown Toronto Holiday Inn in early summer 1982. For McQuirter, Gary MacFarlane was definitely the problem. "He's a pain in the ass until the day he dies," complained McQuirter.[28] It was a view shared by Armand Siksna, McQuirter's acolyte in the Klan, former candidate for the position of mayor of Toronto and a devoted follower of the grand wizard. It would be useful — indeed necessary in their eyes — for MacFarlane to simply disappear from the scene.

"Really?" inquired Constable MacDonald in his undercover persona. I might know a guy, said the constable. If that didn't work out, Armand Siksna said he would be prepared to do what needed to be done.[29] As a demonstration of faith, Siksna put up the cash to pay a contract killer. Constable MacDonald came through with a suitable hitman — undercover OPP constable William Campbell. For a consideration of two thousand dollars in advance, cash, Campbell agreed he could take care of the MacFarlane problem. Planning for the demise of the unaware MacFarlane proceeded over the course of the summer of 1982, much of it in front of hidden police video-cameras in the Holiday Inn.[30]

In the midst of this activity, McQuirter announced he was leaving the Ku Klux Klan as a result of the charges connected to Operation Red Dog. He was scheduled to appear in court in September, so there was some urgency to dealing with MacFarlane. His resignation from the Klan caused barely a ripple of attention in the midst of everything else happening in McQuirter's life.

Planning for the hit on MacFarlane came to a head on August 14, when McQuirter, MacGarry, MacDonald and Campbell met at the Springhurst Avenue house. MacDonald brought along Campbell as a potential drug customer. After some discussion about price and product, a leery MacFarlane agreed to leave with Campbell to go get some illicit Percodan, a controlled opioid used for pain relief. MacFarlane was suspicious of undercover OPP constable Campbell, thinking he was a cop, but went nonetheless.

Once he was away from the others, police officers told MacFarlane he was the target of a murder conspiracy and whisked him away to protective custody. Initially MacFarlane was incredulous. Then the police showed him the video of McQuirter counting out the cash on a hotel room coffee table to the "hit man." At this point, MacFarlane was convinced. To help further the operation, and in so doing take revenge on McQuirter, he gave police his belt buckle and a knife sheath. The undercover officers went back into a meeting with McQuirter and Jean MacGarry. They pulled out the buckle and sheath and pronounced MacFarlane dead.

McQuirter and MacGarry broke out the beer to celebrate. The grand wizard was clearly elated at the outcome of the plan. He tried to maintain a respectful decorum in the face of sudden death, but he couldn't resist. "So did he — this is just out of curiosity — did he struggle?" he asked the bogus killer as they sipped their drinks.[31] McQuirter and MacGarry were arrested in the street outside the Holiday Inn where the murder deal had been sealed. Police seized false documents that included certified cheques in the amount of $134,000, Ontario birth certificates and a Canadian passport. Armand Siksna — who wasn't even on police radar — turned himself in a few days later and confessed to having been involved in the conspiracy.[32]

The sun was steadily setting on the former Sunshine Boy. When the trio came to trial in February 1983, they entered guilty pleas. The trial judge took a particularly dim view of the twenty-four-year-old McQuirter. He was sentenced to eight years in prison for the conspiracy to kill MacFarlane, five years concurrent for conspiracy to forge documents and two years for the conspiracy to overthrow the government of Dominica. "Your participation was criminal, the type of conduct that is abhorrent and cannot be tolerated anywhere in the world," said Judge Patrick Lesage. Charles Yanover also pleaded guilty and received a six-month sentence for his involvement in

Operation Red Dog, plus two more years for plotting to kill a North Korean as part of an unrelated international assassination conspiracy.

Julian Sher later reported that the only known Klansman to attend the sentencing hearing was William Lau Richardson of the Klan Intelligence Agency.[33] He spoke to McQuirter before the session began and slipped away after sentence was pronounced. Co-accused Armand Siksna got six years for the murder conspiracy. The courts seemed to think Jean MacGarry had suffered enough. She received a three-year suspended sentence provided she continued treatments for serious mental and physical problems. James Alexander McQuirter disappeared into the Canadian prison system, eventually emerging to live in a Toronto half-way house in 1989.

Gary MacFarlane, the former head of the Klan's security force, came out of the affair characterized as a potential murder victim, wronged by his romantic partner Jean and his business partner McQuirter. MacGarry even signed over to MacFarlane her interest in the Springhurst Avenue house. It was misplaced empathy. Within months, MacFarlane had a new woman living with him at Springhurst, and in April 1983 they were both charged with murder in the beating death of barber Luigi Quintile.

Police said he was a friend of MacFarlane but had no apparent link to the Klan. His battered body was left in the parking lot of Charles Howitt Public School in the north Toronto suburb of Thornhill, kicked to death and then kicked to pieces after death.[34] MacFarlane was later described in court documents as "a very dangerous man with a serious psychiatric disorder and a psychopath. He would be dangerous to be at large."[35] Gary Eugene MacFarlane was sentenced to life in prison in the spring of 1984.[36] With his incarceration, the last major leadership figure of the revived Ku Klux Klan of Canada was removed from the streets.

# Chapter 14
# TO TRIPOLI AND BEYOND, THE 1980s AND EARLY 1990s

The prison sentences handed to James McQuirter and Wolfgang Droege left the Ku Klux Klan of Canada with several unsolvable problems. McQuirter and Droege, whatever their public reputations, at least had public reputations. They were Canada's rising young racists, with name recognition and a known brand. They were usually available and ready with a useful quote. If the Americans had stylish David Duke, Canadians could counter with James Alexander McQuirter, Sunshine Boy. The rest of the Klan's leadership crew were either unknown, little known or too creepy for prime-time media.

The organizational challenge of running a national group with the leading figures behind bars was almost insurmountable. To complicate matters further, those left behind in the second- and third-level leadership tiers often gave the impression that they should be in jail too. The links that McQuirter and Droege enjoyed with David Duke, Don Black and other American white supremacist leaders had lent legitimacy to the Canadian Klan, at least in the eyes of the followers. Few of the remaining Klan figures in Canada could draw on a similar set of contacts to maintain momentum and recognition from American racists. Finally, it was a hard fact that the louche reputation of the Ku Klux Klan had been reinforced by events. Any claim to be a legitimate political or social group was gone. The Klan was either a criminal organization or an organization of criminals. This was as much a verdict of history as it was of the courts.

The leadership of the Ku Klux Klan in Canada fell to Ann Farmer of Vancouver, an enthusiastic officer in the British Columbia organization. Farmer was brought up in apartheid-era South Africa and had a degree from the University of British Columbia. She also had a high opinion of her own intellectual accomplishments.[1] Although she had both supporters and detractors, one consequence of her emergence as national leader was the splitting away of a number of local B.C. groups unwilling to accept her leadership.

Sociologist Stanley Barrett opined that Farmer was deemed unacceptable as a national leader simply because she was a woman. If that made her unacceptable in Canada, it was almost certainly a deterrent to building effective linkages with American Klan leaders, many of whose views on the place of women were likewise uninformed by modern thinking.

Journalist Warren Kinsella dismissed Farmer as "an ineffective leader."[2] His colleague Julian Sher took a more charitable view, citing descriptions of her supposedly close contacts with Don Black and James Venable, a Georgia lawyer with a long Klan history.[3] Despite her efforts, Farmer was unknown to the general public, the media and the Americans who might have helped shore up the Canadian organization. At base, though, the Ku Klux Klan of Canada was a discredited group with major image issues.

The organization steadily disintegrated, and Farmer could not stop the decay over the course of the two years that she was the Klan's national director. By the time Droege came out of jail in 1984, the national Ku Klux Klan organization had fractured into local fiefdoms. It was obvious the momentum was gone.

Wolfgang Droege had spent his three-year sentence in Sandstone Prison in the northern U.S. state of Minnesota. He passed the time writing letters to the sentencing judge pleading to be released, explaining that his involvement in Red Dog was the result of immature thinking. His girlfriend in Vancouver wrote the judge to say the couple planned to marry when he was released, that Droege was a sweet-tempered teetotaller with a passion for classical music and "no connections to the criminal element." If released, Droege promised the judge, he would do better. In the end, he was released on probation, deported from the United States and barred from re-entering for the next five years.

Wolfgang Droege settled back into life on the west coast, taking over from Ann Farmer as national director of what little remained of national Ku Klux Klan activities. He passed his days at the race track trying to perfect a betting system he had devised while in prison. He went broke. Then he drove a cab. Then he started telling contacts he was thinking about taking over an island in the Caribbean, just not sure which one. When the Vancouver Police Department found out Droege was already driving a taxi, they denied his application for a cab licence.

He slipped back into the United States and headed to Alabama, where friends set him up dealing cocaine and marijuana. He would later say he was making many thousands of dollars a week but only so he could support the cause of white supremacy. He began to mix with members of the Order, the violent right-wing gang that took up arms against what they called the Zionist Occupied Government of the United States. They robbed banks to support themselves and further their goals.

Droege was seen as a hero of the extreme right for his role in Operation Red Dog — and because he hadn't sold out the other team members in return for a lighter prison sentence. He began taking assignments from the Order, including a mission to Huntsville, Alabama, in November 1984 to monitor Jewish leaders there. Droege later claimed the assignment involved the early stages of a plan to assassinate Morris Dees, a local civil rights lawyer and founder of the antiracist Southern Poverty Law Center.[4]

The United States Government's Immigration and Naturalization Service and the FBI were watching. He was picked up with a briefcase carrying a dagger, several ounces of cocaine and $3,700 in cash. Droege pleaded guilty to a range of charges and was sentenced to thirteen years in Lompoc Prison in California. There he waited on the shores of the Pacific Ocean, hoping for early release.

The Klan's Canadian rebirth in the 1980s saw the rise of regional groups and leaders, some skilled and organized, others inept or simply criminal. They followed a familiar pattern of factionalism and fractionalism, particularly after James McQuirter and Wolfgang Droege went to jail.

Splinter groups in Montreal, Winnipeg, Calgary and elsewhere presented themselves as the Ku Klux Klan, but they had no national reach and invariably took their legitimacy from some form of recognition by one of the many rival American Klan factions. Regional leaders like Ivan Ross Macpherson/ Dunsford in Alberta, Michel Larocque in Montreal, John Gilroy in Ontario and Dave Cook, Ann Farmer, Dan Wray and Bryan Taylor in Vancouver became the regional faces of the Klan. These were the restrained racists.

The unrestrained racists were the skinheads who pushed to the front of the Canadian white supremacist scene, impatient with organization and keen to kick somebody in the teeth. They included Bill Harcus, a small-town Manitoba bigot, who shopped around for a place to put his racist ideas into practice.[5] Born in 1971, Harcus came out of Stonewall, Manitoba, and went straight to Winnipeg, where he migrated into neo-Nazi skinhead activity via a series of religious conversions. When he was a child his family belonged to the New Life Baptist Church. Young Bill then moved on to Satanism and finally Christian Identity, the faith of choice for white supremacists in the latter part of the twentieth century. The spiritual home of Christian Identity, the Aryan Nations headquarters in Hayden Lake, Idaho, was a convenient drive from the Canadian border.

It was a destination for an increasing number of Canadian racists, including Klan members. The British Columbia Ku Klux Klan met with the Aryan Nations congregation at Hayden Lake in October 1981.[6] The names of those who attended from the west coast were not publicly known, although James McQuirter and Wolfgang Droege were on the coast that month promoting the national Klan. Another joint meeting was held there in 1984 with about twenty Canadians in the crowd, including Terry Long of Alberta, Carney Nerland of Saskatchewan and assorted racists and neo-fascists from north of the border.[7] The gathering culminated with participants donning Ku Klux Klan robes and cheering the burning of a cross.

Terry Long of Caroline, Alberta, emerged later that year as the Canadian leader of the Aryan Nations, with the stated intention of unveiling "the Jewish nature of Communism and the genocidal intent on the part of the Jew-Communists to destroy the white race."[8] Long, thirty-six years old at the time, was born in Red Deer and brought up in California. He returned to Alberta when he was twenty and graduated in electrical engineering from the University of Alberta. In time, he ended up running a sawmill and turned to Christian Identity as the faith best able to help him make sense of the world. He offered up his property outside Caroline, a hundred kilometres southwest of Red Deer, as the Canadian equivalent of Richard Butler's compound in Idaho.

Terry Long lived close to others with views similar to his own. The nearby town of Eckville had Jim Keegstra teaching Holocaust denial in the high school before and during these years. Keegstra was removed from his job in late 1982 in the midst of a national debate over hate mongering. The dismissal sparked a wave of hate-related activities, including the distribution of Ku Klux Klan posters in Edmonton in May 1983.[9] Terry Long was president of a group called the Christian Defence League, formed in 1983 to support Keegstra.[10] Before that, he had been a member of the provincial Conservative Party, then a founding member of the separatist Western Canada Concept Party. He was defeated as a WCCP candidate in the 1982 election.

Terry Long expressed his faith and political views using a telephone hotline that played hate messages specifically targeting Jews. In July 1989, the Canadian Human Rights Tribunal ordered Long to shut down the telephone operation.[11] He didn't take it well. "In a free society I deserve the right to discriminate against whomever I chose, and they have the right to discriminate against me," he said. "The white man is now officially a second-class citizen in his own country."[12] The view was shared widely in Canada's racist community.

Meanwhile, Bill Harcus in Manitoba was making the rounds of national and international white supremacist circles, looking for a way to make hate work for him. He reached out to Don Andrews, who referred him to like-minded racists around the continent. Harcus travelled to Detroit and Milwaukee to make skinhead contacts. He finally found his future after corresponding with the Missouri KKK, a group with a strong Christian Identity connection. He was determined to create his own Manitoba Knights of the Ku Klux Klan and began looking for followers to help spread the racist message.

He started with two, then found more among the ranks of Winnipeg's racist skinheads. The twenty-year-old Harcus claimed in 1990 to have recruited about thirty members with two cells in Winnipeg and one in the central Manitoba town of Gimli. The Manitoba KKK's activities caught the attention of the Winnipeg Police, which launched an undercover operation to insert two officers into the klavern.

Over the course of several months, the officers came to know Harcus and his activities well. Like Terry Long, Bill Harcus operated a telephone hate line and imported Klan literature across the Canada–U.S. border. The material was distributed at Winnipeg malls, schools, on street corners. Harcus found a seamstress to sew Klan uniforms; he had his own set of grand dragon satin robes. A business opportunity beckoned, selling Klan outfits to other Canadian klaverns. There was interest, particularly from the growing Montreal Klan.

The end for Harcus came in December 1991. The Winnipeg police arrested him and his associate Therou Skryba on charges of violating the promotion of genocide prohibitions in the *Criminal Code*. A trial followed in 1992. By then, Harcus and Skryba were represented by Doug Christie, the Victoria lawyer whose clients included many of the country's better-known bigots and racists. At trial, Christie succeeded in proving that the testimony of one of the Winnipeg police undercover officers was based on surveillance tapes, not written notes based on memory.

The doubt thrown on police evidence put the case in jeopardy, and the charges were stayed. But the publicity and exposure of Harcus's dreams effectively ended the formal existence of the Ku Klux Klan in Manitoba. Harcus went into hiding, changed his name and tried to make a career as a country music performer. He died of a machete wound to the chest in Winnipeg in 2016 after a drug deal went bad.[13]

Back at Terry Long's Aryan Nations camp in Alberta, an increasingly motley crew of racists, skinheads and Nazis began showing up at the gate in the late 1980s. They included Daniel Sims, an Edmonton skinhead, who went on to maim retired Edmonton radio broadcaster Keith Rutherford. Matt McKay was another visitor. The Winnipeg-based member of the Canadian army and Bill Harcus's Manitoba Ku Klux Klan shared stories of beating up Indigenous people and gay people. By the late-1980s, it was clear that the members of the Aryan Nation and the Ku Klux Klan in Canada, at least western Canada, were often the same people.

Carney Nerland was a chubby nineteen-year-old from Prince Albert, Saskatchewan, when he turned up at the July 1984 Aryan Nations World Congress in Hayden Lake, Idaho, along with Terry Long and other Canadians. Nerland was a high-school dropout with a voracious curiosity about Adolf Hitler and the Nazis, a curiosity he later transferred to studying the writings of David Duke. This led him almost inevitably to the gates of the Aryan Nations compound. From there he accepted an invitation to travel to Louisiana, where he worked for Karl Hand, leader of the neo-Nazi group the National Socialist Liberation Front.

Karl Hand was a former organizer with David Duke's Knights of the Ku Klux Klan and a speaker at the 1984 Aryan Nations gathering at Hayden Lake.[14] He was also an old associate of John Ross Taylor, the Toronto Nazi and Klansman. "I've known him for some time," Taylor said in 1981 of his acquaintance with Hand. "He's a fine man. He's standing up for the white race."[15] With first-hand exposure to a culture of guns, Nazis and street-level violence, Nerland returned to Prince Albert in the late 1980s. He was working as a vacuum cleaner salesman when he obtained a licence to open a gun store.

The Northern Pawn and Gun Shop on River Street West in Prince Albert became Nerland's shrine to Hitler and the Nazis. Photos of the führer adorned the walls; Nazi flags draped to the floors. Nerland presented himself as leader of the Saskatchewan Ku Klux Klan, a group that seemed to have only a few members, who showed up for the occasional cross burning.

Nerland was in regular contact with Terry Long, who anointed him in September 1989 as leader of the Aryan Nations in Saskatchewan. Together, they began planning a gathering of white supremacists for the summer of 1990 at Provost, Alberta, just west of the Alberta-Saskatchewan boundary on the road to Red Deer. The two-day Aryan Fest was held on the property of welder Ray Bradley, a Christian Identity believer. It was a spectacle rarely seen in Alberta since the 1930s.

A who's who of western Canadian white supremacists showed up in Provost on September 8, 1990. Terry Long hosted. Bill Harcus arrived in a black Lada with Carney Nerland at the wheel. Racist skinheads and assorted neo-Nazis strutted around the site.[16] Carney Nerland, the gun dealer from Prince Albert, made a splash in sunglasses and a Nazi-styled uniform with a swastika armband. Photos showed him brandishing a large shotgun, scowling, criticizing demonstrators and the media. Guns were pointed and a few discharged into the air. Journalists were assaulted. Death threats were uttered against the media, protesters and anybody else who looked challenging. A cross was burned at night with Nerland and

Harcus representing the Ku Klux Klan in their traditional white robes and cone hoods.

Four months later, on Monday, January 28, 1991, Carney Nerland shot Leo Lachance to death in the snow outside his gun shop in Prince Albert.[17] Lachance was a Cree fur trapper from the Whitefish Reserve northeast of Prince Albert. He was in town to sell furs. The circumstances of his death outside Nerland's shop remained murky in spite of a trial, a commission of inquiry and widespread speculation. The self-styled leader of the Saskatchewan Ku Klux Klan and duly appointed leader of the Aryan Nations in Saskatchewan was charged and pleaded guilty to manslaughter. How and why Nerland shot Lachance was unclear. The Klansman was sentenced to four years in prison to be spent at Stony Mountain Penitentiary in Manitoba. Bill Harcus came to visit him on November 5, 1991. "He is one of the great Klansmen," Harcus told his travelling companion, an undercover Winnipeg police officer. "He's a real man. He's given everything for the cause. He's a real hero."[18]

Carney Nerland was also a real human source for a law enforcement or intelligence service, nobody could say which. On the day of his release from Stony Mountain, an RCMP cruiser picked him up at the gate and whisked him away to a new life in the Witness Protection Program. Some said he worked for the RCMP. Others suggested he was recruited by the U.S. Federal Bureau of Investigation. Who was he sharing information about? The Ku Klux Klan? The Aryan Nations in Canada and the United States? The Brotherhood? Was he working for the Canadian Security Intelligence Service, which was increasingly concerned about the threat from white supremacists? Where, when and how he was recruited, by whom and against whom, remains known only to authorities.

Corporal Matt McKay moved in the same circles as Bill Harcus and Terry Long. McKay was a member of the Princess Patricia's Canadian Light Infantry regiment posted to the Winnipeg Garrison. His activities over the years raised serious and persistent questions about the presence of white supremacists in the Canadian military. McKay was a regular visitor to Terry Long's farm at Caroline, Alberta. He was there as early as October 1988, on leave from the barracks. "Terry Long was really interested in Matt, because Matt was a full-blown white supremacist," recalled a participant in those meetings at Caroline. "And I guess Terry Long liked that because he is so big and can stomp people."[19]

McKay was at Long's compound in March 1990 when Long issued a veiled threat against Keith Rutherford, a retired Edmonton broadcaster. In the 1960s, while working for a radio station, Rutherford had exposed a Nazi war criminal living secretly in Manitoba. Daniel Sims was at the Caroline compound at the same time as McKay. Sims had status in the Ku Klux Klan, Aryan Nations, Aryan Resistance Movement and a handful of other white supremacist organizations in Canada, the United States and Britain. The next month, Sims attacked Keith Rutherford in his Edmonton home and blinded him in one eye, a potent example of the violence that erupted out of Klan circles.

Matt McKay also regularly visited Edmonton, where he and other skinheads would roam the streets looking to terrorize and beat up Indigenous people. This kind of street violence did not stand out as unusual in Edmonton or other western Canadian cities, where Indigenous communities bore the brunt of racial violence. Two decades later, an Alberta report on bias crime written by former Calgary police officer Cam Stewart would conclude that "Aboriginal community members experience significantly more verbal attacks and criminal threats than any other group."[20] Edmonton acquired the label 'Stabmonton,' unfair or not, to describe its street crime climate.

Violence against Indigenous peoples was a regular feature of Ku Klux Klan, skinhead and neo-Nazi activities across the Canadian west in the late twentieth century. Scholars pointed out that such violence had existed in Canada since the mid-nineteenth century.[21] There was ample evidence in the early 1990s that police — let alone skinhead neo-Nazis — had participated in this type of persecution. Two months before Leo Lachance was killed, seventeen-year-old Neil Stonechild froze to death on the night of November 24, 1990, on the outskirts of Saskatoon, a ninety-minute drive down Highway 11 from Prince Albert. A judicial inquiry later concluded that the Indigenous teen was the victim of a "starlight tour" conducted by the Saskatoon Police Service.[22]

The term referred to the police practice of driving Indigenous people in their custody out of the city and abandoning them at night to find their own way home. Or not. Neil Stonechild died in minus twenty-eight-degree

Celsius temperatures. Other police forces were thought to do the same thing, but it seemed to be a practice particular to the Saskatoon police. Ten years later, in the space of two months, three young Indigenous men were taken on starlight tours by the Saskatoon Police service. Only one survived.[23] It was a continuation of a practice that had been known about since at least 1976, one that contributed to the general unease between police and Indigenous peoples across the country.

Mr. Justice David Wright, who conducted the inquiry into Neil Stonechild's death, had a poignant comment on the state of race relations in Saskatchewan: "I was reminded again and again of the chasm that separates Aboriginal and non-Aboriginal people in this city and province," he wrote. "Our two communities do not know each other and do not seem to want to."[24] It was, yet again, an environment ripe for exploitation by racists.

Meanwhile, in September 1992, the *Winnipeg Sun* published a photo of Matt McKay dressed in full skinhead regalia giving a *Sieg Heil* Nazi salute. By then, McKay had transferred to Canadian Forces Base Petawawa in the Ottawa Valley as a corporal in the Canadian Airborne Regiment. He later told one reporter that he had left the Winnipeg racist scene in early 1991 when he realized the potential harm his activities could do to his military career. He told another reporter he abandoned racist activities in September 1990, when "I woke up one day and saw what was going on and said no way, I'm out."[25] The claims were suspect based on later events, but nobody called him on it at the time. Military officials said they were powerless to act since McKay was apparently not involved in illegal activity.

The Airborne Regiment deployed to Somalia in late 1992 as part of a United Nations peacekeeping mission. Corporal Matt McKay went with his unit, even though commanding officer Brigadier-General Ernie Beno was briefed on November 19, 1992, that McKay was under investigation by military police for his alleged involvement in right-wing activities.[26] Four Somalis died at the hands of Airborne personnel during that mission, including a young Somali man, Shedane Abukar Arone. A commission of inquiry into the Somalia mission led to the disbanding of the regiment in 1995.

Corporal McKay was a member of the Airborne Regiment's 2 Commando, which drew most of its members from the Princess Patricia's Canadian Light Infantry. In the early 1980s, before McKay's arrival in the unit, 2

Commando had adopted the Confederate battle flag as its unofficial insignia after a stint of training with U.S. Army airborne units at Fort Bragg, North Carolina. The U.S. army base was notorious during those years for the number of military personnel involved in outside paramilitary groups, including the Ku Klux Klan.

Millions of dollars of weapons, explosives and electronic equipment disappeared from the base's warehouses only to reappear in the hands of white supremacists across the United States.[27] In the years after their stay at Fort Bragg, 2 Commando acquired several members like McKay who were openly racist. The commission of inquiry revealed a unit where members talked of "beating up n-----s". When the unit arrived in Somalia, the soldiers used a variety of offensive terms for the locals.

Pictures of Matt McKay, a Klansman and skinhead, patrolling the streets of the Somali town of Belet Huen with an automatic weapon created an unsettling image. The commission of inquiry later determined that while being held in detention by the Airborne Regiment, Shedane Arone was tortured and beaten to death by Corporal Clayton Matchee. Midway through the attack, Matchee walked over to Matt McKay's tent, got a beer from him, and sat with another soldier to discuss the ways that Arone could be assaulted. Over the following hours, Matchee continued to torture and beat the young Somali until he died.[28]

A video shot by an unknown member of the regiment during the Somalia deployment featured Matt McKay sitting in the shade under an awning, smoking, when approached by the camera. "Corporal McKay, what do you think about the tour?" inquires the videographer. The corporal was forthcoming. "I think it sucks cock man, we ain't killed enough n-----s yet," he says, followed by laughter.[29] The images were later shown on national television. When Matt McKay returned from Somalia, he was posted to Canadian Forces Base Calgary. In 1995, he was "involuntarily discharged" from the army.[30]

The following March the ex-corporal was arrested by the Calgary Police Service tactical unit. McKay and three other men were charged with second-degree murder in the death of Gordon Kuhtey in Winnipeg in June 1991, months after McKay had claimed to have abandoned the racist skinhead scene. The forty-seven-year-old former railway supervisor had been ambushed and beaten at 4:30 a.m. on a riverside walkway where gay men were known to cruise for partners. The beating was seen by many people from a nearby apartment building. "This was bordering almost on a public event," said police spokesman Eric Turner.

Witnesses said four young men dragged Kuhtey to the Assiniboine River and held his head underwater until he died. His body floated away. Police alleged that McKay and his three co-accused were members of a skinhead gang who went out hunting for homosexuals, a tactic used by racist skinheads in other cities. Beatings and robberies of gays were called "fundraisers" by the skinheads, court was told later.[31] One of McKay's co-accused, James Lisik, was kicked out of the military about the same time he was. When the case came to trial in the summer of 1997, the court learned that the Crown's star witness in the case, Laurie White, wasn't even in Winnipeg at the time of the killing. She was in Vancouver, where she cashed a welfare cheque the day of the murder.[32] The Crown was left with no choice. The charges were stayed.[33]

The military career of Matt McKay fed suspicions that the Canadian Armed Forces was a rich recruiting ground for white supremacists. During his time as leader of the Heritage Front in the early 1990s, Wolfgang Droege told a story to a CBC researcher about a small Klan cell operating near Canadian Forces Base Petawawa in the Ottawa Valley.[34] A briefing note prepared by the Canadian Security Intelligence Service for then Solicitor General Herb Gray quoted Droege as saying the leader of the cell was affiliated with a Quebec group linked to a KKK faction in the United States. Droege said he was prepared to be interviewed by the CBC but would have to be vague about military members. Nothing came of the story except an unsubstantiated allegation that CSIS was investigating the CBC. Droege was equally coy in referring to military members in other interviews. He told Salim Jiwa of the *Vancouver Province* newspaper in 1998 that there were many Heritage Front members in the military, but they kept a low profile out of fear of discovery.[35]

The reality was that white supremacists actively sought military experience to prepare for an anticipated race war, known as the "boogaloo," a staple belief in the extreme right wing for decades. Beginning in the 1980s and well into the 2010s, the Canadian Armed Forces experienced regular cases of infiltration by individuals or groups with racist links.[36] In 1997, twenty-five-year-old Corporal Nathan Leblanc was released from the military after hate literature was found in his quarters at CFB Petawawa. Four other privates in his unit were also identified as racists.

A few weeks later, in January 1998, Leblanc was charged, along with three other neo-Nazis, in the beating death of Nirmal Singh Gill, sixty-five, in the parking lot of the Guru Nanak Sikh temple in Surrey, British Columbia. Gill was the temple caretaker. Leblanc was convicted and sentenced to twelve years in jail. In 2003, military police launched an investigation into alleged links to white supremacist groups by six Canadian Forces members. Military police alleged in 2018 that several dozen CF members had been involved with hate groups over the previous five years.[37] These activities were said not to pose a threat to the Canadian Armed Forces. The public was left to wonder whether they posed a wider threat to Canadian society generally.

* * *

Wolfgang Droege, former national director of the Ku Klux Klan, turned up in Toronto in late April 1989.[38] He had been paroled from Lompoc Prison in California on April 21 and deported to Canada, again. He had nothing. Don Andrews hosted a Nationalist Party meeting at his Toronto home where Droege was introduced as an old friend. The right-wing community rallied to find him a place to stay, food and work. Alan Overfield, who had been a member of the Edmund Burke Society twenty years before, gave him a part-time job working for his bailiff company.

But Wolfgang Droege had yet another dream, formulated while he was in Lompoc Prison, observing the evolution of the white supremacist movement back home in Canada. He wanted to unite the fractious remnants of the Canadian Ku Klux Klan and the growing Aryan Nations group into a single organization to advocate for white supremacy in Canada. This made some sense given what was happening in white supremacist circles in western Canada with individuals holding memberships in both the Klan and the Aryan Nations.

Droege put his latest dream on hold in the summer of 1989, when he accepted an invitation from his benefactor, Don Andrews, and the Nationalist Party. The party had been accepting money for years from the Libyan government of dictator Muammar Gaddafi.[39] The Libyan leader was notorious for lavishing money and support on Western groups he felt could help prop up the credibility of his oil-rich Arab nationalist movement. The Nationalist Party was one such organization.

Don Andrews had already sent one delegation to Libya in 1987. It was a bizarre group that included left-wingers, right-wingers and at least one journalist, Christoph Lehmann-Halens from the *Ottawa Citizen*. During the stay, Lehmann-Halens died under mysterious circumstances, when he fell from the roof of the group's hotel in Tripoli. Suicide was offered by the Libyans as an explanation, but many were skeptical. Christoph Lehmann-Halens's death remained unexplained.

In the summer of 1989, Don Andrews was putting together another trip to Libya at the invitation of the Gaddafi government to mark the dictator's twentieth anniversary in power. The seventeen-member Canadian delegation was another mix of incongruous travellers, but unlike the 1987 group, they were all resolutely identified with the extreme right wing — mostly but not exclusively members of the Nationalist Party. In fact, the bar was set relatively low for participation. "Most people were chosen because they would not embarrass Andrews and his Party," investigators reported later. "Those who owned luggage were also favoured."[40] Wolfgang Droege qualified. So did Grant Bristow, who had emerged as a leading figure in Andrews's circle. They set off for Rome, where Droege was questioned by police before being allowed to continue on to Malta. There, they caught a ship to Tripoli, with Droege and Bristow sharing a cabin.

There was to be a celebratory parade in Tripoli to honour the Libyan strongman. Participants were expected to wear uniforms. Droege was opposed, as was Bristow, who didn't want to be photographed in a Libyan uniform. The group split along loyalty lines, with Droege and Bristow on one side, opposed to those who supported Andrews and the Libyan hosts on the other. After a bitter and divisive argument, the group decided not to wear the uniforms.

The trip home was equally fraught. In Rome, the group abruptly realized they would be transiting through Chicago before arriving in Toronto. Droege sat beside Grant Bristow on the plane and confided his concerns about the Chicago stop. He had just been deported from the United States in April and was barred from returning. What was going to happen in Chicago? "We'll probably get arrested," Bristow replied.

They were. And they were strip-searched. They called Don Andrews for guidance. He instructed the others to come home, but Grant Bristow was assigned to stay in Chicago and get a lawyer for Droege, who was being held in detention. After negotiations, the American authorities agreed to drive Droege to Niagara Falls, where he caught a bus to Toronto. When he got back at 6 a.m., Droege called Andrews, who invited him over to his house for breakfast. A policeman was with Andrews when Droege arrived, a coincidence that caused many to question Andrews's role in the entire Libya trip. By this point, Droege and others had had enough of the Nationalist Party.

Two months later, Wolfgang Droege, former leader of the Ku Klux Klan of Canada, deputy to the former grand wizard of the same Klan and associate of white supremacists across North America and beyond, announced the creation of the Heritage Front, a new group dedicated to racist right-wing goals. The Heritage Front became a direct descendant of the Ku Klux Klan, with its principal leader shaped and formed in the Klan experience. He was supported by a small group of familiars, who included Grant Bristow, his travelling companion to Libya.

The front's goals included uniting Canada's white supremacist groups under one organization, creating a whites-only homeland in some unspecified geographic area of Canada, taking over the city government of Peterborough, Ontario, and legislating racist measures in its bylaws. This would be accompanied by funding initiatives, such as soliciting money from the Libyan government, robbing Black drug dealers and ambushing armoured cars.

The Heritage Front attracted members from across the country, including drawing members away from Don Andrews's Nationalist Party. The Canadian Security Intelligence Service was kept abreast of these aspirations by Grant Bristow, who was a long-time human source. Droege was under close CSIS surveillance during these years, with his mail and telephone monitored.[41] Bristow even accompanied Droege in March 1991 on a visit to Dachau, the former Nazi concentration camp outside Munich, Germany.[42] With this visit, Droege was scarcely two hundred kilometres from his birthplace in Forchheim, Bavaria.

The growth of white supremacist organizations was met in Toronto in the early 1990s by the formation of Klan Busters, an initiative led out of the Native Canadian Centre of Toronto.[43] By then, the Ku Klux Klan had been supplanted by the Heritage Front led by Wolfgang Droege, who had learned his disruptive tactics from the Ku Klux Klan and the Western Guard. The anti-racism coordinator with the centre was Rodney Bobiwash, an Anishinaabe activist who had lost at least one academic job for his role in Indigenous protests.

Wolfgang Droege's activities sparked Bobiwash's creation of Klan Busters and the establishment of an antiracism hotline. Droege's people in turn set up their own hotline. What ensued was a tit-for-tat round of hacking into each other's answering machines, altering messages and taking the names and phone numbers of callers.[44] The result was an on-going harassment campaign against Bobiwash and anti-Klan activists and supporters by white supremacists. Bobiwash was under police protection as a result.

The Heritage Front was an active, violence-tinged organization during its heyday. With Droege as the front man and a cast of characters that included Grant Bristow in the background, the Heritage Front became the leading right-wing organization in Canada. Bristow and other Heritage Front leaders actively targeted Jews and Jewish organizations like the Canadian Jewish Congress, antiracist organizers and minority group members. In 1994, Grant Bristow's role as a CSIS source was revealed by the *Toronto Sun*. There were no secrets in the Heritage Front that weren't known to the authorities. The Heritage Front folded and Droege faded from public sight.

The death of John Ross Taylor passed almost unnoticed in the midst of public controversies over the Heritage Front, Grant Bristow and racist skinheads in the Canadian military. The eighty-year-old old Nazi, veteran of 1930s fascist movements, the Western Guard and the Ku Klux Klan, had moved to Alberta to be close to new colleagues in the Aryan Nations, among them Terry Long. Taylor succumbed to a fatal heart attack in an Edmonton boarding house in early November 1994.[45] His passing drew little comment in the midst of the other hate news of the day.

# Chapter 15
# LE KLAN IN QUEBEC, 1990s

The most vibrant and unexpected manifestation of Ku Klux Klan activity in Canada during the 1990s skinhead era came in Montreal. The province of Quebec was not traditional Klan territory, with the possible exception of the largely anglophone Eastern Townships. But even there, the Orange Lodge had exerted only minimal influence during the first two decades of the twentieth century, so there was no natural foundation on which to build a Ku Klux Klan organization.[1] If anything, during the 1920s and later, the province's French-speaking, Catholic population saw itself as a potential victim of the Ku Klux Klan.[2]

Newspaper reports in 1921 that a klavern had been formed in Montreal sounded like the efforts of a recruiting kleagle to drum up publicity. The reality was that a small group "in a state of semi-organization" had applied to Atlanta for a Klan charter, but they wanted certain exemptions from the standard requirements. They asked to be excluded from swearing an oath of allegiance to the United States and that Montreal members be excused "from all persecutions of Catholic members of society."[3] There is no evidence a charter was issued for a Montreal klavern. To do so would have meant denying key elements of the Klan's myth — American patriotism and anti-Catholicism.

Rumours that the Klan was responsible for a fire at the St. Sulpice Monastery north of Montreal in early December 1922 were never substantiated either historically or forensically.[4] William Simmons went so far as to send a telegram from Atlanta to the Montreal press denying any Klan involvement in a spate of recent fires in the province. But the destruction of the Quebec City Basilica in a fire two weeks later on December 22, 1922 continued to feed speculation about Klan activities in the province.

The province's fire marshall, Eugene Leclerc, became impatient with these loose interpretations of the facts.[5] After an extensive investigation of the Basilica fire, he ruled out a gas leak, defective wiring or "any outside agency" as the cause of the blaze. It was a clear case of spontaneous combustion in the basement of the church. Leclerc reviewed the history of religious institutions in the province destroyed by fire over the previous ten years. There had been fifty-six such cases, and of these only four or five remained unexplained. Leclerc placed the blame for these fires on church wardens who "do not pay enough attention to the matter of fire protection and holds them morally responsible for many of those fires."

So, while Quebec had its extremists — Adrien Arcand and his Fascists in the 1930s, the Front de Liberation du Québec (FLQ) in the 1960s and 1970s — there was no historical record of an organized Ku Klux Klan presence in the province until the late 1980s. The Klan came to the fore in Montreal in the midst of exacerbated racial, linguistic and political tensions.

White, Black, Middle Eastern and Indigenous youth regularly clashed in the bars, parks and streets of Montreal over racial animosities, sometimes with an overlay of French-English linguistic tensions, often fueled by beer. Into this mix came the skinheads: white, English-speaking, French-speaking, some the children of immigrants, parroting the racial ideologies of Europe and America and living the local tensions exacerbated by the threat of Quebec separatism. Their leader was an unemployed security guard named Michel Larocque, a flamboyant, media-friendly, mid-thirties white supremacist with strong organizational abilities and sense of Quebec's unique identity.[6]

His informal leadership of street skinheads took form and direction as he sought links with like-minded white supremacists in the United States. His skinheads became a formal branch of the invisible empire, Knights of the Ku Klux Klan, one of the rump organizations left over from David Duke's old organization. The group that Larocque affiliated with in the late 1980s was led by James Farrands, a tool-and-die maker from Shelton,

Connecticut. It was Farrands's faction that Wolfgang Droege would later allege had a small military Klan cell operating near Petawawa.

Farrands was an unusual Klansman — he was Roman Catholic and based in the northeast United States, not the usual southern U.S. location. But he had an organization that stretched across the United States and, with Larocque's help, into Canada. Organizational support for Larocque's newly minted klavern came in the person of Thomas Herman, a former New Hampshire police officer who was fired after his picture was printed in a local newspaper dressed in his Klan robes handing out candy to kids at Hallowe'en.[7] Larocque's Klan had all the trappings of the real thing — robes, regalia, passwords, cell structure. It also had a growing membership on the streets of Montreal and other Quebec cities.

Alain Roy came to Montreal from the all-white, mostly French-speaking suburban town of Boisbriand north of the city. From his early years, he had absorbed the message that Jews — traditional targets of the Quebec nationalist movement — were the source of Quebec's social ills and political impotence. With no education to speak of, he moved to Montreal in 1987 when he was twenty and worked as a mover and delivery truck driver.

Roy later recounted to journalist Warren Kinsella how in late June 1989, he and four friends had a street fight with a gang of Arab youths outside a Montreal North Metro station. He served a six-month jail sentence as a result. When he came out of jail in early 1990, he was already a seasoned racist with a couple of years of exposure to Michel Larocque and the Klan's ideology. Alain Roy became the exalted cyclops of the Montreal KKK.

Racial tensions were running high in the summer of 1990, and then they went higher yet. A confrontation between the Kanesatake Mohawk First Nation at Oka, northwest of Montreal, turned violent when the provincial police tried to break an Indigenous blockade that was set up outside a golf course to protect traditional lands. The Mohawk Warrior Society (MWS), an Indigenous self-defence organization with access to weapons, fought back when police tried to breach the blockade. A Sûreté du Québec officer was killed during an exchange of gunfire, by whose bullet was never established. The resulting standoff saw police and eventually the Canadian army eye-to-eye with the MWS.

Downstream at Kahnawake, a Mohawk community on the banks of the St. Lawrence River south of Montreal, the Mercier Bridge, a major cross-river link for Montreal commuters, was blocked by the local MWS in solidarity with the Oka resisters. The Kahnawake confrontation stirred local white anger that eventually degenerated into mob violence over the course of that hot, tension-filled summer.

Relations between the Mohawks and the neighbouring white communities were traditionally cordial but not warm. The Mohawks were predominantly English-speaking in the midst of a French-speaking province. The national Meech Lake Accord in June saw constitutional proposals defeated that would have enhanced Quebec's powers in Canada. Emotions among nationalist Québécois were raw from the setback. The Mohawks had been resolutely opposed to the amendments, seeing them as a threat to their Indigenous constitutional rights. The Oka Crisis took Mohawk-Québécois relations to a new low. This was fertile ground for white supremacists, in many ways similar to the situation in western Canada.

Michel Larocque was alert to the possibilities. He and Alain Roy began visiting the scene of confrontations at the Mercier Bridge during July, where angry crowds of white residents from nearby Chateauguay would gather to watch police officers and armed MWS warriors glare at each other across the barricades. The Klansmen began distributing anti-Mohawk pamphlets to the predominantly white onlookers, highlighting their presence with placards urging the Quebec government to take a hard line. Their conduct was later described by military historian Timothy Winegard as "loutish behaviour," a polite term for what was about to happen.[8]

A local talk radio personality, Gilles Proulx of station CJMS, attacked the Mohawks on-air for their blockade of the bridge. Throughout the increasingly tense summer weeks, he used his show to voice subtle — and not so subtle — racist opinions. These echoed the views of many Chateauguay residents, who took their cues from another local leader, real estate agent Yvon Poitras, a forty-seven-year-old former police officer with the Sûreté du Québec.

With rowdy crowds behind him, Poitras called on governments, the police and the army to clear MWS barricades from the Mercier Bridge. On August 1, 1990, Poitras led a march of ten thousand angry whites through the streets of Chateauguay, calling for force to be used to open the Mercier. The increasingly agitated crowd moved on to blockade the Champlain

Bridge, a neighbouring bridge to Montreal that had remained open throughout the summer. It took police a day to negotiate its re-opening.[9]

Trapped in their own community, it became clear to Mohawk leaders that it was important to remove vulnerable residents from what was an increasingly hostile environment. Alwyn Morris, a Mohawk leader from Kahnawake, former Olympic athlete and member of the Order of Canada, met with police to organize the safe evacuation of about one hundred women, children and old people. They set off in a caravan of cars on the afternoon of August 28, headed north for the Mercier Bridge bound for Montreal.

The Klan assured that the evacuation would be anything but peaceful. Michel Larocque, Alain Roy and more than a dozen Klan members were waiting at the north end of the bridge. The Mohawk motorcade passed through the MWS barricades on the south end and ventured onto the bridge over the St. Lawrence River. The Sûreté du Québec halted the caravan in the middle of the bridge. Under the hot sun, the cars were held in place for two hours as the Sûreté threw open trunks, searched vehicles and checked identities. Meanwhile, radio host Gilles Proulx had been alerted to the evacuation and broadcast the news, urging whites to gather at the north end of the bridge to greet the cavalcade. Finally, the police waved the Mohawk caravan forward.

A large crowd of white people collected at the north exit from the bridge in the suburb of LaSalle, watching the Mohawks negotiate their way through the police line. "About twenty young men in shorts and tank tops who were standing on the west side of the road scrambled onto a nearby dirt mound and began picking up rocks, bricks other bits of debris and hurling them at the cars as they drove by," wrote journalists Geoffrey York and Loreen Pindera in their book on the Oka Crisis.[10] These were Klan members, reinforced by angry local whites. Volleys of large rocks and jagged pieces of asphalt pelted the cars full of fleeing Mohawks. Police officers from the Sûreté du Québec stood by and watched. Before it was over, the media estimated that three hundred people joined the Klan in attacking the convoy.

Michael Orsini was a junior reporter at the *Montreal Gazette,* sent out to cover the Mercier Bridge confrontation. He described a harrowing scene of passing Mohawk cars "filled with frightened children staring at the small crowd shouting obscenities." It became much worse. "I recall a man in his fifties, beads of sweat streaming down the side of his face, ambling toward a small hill to collect some rocks suitably big enough to smash a few windshields. Each time a rock was met with the sound of broken glass, a small group watching on the sidelines cheered on the rock throwers," recalled Orsini.[11]

There were serious injuries. Six Mohawks, including a seventy-six-year-old man and a young child, were hurt. "A chunk of concrete nearly the size of a soccer ball smashed through the window behind me and landed on my father's chest," recalled Don Horne, who was driving a car through the mob. "He was covered in broken glass . . . he was bleeding all over."[12]

An unnamed Canadian Forces soldier at the barricades watched the violence aghast. "The cops didn't do anything or wouldn't do anything," he remembered. "The amount of hatred was just incredible."[13] A week later, Joe Armstrong, a seventy-one-year-old Mohawk man and Second World War veteran who had come through the gauntlet on the Mercier Bridge, died in hospital of a heart attack.

Many Mohawks believed Joe Armstrong died as a result of the stress of the evacuation and his encounter with the mob at the north end of the Mercier Bridge. Armstrong was a combat veteran who had served with the Princess Patricia's Canadian Light Infantry regiment. His death prompted a statement from his comrades at Royal Canadian Legion Branch 219 in Kahnawake. "The people responsible for this barrage . . . will live with it for the rest of their lives and answer to the Creator," said their memorial press release.[14]

The spectacle of a Klan-led mob attacking cars full of fleeing Mohawks while cameras documented the scene attracted national and international condemnation. Alain Roy of the Klan loved it. "We made people pay attention to us," he told Warren Kinsella. His version of the event was that a media organization had paid the Klan to throw things at the barricades, but all evidence suggested the Klan — and the anti-Mohawk mobs of local white residents — would have done it even if they weren't paid.

While the Klan was stoning Mohawks on the Mercier Bridge, three small planes landed on a road on the Kahnawake reserve, took on board passengers and departed for American airspace a few minutes' flying time away.[15] Military observation posts counted as many as fifteen such flights, suspected of carrying heavy weapons and warriors away from Canadian authorities.[16] A suspicious mind might think the Klan's Mercier Bridge attack was a planned diversion to draw attention away from the air evacuation of persons unknown. More likely, though, it was the MWS taking advantage of an ugly spectacle to get away.

Public and political condemnation followed the Mohawk stoning, but Larocque and Roy were oblivious. For them, the Mercier Bridge attack provided unexpected publicity that attracted attention, new members and gave them status as the pre-eminent white supremacist organization in the city, if not the country. "We are starting to link with other groups in other provinces, and we are learning good communications," Larocque said. "Me and my people, we're not going to be stopped. Money is not an object." The Oka barricades went down in late September, and relative calm returned to the Montreal region.

The Klan's early successes in Quebec included the creation in the late 1980s of a klavern in Sherbrooke, Quebec, a small city about one hundred and fifty kilometres east of Montreal, with easy access to the American border. The KKK leader in Sherbrooke was Eric Vachon, an aggressive skinhead who was also affiliated with James Farrands and his Klan organization. In the heady days after the Mercier Bridge attack, Larocque, a strong Quebec nationalist, claimed to have found evidence that James Farrands was favouring Vachon, who had supported the federalist side in the referendum earlier in the year. "I learned that Farrands was trying to favour the Sherbrooke takeover of Montreal, at my expense," said Larocque. "They interfered in our affairs."

More generally, Larocque found Farrands lacking in political credibility. By the summer of 1991, Farrands had moved his headquarters from Connecticut to Klan-friendly North Carolina. In his magazine, the *Klansman,* which was published in the United States, Farrands wrote that the Klan's white supremacist views could be a unifying factor in relations between Canada's anglophones and francophones. The Klan could solidify opposition to the Jews. Farrands attributed Canada's recent constitutional turmoil to "a plan by the Jews to further divide Canada." Larocque was dismissive. "That's silly," he told a journalist. "It doesn't have [anything] to do with the Jews."[17] That was enough for Larocque. He denounced Farrands as an alcoholic and a drug user, and pulled his local Montreal klavern out of the U.S. organization.

The Montreal Klan began to go down a familiar path. First, Larocque changed the name of his group to Longitude 74 KKK, so-called because Montreal sits on the seventy-fourth line of longitude. Then he affiliated with another Klan organization based in the Ozark Mountains near Harrison, Arkansas. This group was led by Thom Robb, an ordained Baptist minister with strong Christian Identity beliefs, who had his own set of imperatives for his Klan followers.

Robb was death — literally — on homosexuals. He regularly and publicly called for their execution, basing his belief on the Bible.[18] "We must endorse and support the law of God, which calls for the death penalty to the faggot slime," Robb was quoted. "We endorse and seek the execution of the homosexuals."[19] The Arkansas Klan was a direct descendant of Don Black's Knights of the Ku Klux Klan organization. After assuming a leadership role in Black's group, Robb had shifted the headquarters from Tuscumbia, Alabama, to Arkansas in the mid-1980s.

Next, Larocque and Alain Roy began organizing Montreal's skinheads into a group called White Power Canada, which Roy described as "a junior Ku Klux Klan club" that would fight in the streets but not implicate Larocque or Roy. Events would demonstrate how well the strategy worked. The same events seemed to show the influence of Thom Robb's thinking on the Montreal Klan.

Meanwhile, Eric Vachon's klavern in Sherbrooke was increasingly active. By the spring of 1991, the group was bringing Klan literature across the American border and distributing it throughout the Eastern Townships and into the Montreal suburbs. One of the publications was the *Klansman,* which officials said contained passages that violated the hate propaganda provisions of the *Criminal Code.*

In November 1991, the Sûreté du Québec arrested Vachon and two other young men crossing the U.S. border into Canada in the bush near Stanhope, Quebec. They pleaded guilty to illegal importation of hate literature and walked away with five-hundred-dollar fines. Six months later, Vachon was convicted of assault after attacking an anti-racist activist in a Sherbrooke bar, then ripping out the surgically implanted hairpiece of bar owner Normand Martin when he tried to break up the fight. A fine of $350 and six months of probation ended this typical Klan fracas.[20]

The White Power Canada presence on Montreal streets led to large-scale brawls with minority and anti-racist youth. The violence escalated. On November 29, 1992, four skinheads from White Power Canada — the leader was fifteen years old — beat a man to death in Montreal's Angrignon Park because they thought he was gay. Yves Lalonde, fifty-one, was robbed and beaten to death with a bat and tree limbs.

The four were arrested and charged with murder. "You live like an animal," Youth Court Judge Normand Lafond said later when sentencing a sixteen-year-old who had wielded a tree limb. "You have an inhumane attitude." Crown Attorney Reynald Bernier said the fifteen-year-old who used the baseball bat in the attack "is a danger to all citizens who don't fit into his racist philosophy because of their clothes, sex or skin colour." Both were sentenced to three years in reformatory and two years probation under the *Young Offenders Act*.[21]

Two weeks after Lalonde's killing, another man was beaten to death at a highway rest stop near Joliette, north of Montreal. The rest stop was reputed to be a meeting place for gay men. White Power Canada skinheads began patrolling the site as part of a Klan-inspired war on homosexuality. Daniel Lacombe, thirty-seven, a high school teacher, was beat on the head until he suffered a fatal aneurysm. Five WPC teens were charged with manslaughter, aggravated assault and conspiracy to commit a criminal act. They eventually pleaded guilty to second-degree murder.

The killings came at a time when the attitude of the Montreal police towards gays was under close scrutiny. If police in the west were antagonistic towards Indigenous people, there was concern that police in Montreal had a similar relationship with the gay community. There were complaints that police investigations into gay-bashing and killings were given little to no priority.

Worse, the Montreal police service suffered from a reputation for brutality against gays, a view cemented by the July 1990 raid on the so-called Sex Garage. The gay club near Old Montreal was surrounded by as many as forty officers, who removed their name tags and battered patrons with truncheons as they came out of the bar's only exit. It was the latest in a series of violent raids on gay clubs ranging from the late 1970s to the early 1990s.

The Montreal Klan continued its descent into violence. In October 1991, Larocque was charged with multiple offenses after police were called to his Rachel Street apartment in east-end Montreal — assault, possession of a prohibited weapon, obstructing a police officer and uttering threats. Three months later, Michel Larocque and Alain Roy led a gang of almost forty skinheads on a mission to Rue Cuvillier in the Hochelaga-Maisonneuve district of the east end.

They were shadowed by Montreal police who, logically, wondered what the group was doing and where they were headed when they met up at L'Assomption Metro Station. So they followed them. The group of mostly teenage skinheads, plus Larocque and Roy, gathered outside an apartment building where five Somali men lived. The five were said to have beaten some skinheads a few weeks before. This was a revenge mission.

One of the skinheads in the crowd, Martin Bellehumeur, carried a bag. Bellehumeur, twenty, was studying to become a firefighter, but that did not begin to explain why his bag contained three beer bottles full of gasoline. As the crowd loitered outside the Somalis' apartment building, police watched as Bellehumeur placed the bag of Molotov cocktails against the wall of a building opposite the Somali men's residence. The police had seen enough. They arrested the lot. Charges were considered. Larocque and Roy were obvious candidates, but in the end the Crown attorney determined that only Bellehumeur would be charged.

At trial, the aspiring firefighter said he was not a member of the Ku Klux Klan. He knew Larocque and Roy as acquaintances who lived in the same neighbourhood as he did. He admitted that he carried the bag with the beer bottles because an "aggressive" Larocque forced him to do it. Bellehumeur was sentenced to jail for six months for possession of explosive materials.[22] Larocque and Roy escaped prosecution. And then Larocque was acquitted of the charges against him from October 1991 when the court could not ascertain, exactly, what he had said to the police that was deemed to constitute a threat.

Photographer André Querry was a witness to the rise of white supremacist activity in Montreal during the 1990s. He was a familiar figure at demonstrations. But he was also aligned with social groups that grew in opposition to the skinheads and the Klan. In 1993, he became a Klan target. He was attacked by Klan members while passing out pamphlets warning residents in a Montreal neighbourhood of an upcoming Klan event. "They attacked me because of my sexual orientation," he recalled later, another victim of the Klan's hate campaign against gays. The front door of his building was spray-painted with "KKK" and the Klan's cross-hair sniper symbol in July 1993. The warning was clear.

One of the more inexplicable eruptions by the Ku Klux Klan into the public eye — with a Quebec connection — occurred in January 1993 in Georgetown, Ontario, a small town northwest of Toronto. With no warning and no explanations, seven Klan members appeared on downtown streets in full white-robe regalia and hoods to hand out pamphlets.[23] "Why they came here I have no idea, absolutely none," local councillor Anne Currie said later.

The handouts in English and French complained about "anti-white movies," gun control and "high taxes for the minority welfare." At least one of the cars they arrived in had Quebec licence plates, suggesting this was some kind of field trip for the Quebec Klan, reasons unknown. The police took names, ran licence plates and basically let them go about their business. "Like any other group, they have the right to exercise their — if you will — beliefs," said Staff Sergeant Don Cousens of the Halton Regional Police. Local residents had a different view. Passersby began pounding on one of the cars and ripped the white hood off one the Klan members. The seven Klansmen drove away without explanation soon after, leaving residents mystified.

The only other Klan manifestations in Georgetown in recent memory involved a local man, Craig Harrison, who came to police attention in 1989. He had burned a cross in his driveway "and stated at the time he was practicing his religion, a protest against Blacks, Jews and Pakistanis," according to the Crown prosecutor.[24] In 1996, three years after the Klan visit to Georgetown, Harrison was sentenced to two-years-less-a-day in jail for beating up a local shop owner, Michael Wong, on the street outside his store. A decade later, Harrison was the subject of a cease and desist order and fined one thousand dollars by the Canadian Human Rights Tribunal for having posted hateful content to the Freedom Site, a white supremacist Internet platform. The fine was issued primarily because of the violent nature of the posts.[25]

Meanwhile back in Quebec, with two murders, a failed fire bombing, countless assaults, threats and related criminal charges on their records, the members of the Montreal Ku Klux Klan, Longtitude 74 and White Power Canada began fading from the racist scene towards the end of the 1990s. Prison took its toll. Official scrutiny hampered organizational efforts. Street fighters aged. But the ideas behind the Ku Klux Klan endured in Quebec society as they did elsewhere in Canada. Almost thirty years after the Mercier Bridge attack on the Mohawks of Kahnawake, Michel Larocque emerged to join demonstrations mounted by La Meute (the Wolf Pack), a populist, anti-immigrant, white supremacist group active in Quebec. To demonstrate his solidarity, Michel Larocque posed for photos with a Wolf Pack tattoo on his hand.

* * *

The footnotes to the late twentieth-century Klan era did not end with Michel Larocque. James McQuirter also flashed briefly in the public eye almost thirty years after he went to jail. Journalist Stewart Bell, chronicler of the ill-fated plot to invade Dominica, talked to him in 2009 about life after hate.[26] "These ideas are anathema to me now, to such a degree that even thinking about them is abhorrent to me," said the fifty-year-old McQuirter. "When I read or think about that time in my past, it's like reading about someone else." During the interview, McQuirter apologized.

> *The reason that I haven't done so publicly before now was not because I am not apologetic for my past, but as I am no longer that person anymore, and therefore I find it difficult to apologize on behalf of someone I no longer am. It is very hard to acknowledge that part of my life . . . However, I see the need to apologize publicly, as having not doing so may appear to others as me trying to minimize my past.*

About the effect his words and actions had on Klan targets during the 1980s, McQuirter said, "I never thought about the impact. I don't think my sense of empathy was fully developed." Always disciplined and fastidious about his appearance, McQuiter had adapted to his circumstances in jail. He read widely, considered race and the role of individuals in society.

> *Prison allowed me the time to sort out my mistakes and understand fatal flaws in my beliefs. Gradually I changed. Prison turned out to be a good experience for me. I finally had a good night's sleep. I think it saved my life. Had I continued the way I was going, I'm sure I'd not be alive today.*

He was paroled in 1989, about the same time Wolfgang Droege was released from jail in California. Back in Canada, full of ideas for the future, the leader of the new Heritage Front gave him a call. Want in, Droege asked? No, not interested, said McQuirter. He went on to work in "multi-level marketing" (a euphemism for pyramid sales) selling water filters, using his charm, leadership and communication skills to make what he said was a good living. He developed ideas about marketing, wealth and how to achieve a better life, something he had obviously been seeking during his Klan years.

He adopted the pen name James Tavian Alexander and wrote books on how to gain wealth, change your life and create a healthy lifestyle. McQuirter claimed to have lived in Paris, Rome and then Panama. He was there when the façade fell. A local journalist there checked him out when he seemed discomfited at their meeting, discovered his background and published the story. With time, McQuirter was philosophical about the disclosure.

> *The secret is out, yes, but the secret is not that I held abhorrent views, and hurt so many people. The secret is that anyone who feels that what they are is not who they want to be, can change . . . I'm living proof that change can happen.*

A return to Toronto brought more change. He moved in with his girlfriend, a raw food enthusiast, who drew McQuirter into a new lifestyle. He wrote articles and books on the benefits of raw food. He took photos, made a music video. Then he was diagnosed with throat cancer and survived. His raw food diet, he asserted, contributed to his recovery. In March 2009, the National Parole Board granted him a pardon for his crimes, saying he had remained "free of any conviction since completing the sentence and was of good conduct and that the convictions should no longer reflect adversely on his character."

His fate was far different from Wolfgang Droege's. Racist, drug dealer, relentless dreamer, Wolfgang Droege died in his underwear on the afternoon of Wednesday, April 13, 2005, on the stairwell of his Toronto apartment building with .22-calibre bullets in his chest and the back of his head. His killer was a delusional cocaine customer who believed Droege was controlling him through his computer. The death of fifty-five-year-old Wolfgang Droege was a violent footnote to the Ku Klux Klan's return to Canada in the twentieth century.

# Chapter 16
# KLAN ONLINE IN THE 2000s

The Ku Klux Klan in the first two decades of the twenty-first century was old school, a cliché, a symbol. The Klan organizations that claimed to exist in Canada in the new century were almost always the creation of individuals who fancied themselves the newest grand dragon or imperial wizard. In the Canadian hate sphere, legitimacy flowed from recognition by, or affiliation with, a U.S.-based Klan group. But in almost all cases, the twenty-first-century Klan lived largely in cyberspace with Internet links that facilitated the targeting of victims, vilification of rivals and easy access to a universe of hate.

There were early signs that the Klan would go in this direction. Many advantages flowed from operating in cyberspace. No need to wear a cone-shaped hood and robes in a public place to display your affiliation and attract attention. No need to use a real name, meet in a real place, distribute your propaganda on the street. "Racist groups have been historically highly skilled, early adopters of new technologies," wrote Australian academic Ana-Maria Bliuc.[1] A white hood was irrelevant when the Klan and similar organizations could do their business in the anonymity of computer circuitry.

The Ku Klux Klan came quickly to telephony as a way of spreading hate propaganda. Both the Canadian and American Klans used telephone hate lines in the late twentieth century. The public could call in to hear recorded hate messages, leave contact details to receive literature or inquire about how to join Klan ranks. These efforts were deplored by the public and politicians. In Canada, the technique became the trigger for multiple charges under the hate propaganda provisions of the *Criminal Code* and s. 13 of the *Canadian Human Rights Act*. Passed by Parliament in 1977, the *Human Rights Act* was an especially timely response to the spread of telephone hate lines.

By the late 1980s, with the advent of the Internet, enterprising individuals in the Klan and other racist organizations began to exploit the new technology. Bill Harcus, the young self-styled grand wizard of the Manitoba Ku Klux Klan, gave serious thought in 1990 about how to move beyond telephone hate line techniques, particularly after the Canadian Human Rights Commission shut down his phone operation.[2] He built on his contacts with Louis Beam, Jr., the erstwhile grand dragon of the Texas KKK, to try and set up a computerized bulletin board for white supremacists to share information and coordinate activities in Canada and the United States.[3]

The Aryan Nations operated a computer bulletin board in the mid-1980s to distribute their white supremacist message, an innovation inspired by Louis Beam.[4] The head of the Aryan Nations' Canadian affiliate, Terry Long, avoided customs and criminal restrictions on hate propaganda by using the Aryan Nation's computer network to transmit banned materials across the international border. "The computer system is a beautiful solution, because if you have a modem and a printer, you can get all of this information in your own home," Long exulted in 1984, pointing to the future of cyber propaganda.[5]

The following year, Long advertised that he could provide access to computerized data banks containing lists of so-called "race traitors." This was an unsettling assertion from a man who was also quoted as saying all Jews should be hung for treason.[6] The "index of traitors" was again the creation of Louis Beam, even if Terry Long was the portal through which aspiring race warriors could gain access.[7] The index was a list of anti-Klan groups and individuals with their names and addresses as well as those of federal judges, federal agents and anybody else — mostly Americans — assessed as a threat to the white power movement, so-called.

A guru of the American white supremacist world, Louis Beam was notorious for the range and depth of his commitment to racism and violence.[8] Beam served in the Vietnam War for eighteen months in the late 1960s as a machine gunner on U.S. Army Huey attack helicopters. When he came home in 1968, he promptly joined the Texas chapter of the United Klans of America, an Alabama-based group that was responsible for repeated attacks on civil rights workers during the 1950s and 1960s. When David Duke started up the Knights of the Ku Klux Klan in 1975, Beam shifted his allegiances and eventually became the grand dragon for Texas in Duke's organization. After several violent and highly publicized racist confrontations, Beam moved to Idaho in the early 1980s to live at the Aryan Nations compound at Hayden Lake.

The Aryan Nations camp gave him a platform for his violent ideas on race war. Based on the assumption of an apocalyptic world after a nuclear exchange between America and the Soviet Union, Beam hypothesized a future where prepared white supremacists would seize tracts of North America to create a whites-only homeland. To help achieve that goal, Beam advised white supremacist and racist groups on violence, security measures and technology. In July 1984, for example, Beam instructed assembled racists at the Aryan Nations World Congress on building pipe bombs and converting assault rifles to full automatic mode. The Canadian participants included Terry Long and Carney Nerland, future gun shop owner.[9] The same year, Beam and two associates established the Aryan Nations Liberty Net, probably the world's first white supremacist online bulletin board. In fact, the Liberty Net was a system of close to a dozen bulletin boards that allowed white supremacists to spread propaganda and communicate and coordinate their activities.[10]

As U.S. authorities cracked down on the extreme right wing during the 1980s, Beam observed the efficiency of their investigations against structured, hierarchical organizations that relied on regular contacts and communications to achieve their goals. In response, he sat down and produced a series of articles on the merits of "leaderless resistance." The resistance he envisaged would be comprised of so-called "phantom cells" of one to six members, with individual members acting on their own initiative rather than in response to orders issued through a command hierarchy that was vulnerable to penetration and disruption. "The basic idea was to avoid the destruction of revolutionary organizations when they were infiltrated or in other ways compromised by law enforcement officials, limiting damage to a single cell at most," concluded Klan watchers at the Southern Poverty Law Centre. Individuals acting alone, not organizations acting in coordination, would be the way to frustrate the agents of the supposed Zionist Occupied Government.[11]

The Internet and new methods of communication were ideal for promoting the idea and the practice of leaderless resistance. As Terry Long predicted, individuals could receive their racist information in their own homes on computer networks. They could reach out to others with similar ideas, also from the privacy of their homes. No physical meetings, no facial identification, no real names need enter into the relationship. Encryption and private chat rooms enhanced anonymity. Individuals could choose to act alone, or they could coordinate with anonymous associates to undertake racist activities.

Louis Beam and leaderless resistance were made for the booming World Wide Web. The white supremacist community moved quickly into the cyber universe. "The Internet affords the Klan a unique opportunity to get into the living room of Middle America and allows us access to young kids," observed Thom Robb, the KKK imperial wizard from Arkansas, whose condemnation of gays seemed to have motivated neo-Nazi skinheads in the Montreal Klan in the early 1990s.[12]

A familiar figure emerged in the forefront of technology services for racists. Don Black was David Duke's successor in 1979 as the imperial wizard of the Louisiana-based Knights of the Ku Klux Klan. He was drawn into the folly that was Operation Red Dog, eventually ending up in the parking lot at the Harbor Inn Marina in New Orleans on the night of April 27, 1981, staring into the police floodlights. Like Wolfgang Droege, Don Black went to jail, not Dominica, convicted of violating the neutrality provisions of American law.[13] He presented himself at his trial in the style of David Duke, dressed in three-piece suits, well-groomed and well-spoken. Asked questions, the twenty-seven-year-old talked and talked and talked until the judge told him to cut it short. But all the talk made no difference to the jury.[14] He was sent down.

Prison gave Don Black new skills to supplement his lifetime avocation as a hatemonger. Black had first encountered computers at the Marshall Space Flight Center in Huntsville, Alabama, where he visited as a child. Later, when he lived with David Duke, he tinkered with the imperial wizard's personal computer. He also featured in Duke's personal life, marrying Chloe

Duke after she and David divorced in the early 1980s. But spending three years in Big Spring minimum-security federal prison in Texas gave Black an insight into what the future held for white supremacist organizing.

He began taking computer science programming courses in jail and spending long stretches of time fiddling with a Radio Shack TRS-80 computer. When he came out of prison, David Duke met him at the prison gate and flew with him back to Birmingham, Alabama. Life changed. He quit the Klan, claiming it was too violent. He married Chloe in 1988. David Duke was the best man at Don and Chloe's wedding, and later took on the role of a mentor to their son Derek.[15] Don Black ran for a U.S. senate seat in Alabama as a candidate for the rarely-heard-of Populist Party. He was arrested during civil rights demonstrations in Georgia for illegally blocking a highway. He talked publicly about recruiting, training and dispatching anti-Communist Klan mercenaries to Nicaragua to fight against the socialist government there.[16] A move to Florida to become a stockbroker stalled when the state brokerage industry refused to license him because of his links with David Duke.

He was among friends in Florida. The Southern Poverty Law Center estimated that in the mid-1990s there were thirty-three Klan groups and seventy-two armed militia groups of diverse stripes in Florida, more than in any other state of the United States. The racial and religious mix that characterized Florida society were seen as a hothouse culture that promoted white supremacist and neo-Nazi activities. Canadians would remember that Charles Lewis Fowler and Pat Emmons had migrated there a half-century earlier, following their Klan misadventures in Ontario and Saskatchewan.

Don and Chloe Black came to ground in West Palm Beach, Florida, in a smallish house in a mixed-race neighbourhood. Don launched a one-man computer services company managing databases, designing bulletin boards and websites. He converted the master bedroom of his house into his world headquarters — literally — and launched Stormfront.org on March 27, 1995. With the passing of years, Stormfront became the Internet's pre-eminent racist, white supremacist, neo-Nazi website, hosting the full spectrum of hate-based groups, but with a particular affinity for the diverse pathological universe of the Ku Klux Klan.

In doing so, Don Black became not just an American hate-monger but an international hate-monger with a chilling perspective on the future of the United States. "We see the breakup coming in about twenty years," he told journalist David Abel in 1998. "It's a natural progression of events." This timeline would put disintegration midway through the disastrous term of U.S. President Donald Trump. It was a timeline that gave observers something to think about as the United States struggled with the racist policies and pronouncements of the erratic New York real estate developer who was elected president in 2016.

Black was enthusiastic about Stormfront's ability to shape future events. "The Internet is a means of planting seeds for the future," he told Abel. Young people, disaffected middle-class Americans, the oppressed white population could find their views on Stormfront and be guided accordingly. By the end of the twentieth century, there were hundreds of racist websites, but Stormfront, organized with national sections for the Canadians, the British, the Australians and others, became the unequivocal leader of the hate-mongering Internet pack.

The potential of cyber-hate was not lost on Canadian white supremacists. Among the young people drawn into Wolfgang Droege's Heritage Front in 1990 was fifteen-year-old Marc Lemire from Toronto. Lemire had a troubled background remarkably similar to James McQuirter and Droege himself. He found an intellectual and political home with Droege, Grant Bristow and the other leadership figures of the Heritage Front. He also brought interests and skills in the world of computers and information technology. By 1994, he was at the forefront of the Heritage Front's foray into establishing a cyber presence. "With few exceptions, the Internet equips the right wing with an uncensored medium where they are able to espouse their views freely and openly without reprisal," concluded an early Canadian study of how extremists were using new technologies.[17]

The first noteworthy cyber presence of Canadian racists involved an online organization called the Canadian Patriots Network (CPN), which was devoted to bringing right-wing groups together in a centralized cyber network. Over the course of the late 1990s, the CPN evolved into a platform called the Freedom Site, where the likes of Craig Harrison of Georgetown, Ontario, posted vitriolic and threatening messages against minorities of all kinds.[18] Under Lemire's guidance, the Freedom Site initially hosted five organizations including the

Heritage Front and groups promoted by long-time right-wing figure Paul Fromm. The Freedom Site's extremist content made Internet service provider (ISP) companies nervous. After moving from company to company, the site ended up on an Internet service provider in Oliver, British Columbia.

The ISP in Oliver, Fairview Technologies, was owned and operated by Bernard Klatt, an individual with a deeply held commitment to free speech if not the ideologies he hosted. The site had a local business base, but it soon became home to hate groups from around the globe, including the Heritage Front. After public denunciations and protest, British Columbia Telephones, which provided Internet access to the company, threatened to impose restrictions on its operations. In response, Canadian hate organizations began shifting their websites to the United States and other countries, effectively making it difficult for Canadian authorities to take action against them.[19] The law governing the Canadian Human Rights Commission was amended in late 2001 to explicitly give the commission jurisdiction over "matters communicated by means of the Internet." Any ambiguity concerning the commission's reach over the cyber world was settled beyond doubt.[20] Six months later, in June 2002, Marc Lemire officially joined Stormfront.org, where he encouraged visitors to click over to the Freedom Site for a Canadian perspective.[21]

The ability to reach individuals with an interest in white supremacy, as predicted by Terry Long, was a huge benefit to Ku Klux Klan recruiters, and these benefits were obvious early. Chris Waters of Regina offers a case in point.[22] He joined the Brotherhood of Klans, an Ohio-based faction of the Klan, in 2001 after chatting online with other BOK members. Seven years later, he was identified as the grand dragon of Realm Number 51 in Regina and a self-identified leading member of the BOK in Saskatchewan. He claimed two hundred and fifty members in the province and thirty-five hundred across the country. Online detractors noted that he was a recent arrival from Ontario and had spent much of his time in the province collecting welfare. How much any of this was based in reality remained an open question, as was the case with many claims made on the Internet.

Stormfront.org as a racist online platform offered advantages to Canadian visitors. There was a dedicated Stormfront Canada subsection, where a Canadian visitor could sign up for an account with a user name. Anonymity was assured. The aspiring Canadian white supremacist could then reach out to like-minded countrymen — and presumably women — although most participants appeared to be men. The site warned readers that not everybody on it was their friend: "You are advised to be cautious and thoughtful, both in anything you say on this forum, and in anything you do in Canada." To make the point even clearer, the Stormfront Canada moderator, going by the name Leto Atreides II, reminded visitors of specific *Criminal Code* provisions (i.e., s. 318 Advocating genocide; s. 319 Public incitement of hatred, and associated penalties) as well as *Human Rights Acts*. "Canada does not have freedom of speech," advised Leto. "Canada is dominated by powerful, wealthy entities whom *[sic]* oppose the survival and liberty of the White race."

Leto Atreides II was identified by academic Barbara Perry as the online persona of a notorious Edmonton racist named Keith Francis William "Bill" Noble, a member of several white supremacist groups including the National Socialist Party of Canada but not, apparently, the Ku Klux Klan.[23] Originally from Fort St. John in British Columbia, Noble moved to Edmonton, where he was arrested in 2006 and charged with wilful promotion of hatred on the basis of material posted on his personal website. He was sentenced to four months in jail followed by three years of probation. Leto's admonishment to Stormfront users to be mindful of Canada's anti-hate laws was obviously based on hard-won personal experience.

The creation of online venues like Stormfront Canada was met by opposing online communities dedicated to monitoring and publicizing racist activities and individuals. The Anti-Racist Coalition (ARC), an online group of anonymous reporters, provided a running update on the people and events that made up the racist, white supremacist community in Canada. Names, dates, places, activities, photos and videos filled the group's web pages. It was the kind of detail that made it impossible to deny the existence of a community of hate. The ARC website tracked neo-Nazis, skinheads and the occasional retro Klansman across the decades, following them from the streets to their media eruptions and in some cases on to jail. A west coast group called Stop Racism performed a similar role but at a higher level of surveillance, remarking on trends and their meaning rather than the forensic details of racism in action.

The Canadian Anti-Hate Network (CAHN) took on a similar role, with commentaries on trends and analysis of prominent hate indicators. With a broadly based board of directors made up of well-known community leaders and activists, the CAHN had political heft. With the likes of Bernie Farber, a former leader of the Canadian Jewish Congress, on the board, the CAHN was able to guide public discourse on the state of hate in the country. Ottawa civil rights lawyer Richard Warman, also a member of the CAHN's board of directors, had the distinction during the early twenty-first century of launching more than a dozen actions under s. 13 of the *Canadian Human Rights Act* that led to the shutting down of Internet hate sites or bulletin boards.

This remedy to online hate disappeared when the Conservative government of Stephen Harper accepted a private member's bill in 2013 sponsored by Alberta MP Brian Storseth. The bill killed s. 13 of the *Act,* removing the ability of individuals to seek redress against cyber hate. The amendment was defended by the Conservative Party and its supporters as removing an unnecessary limit on free speech. The measure left only cumbersome *Criminal Code* charges as a legal tool to stop hate propaganda. The *Charter of Rights and Freedoms,* with its enshrined fundamental freedoms and equality rights, continued to enjoy the same high level of public approval and support it had enjoyed from its earliest days in 1981.[24]

As in the civilian world, the Canadian military saw its members targeted by online white supremacist recruiters. The Canadian Forces' Military Police Intelligence Unit noted in 2018 that racist and white supremacist groups were active users of the Internet. "Online communities provide a venue to share and expand their ideologies and allow connections with a potential for recruitment, as well as 'lone actor' activity," the military police reported.[25] "Prominent social media platforms have played a role in the proliferation of certain hate groups and their ability to attract members."

Canadian Forces members were as susceptible as civilians. For some groups, the attraction of the military stemmed from access to military training, which would prepare them to wage race war. For others, it was the fellowship of other racists in a protected atmosphere similar to 2 Commando of the disbanded Canadian Airborne Regiment. There were ample cases to consider. A young soldier was disciplined in 2011 for posting comments on a racist website. At least one former soldier from Nova Scotia was identified in 2018 as an active online member of the Atomwaffen Division, an extreme violence-prone neo-Nazi organization based in the United States.[26] The Atomwaffen Division in Canada was described by the military police as "few in number and are not believed to have a national footprint."[27] In Winnipeg, a master corporal in the CF army reserves was identified by the media in late summer 2019 as a member of a U.S.-based hate group called the Base that encouraged its members to join the military for combat training.[28] He disappeared from Manitoba, slipping across the border into the United States, where he was arrested in January 2020, along with other Base members plotting armed insurrection for what they hoped would be the prelude to race war.

The election of Donald Trump as president of the United States in November 2016 ignited a wave of white supremacist and racist activity. With a campaign steeped in populism and white nationalism, Trump attracted the support of the likes of David Duke, Don Black and other figures in the extreme right wing. Their messages of support and racism were magnified through the Internet and social media platforms. In Canada, academics Barbara Perry and Ryan Scrivens, who studied right-wing extremism, argued that the Trump victory "galvanized Canadian-based white supremacist ideologies, identities, movements and practices."[29] They asserted that the resurgence of right-wing extremism in Canada was "symptomatic of the continuing legacy of white supremacy." The history of the Ku Klux Klan in Canada with its deep and recurring episodes stood as strong evidence for the argument.

Events in the aftermath of the Trump victory spoke to the enabling nature of the relentless and crude hate flowing north to Canada. The months after Trump's election and inauguration saw a spike in anti-immigrant, anti-Muslim, anti-Black and homophobic incidents and attacks across the country, many of them referencing the Ku Klux Klan but without real Klan organizations to back them. The culmination came on January 29, 2017, when Alexandre Bissonnette attacked the Centre Culturel Islamique de Québec in Ste-Foy, shooting six Muslim men to death and wounding nineteen others. Bissonnette's social media statements explicitly referred to the Trump victory and anti-Islamic propaganda found on the Internet.

Six months later, American white supremacists had been emboldened by

Trump's presence in the White House. David Duke congratulated Donald Trump on his election. Don Black saw the traffic on Stormfront streak straight up on election night. There was a sense among white nationalists that their time had come. New leaders, new groups, new extremes appeared on the political landscape. Charlottesville, a college town in Virginia, was in the midst of a controversy over removing a century-old Confederate statue from its main square. Extreme right-wing groups across America called for a "Unite the Right" rally to be held in Charlottesville on August 12, 2017. They came from across the United States. And Canada.

A few days before the rally, an anonymous leader in Montreal's extreme right wing signed on to a closed chat group of white supremacists to advise his American contacts that a delegation was planning to travel to Virginia.[30] "We are about twenty guys driving through the border from Canada and we obviously will not be able to bring protective gear like shields and so on through the border agents," he wrote. "If you've got extra ones, some of our members are interested in buying them from you over there." The group left for Virginia soon after.

They arrived in Charlottesville in time to participate in a torchlight parade on the night of August 11 that saw thousands of mostly young men celebrate their white hate with noisy bravado. The next day, white supremacists flooded into the streets of Charlottesville and were met by thousands of counter-demonstrators. Street fights followed. People were hurt, some badly. A car driven by an Ohio Klansman, James Fields, crashed into a crowd of demonstrators at high speed. Bodies flew. Heather Heyer, a librarian protesting against the white supremacists, was killed. Donald Trump, the president of the United States, took several days to acknowledge that something bad might have happened in Charlottesville. The nature and tone of the Trump presidency's white nationalism was fixed in history.

The Canadians at Charlottesville were largely drawn from La Meute (the Wolf Pack), a Quebec-based group put together in 2015 to protest Canada's acceptance of thirty thousand refugees from war-torn Syria. The new Liberal Prime Minister Justin Trudeau welcomed the newcomers, a major policy change from the unpopular right-wing government of his predecessor, Stephen Harper. La Meute was organized by two former soldiers, Eric Venne and Patrick Beaudry.[31]

In the following years, La Meute became one of the fastest-growing populist movements in the province of Quebec. Shawn Beauvois-MacDonald was a member of La Meute, and he went to Charlottesville. Vincent Belanger-Mercure said he went to Virginia on his own, just for fun. But he supported the white race message the event conveyed.[32] The online organizer who wanted to buy shields for his group was subsequently identified as an elusive character who went by the cover name Zeiger. The *Montreal Gazette* concluded that he was probably Gabriel Sohier Chaput, a computer nerd with a handlebar moustache from east-end Montreal with a following of a few dozen misogynist, poorly socialized white men.

La Meute was only one of several new right-wing extremist groups that surfaced in Canada during the first two decades of the new century. There were the Soldiers (or Sons) of Odin, a group that originated in Finland and appeared in Canada in 2016. The group claimed to be concerned with countering street crime but gained a reputation for anti-immigrant, anti-Muslim rhetoric and protests. Blood and Honour and its affiliate Combat 18 were violent neo-Nazi groups with links to an international array of hate groups. Both organizations were named as terrorist entities by the Canadian government in 2019 and banned. The Base was a neo-Nazi white supremacist group formed in 2018. It had a presence in Canada — primarily Winnipeg — where a Canadian Forces reserve soldier was accused of recruiting for the group. And there were others.

* * *

But they were not the Ku Klux Klan. In fact, by the end of the second decade of the twenty-first century, there was no formal organization extant with the name of Ku Klux Klan of Canada. From time to time, individuals presented themselves online or in the media or in court as Klan leaders and members but they were typically deluded, drunk or drug-addled. Their credibility, if any, was drawn from some form of recognition from an American Klan faction. And in the United States, the number of Klan organizations and Klan members was said to be in decline, even in the hospitable environment created by the Trump presidency. Antiracist forces in Canada and elsewhere took heart, but the hate persisted.

The posts by visitors to Stormfront Canada in late 2019 were sometimes plaintive, sometimes ignorant, sometimes illiterate. User TMWTB28 was "trying to find a kkk group here in Vancouver . . . all of the sites have been taken down any help would be great." Wheres Whitey responded that "I don't think any such groups exist." On the east coast, somebody asked if there were participants from Newfoundland. Bigpatrick710 replied "It's all whites here b'y everthings good." SangiusCivitasPatria was in New Brunswick "and would like to meet others." A general query about the "Whitest City in Canada?" generated a burst of responses. Sonofeurope summed up many of them: "The Maritimes are still pretty white, Except for Halifax. Charlottetown, Fredericton, St. John's [NL] are good candidates." Anywhere near a First Nations reserve was deemed unacceptably tainted. Anti-Muslim, anti-Jewish, anti-immigrant rants were the norm.

The responses to a query from cjag ("Anyone here in the GTA?") included a chilling post with Nazi overtones from SSGalizien:

> *Grew up here and not particularly fond of my multicultural environment but I know I have to stay here and make a little more money from the Globalists in order to one day use it against them. This is the sacrifice I need to make for National Socialism . . . I believe in ridding the GTA of non-White parasites and the implementation of a Northern Ontario Living Space (Lebensraum), liquidating Crown Land and selling it to Canadians.*

The post prompted others to agree with the goal but question how it would be achieved.

The Ku Klux Klan possessed brand recognition, even if the organization was elusive outside the Internet. "The Klan's symbols and its very name remain shorthand for white supremacy, bigotry and hate," wrote Kristofer Allerfeldt in the *Conversation* in 2019.[33] "The Klan hood is still one of the most widely recognized symbols of hate. Yes, it is old-fashioned and certainly, it is impractical. But surely that's the point." The Klan symbols were statements of intent, a position, a demand for attention, a call to fear. They had been used as such for more than one hundred and fifty years, and were not likely to die soon.

For Canadians, the Ku Klux Klan symbols have meant something sinister for a century — instantly recognizable sources of hate, generators of fear. That the symbols and the ceremonies were largely the creation of Hollywood and a gang of scammers from the American South made little difference. A white hood, a flaming cross and the letters KKK were capable of stirring fear, threats and "bloody murder" in the words of a 1920s Canadian journalist. Hate, intimidation, suppression and worse. This is the legacy of the Ku Klux Klan in Canada.

# ACKNOWLEDGEMENTS

I wish to acknowledge the efforts of several authors and journalists whose work is cited frequently in this book, and without whom we would know much less than we do about the Ku Klux Klan in Canada. They include: William Peter Baergen, Stanley Barrett, Stewart Bell, Warren Kinsella, James Pitsula, Patrick Richards and Julian Sher.

An under-valued and under-appreciated public resource in Canada are the various archival institutions that document our national life at the local, regional, provincial and national levels. The staff members of several archives provided amazing service in the course of my research. They included the archives of New Brunswick, Ontario, Saskatchewan, Alberta, British Columbia, Vancouver, Edmonton, Toronto, Elgin County (Ontario) and Belleville and Hastings County (Ontario). I thank them.

The last phase of preparing this book for publication occurred in the midst of the 2020 COVID-19 pandemic. Notwithstanding the circumstances, the staff of Formac Books, particularly acquisitions editor David Gray-Donald, persevered in the face of several challenges, including an author with a limited capacity to master technology. I wish to make a special acknowledgement of my late friend Frank Clarke whose research support several years ago is not forgotten. Finally, I want to thank Wanda Taylor of Formac who launched me back into a world I thought was behind me. Our times demanded I go there.

# ENDNOTES

## Preface

1. Alexi Zentner, "I'm a Canadian Living in the U.S. What's Happening There Could Happen Here Too," *Globe and Mail*, July 4, 2019.

## Chapter 1

1. *Vancouver Sun*, Jan. 8, 2016.
2. Toronto *Globe*, Sept. 21, 1915.
3. Toronto *Globe*, Oct. 2, 1915.
4. For example, see Toronto *Globe*, May 7, 1912; May 13, 1916; June 6, 1917.
5. "Col. George T. Denison in Louisville." Toronto *Globe*, May 13, 1916.
6. Oscar Kinchen. *Confederate Operations in Canada and the North* (North Quincy, Mass.: Christopher Publishing House, 1970), pp. 122, 196.
7. A pseudo-archaeological belief that the people of the British Isles are the direct descendants of the Ten Lost Tribes of ancient Israel.
8. Toronto *Globe*, Dec, 11, 1915.
9. *Canadian Men and Women of the Time* (Toronto: W. Briggs, 1912), p. 882.
10. Toronto *Globe*, March 1, 1917.
11. Toronto *Globe*, Dec. 15, 1917; Dec. 24, 1917; Dec. 26, 1917.
12. Raymond A. Cook, *Thomas Dixon* (New York: Twayne Publishers, 1974), p. 23.
13. Katherine J. Lennard, "Uniform Threat: Manufacturing the Ku Klux Klan's Visible Empire" (PhD dissertation, University of Michigan, 2017), pp. 152–53.
14. Kenneth Jackson, *The Klan in the City* (New York: Oxford University Press, 1967).
15. Reuben Maury, *The Wars of the Godly* (New York: Robert M. McBride & Co., 1928), p. 273.
16. Ibid., p. 273.
17. Tom Rice, *White Robes Silver Screens: Movies and the Making of the Ku Klux Klan* (Bloomington: Indiana University Press, 2015), p. xi.
18. Maury, *The Wars*, pp. 274–75.
19. Glen Williams, *Blood Must Tell: Debating Race and Identity in the Canadian House of Commons, 1880–1925* (Ottawa: willowBX Press, 2014).

20. Canada, Privy Council, Order-in-Council 1911-1324.
21. Rachel Alken, "Senate Motions to Scrap 1918 'Colour Bar' on Black Medical Students," *Queen's Journal*, Sept. 28, 2018.
22. Sarah-Jane Mathieu, *North of the Color Line: Migration and Black Resistance in Canada 1870–1955* (Chapel Hill: University of North Carolina Press, 2010), p. 169.
23. Toronto *Globe*, Sept. 15, 1915; Sept. 20, 1915.
24. Adrienne Shadd, *The Long Journey from Tollgate to Parkway* (Toronto: National Heritage Books, 2010), p. 213.
25. Donald Smith. *Calgary's Grand Story* (Calgary: University of Calgary Press, 2005), p. 156.
26. James W. St. G. Walker. "The Law's Confirmation of Racial Inferiority: *Christie v. York*," in Barrington Walker, ed. *The African Canadian Legal Odyssey: Historical Essays* (Toronto: Osgoode Society for Canadian Legal History / University of Toronto Press, 2012), pp. 243–323.
27. Toronto *Globe*, Sept. 24, 1915.
28. Paul S. Moore. "Movie Palaces on Canadian Downtown Main Streets: Montreal, Toronto and Vancouver," *Urban History Review* 32, no. 2 (Spring 2004): 18, fn 35. The rebuilt Princess Theatre was the site of the fatal punch in October 1926 that caused the death of famous escape artist Harry Houdini.
29. Greg Marquis. "A War Within a War: Canadian Reactions to D.W. Griffith's *The Birth of a Nation*," *Social History* 47, no. 94 (June 2014): 437.
30. Jessica Leeder. "Black on the Battlefield: Canada's Forgotten First World War Battalion," *Globe and Mail*. Nov. 9, 2018.
31. Marquis, "War Within a War," 438.
32. Robin Winks, *The Blacks in Canada* (New Haven, Conn.: Yale University Press, 1971), p. 325.
33. Charles Foster, *Stardust and Shadows: Canadians in Early Hollywood* (Toronto: Dundurn. 2000).
34. Charles O. Jackson. "William J. Simmons: A Career in Klu Kluxism," *Georgia Historical Quarterly* 50, no. 4 (December 1966): 357.
35. Daniel Okrent, *Last Call: The Rise and Fall of Prohibition* (New York: Scribner, 2010), p. 244.
36. A kleagle is an officer of the Ku Klux Klan whose main role is to recruit new members and must maintain the three guiding principles; recruit, maintain control and safeguard.
37. David Chalmers, *Notes on Writing the History of the Ku Klux Klan* (Tallahassee: University Press of Florida, 2013), p. 15.

38. George Lewis, "'An Amorphous Code': The Ku Klux Klan and Un-Americanism, 1915–1965," *Journal of American Studies* 47, no. 4 (November 2013): 978.
39. Linda Gordon, *The Second Coming of the KKK: The Ku Klux Klan of the 1920s and the American Political Tradition* (New York: Liveright, 2017), p. 101.
40. United States Congress, House of Representatives, 67th Congress, 1st Session, Committee on Rules (Washington, 1921).
41. United States Congress, Senate, 68th Congress, 1st Session, *Hearings Before a Subcommittee of the Committee on Privileges and Elections* (Washington, 1924).
42. Southern Poverty Law Center, Klanwatch Project, *Ku Klux Klan: A History of Racism* (Montgomery, Ala.: Southern Poverty Law Center, 2011), retrieved from https://www.splcenter.org/20110228/ku-klux-klan-history-racism
43. C.L. Fowler, *The Ku Klux Klan: Its Origin, Meaning and Scope of Operation* (Atlanta, Ga.: Author, 1922). The praise for Edward Young Clarke is found in the Tribute section.
44. C.O. Jackson, "William J, Simmons," p. 361.
45. Okrent, *Last Call*, p. 244.
46. Toronto *Globe*, Jan. 14, 1921.

## Chapter 2

1. James Pitsula, *Keeping Canada British: The Ku Klux Klan in 1920s Saskatchewan* (Vancouver: UBC Press, 2013), p. 7.
2. Colin McFarquhar. "The Black Occupational Structure in Late Nineteenth Century Ontario: Evidence from the Census" in *Racism, Eh?: A Critical Inter-Disciplinary Anthology of Race and Racism in Canada*, ed. Camille A. Nelson and Charmane A. Nelson (Concord, Ont.: Captus Press, 2004), p. 51.
3. Toronto *Globe*, June 15, 1920.
4. Martin Robin, *Shades of Right: Nativist and Fascist Politics in Canada, 1920–1940* (Toronto: University of Toronto Press, 1992), p. 12.
5. Kenneth Jackson, *The Klan in the City* (New York: Oxford University Press, 1967), p. 173.
6. Cecil Houston and William J. Smyth, *The Sash Canada Wore: A Historical Geography of the Orange Order in Canada* (Toronto: University of Toronto Press, 1980), p. 154.
7. Cyril Levitt and William Shaffir, *The Riot at Christie Pits*, 2nd ed. (Toronto: New Jewish Press / University of Toronto Press, 2018), p. 11.

8. Houston and Smyth, *Sash Canada Wore*, p. 165.
9. Lincoln Alexander and Herb Shoveller, *"Go to School, You're a Little Black Boy": The Honourable Lincoln M. Alexander* (Toronto: Dundurn, 2006), p. 17.
10. Keith S. Henry, *Black Politics in Toronto Since World War I* (Toronto: Multicultural History Society of Ontario, 1981), p. 3.
11. John Cooper, *Rapid Ray: The Story of Ray Lewis* (Toronto: Tundra Books, 2002), p. 63.
12. Adrienne Shadd, *The Long Journey from Tollgate to Parkway* (Toronto: National Heritage Books, 2010), p. 233.
13. Levitt and Shaffir, *Riot at Christie Pits*, pp. xxiv, 15.
14. The following account of Matthew Bullock's story is drawn primarily from Sarah-Jane Mathieu, *North of the Color Line: Migration and Black Resistance in Canada 1870–1955* (Chapel Hill: University of North Carolina Press, 2010); and John Weaver,"Black Man, White Justice: The Extradition of Matthew Bullock, an African-American Residing in Ontario, 1922," *Osgoode Hall Law Journal* 34, no. 4 (Winter 1996).
15. Weaver, "Black Man, White Justice."
16. Charles Alexander, "White-Robed Reformers: The Ku Klux Klan Comes to Arkansas, 1921–1922," *Arkansas Historical Quarterly*, 22, no 1 (Spring 1963): 8–23.
17. Mathieu, *Color Line*, pp. 171–82.
18. "No Klan Plot To Kidnap Bullock." Toronto *Globe*, May 1, 1922.
19. "Police Protection for Matt. Bullock." *Ottawa Citizen*, March 20, 1922.
20. Mathieu, *Color Line*, p. 182.
21. Matthew Bullock. Death Certificate #40164, 1982. North Carolina. Ancestry.com
22. William Calderwood, "The Rise and Fall of the Ku Klux Klan in Saskatchewan" (master's thesis, University of Saskatchewan, 1968), pp. 16–17; Evelyn Wrench, "The English-Speaking World," *Spectator*. March 24, 1923, pp. 506–7.
23. Houston and Smyth, *Sash Canada Wore*, p. 155.
24. "Canada's 'Keep-Out' to Klanism," *Literary Digest*, Feb. 3, 1923, p. 20; "The Ku Klux Klan," *Canadian Annual Review*, 1923, pp. 82–83.
25. "Not Wanted in Canada," *Ottawa Citizen*, Oct. 4, 1921.
26. "Branch of Ku Klux Klan at London, Ont.," *Ottawa Citizen*, Dec. 15, 1922.
27. Irwin Hignett, Regimental number 67488, Canadian Expeditionary

Force (CEF), Personnel record, RG150, Accession 1992–93/166, Box 4338-44, Library and Archives Canada.

28. Toronto *Globe*, March 15, 1923.
29. These incidents were recounted in letters to the author in the late 1980s from an individual who, despite the passage of years, asked for anonymity.
30. John Weaver, *Crimes, Constables and Courts: Order and Transgression in a Canadian City 1816–1970* (Montreal and Kingston: McGill-Queen's University Press, 1995), pp. 115–16.
31. Ibid., p. 116.
32. Toronto *Globe*, Nov. 19, 1924.
33. Shawn Lay, *Hooded Knights on the Niagara: The Ku Klux Klan in Buffalo, New York* (New York: New York University Press, 1995).
34. Toronto *Globe*, Nov. 20, 1924.
35. "Flaming Cross on Hill at Hamilton," *Ottawa Citizen*, Oct. 13, 1924.
36. Toronto *Globe*, Nov. 17, 1924.
37. Toronto *Globe*, Nov. 16, 1924.
38. Raney Bench, *Maine's Gone Mad: The Rising of the Klan*, (2018), p. 8, retrieved from https://mdihistory.org/wp-content/uploads/Maines-Gone-Mad-The-Rising-of-the-Klan_ocr.pdf
39. Anthony Slide, *The New Historical Dictionary of the American Film Industry* (Lanham, Md.: Scarecrow Press, 1998), p. 123.
40. Anthony Slide, *American Racist: The Life and Films of Thomas Dixon* (Lexington, Ky.: University Press of Kentucky, 2004), p. 126.
41. Details on the Farnsworth family are found in Ancestry.ca. Frank Eugene Farnsworth applied for United States passports in 1910 and 1916. Both applications provide details of his occupations and travels. See also Mark Paul Richard, "'Why Don't You Be a Klansman?': Anglo-Canadian Support for the Ku Klux Klan Movement in 1920s New England," *American Review of Canadian Studies* 40, no. 4 (2010).
42. Bench, *Maine's Gone Mad*, p. 9.
43. *Toronto Star*, Sept. 15, 1923, quoted in Richard, "'Why Don't You Be A Klansman?'"
44. Richard, "'Why Don't You Be A Klansman?'"
45. Thomas Acheson. "Denominationalism In A Loyalist County: A Social History of Charlotte 1783–1940" (master's thesis, University of New Brunswick, 1964), p. 293.
46. Michel Boudreau, *City of Order: Crime and Society in Halifax, 1918–1935* (Vancouver: UBC Press, 2012), pp. 160–65.

47. Patricia Roy, "The Oriental 'Menace' in British Columbia," in *The Twenties in Canada*, ed. S.M. Trofimenkoff (Ottawa: National Museum of Man, 1972).
48. Julie F. Gilmour, *Trouble on Main Street: Mackenzie King, Reason, Race and the 1907 Vancouver Riots* (Toronto: Penguin, 2014), p. 135.
49. Glen Williams, *Blood Must Tell: Debating Race and Identity in the Canadian House of Commons, 1880–1925* (Ottawa: willowBX Press, 2014).
50. Gillian Creese, "Organizing against Racism in the Workplace: Chinese Workers in Vancouver before the Second World War," in *Racism in Canada*, ed. Ormand McKague (Saskatoon: Fifth House, 1991).
51. Trevor Griffey, *History of the KKK in Washington State* (Seattle: University of Washington, Seattle Civil Rights & Labor History Project, 2007), retrieved from https://depts.washington.edu/civilr/kkk_history.htm
52. David Chalmers, *Hooded Americanism*, (Chicago: Quadrangle, 1968), p. 86.
53. Kenneth Jackson, *The Klan in the City* (New York: Oxford University Press, 1967), pp. 211–12.
54. "Vancouver May Have Ku Klux Klan Branch," *Ottawa Citizen*, May 3, 1924.
55. Chalmers, *Hooded Americanism*, p. 91.
56. Lani Russwurm, *The History of the Ku Klux Klan in Vancouver* (2017), retrieved from https://forbiddenvancouver.ca/blog/kkk-history-vancouver.
57. Tom Henson, "Ku Klux Klan in Western Canada," *Alberta History* (Autumn 1977), p. 2
58. William Peter Baergen, *The Ku Klux Klan in Central Alberta* (Red Deer, Alta.: Central Alberta Historical Society, 2000), pp. 102–7.
59. Discharge Papers, A/Cpl. Harry Humble, Regimental #M/2202520. Ancestry.com.
60. *Hanna Herald*, Oct. 13, 1927.
61. "Calgary Now Has Members of Klan," *Ottawa Citizen*, Dec. 6, 1924.

## Chapter 3

1. Portions of Chapters 2–5 appeared in my article "A Public Nuisance: The Ku Klux Klan in Ontario 1923–27," *Journal of Canadian Studies* 30, no. 3 (Fall 1995): 156–74.
2. *Wall Street Journal*, Dec. 20, 1920, p. 12.

3. P.M. Richards, "How the Ku Klux Klan Came to Canada," *Saturday Night*, June 26, 1926.
4. P.M. Richards, "Claims of the Ku Klux Klan," *Saturday Night*, July 17, 1926.
5. William Calderwood, "The Rise and Fall of the Ku Klux Klan in Saskatchewan" (master's thesis, University of Saskatchewan, 1968), p. 15.
6. "Helen Barclay Hawkins," United States Bureau of the Census. Thirteenth Census of the United States. Alabama. Jefferson County, Birmingham City. Sheet 16A. U.S. Census, 1910. Ancestry.com.
7. John T. Kneebone, "Ku Klux Klan in Virginia," *Encyclopedia Virginia*, Virginia Humanities, Nov. 4, 2016, https://www.encyclopediavirginia.org.
8. C.H. Higginbotham, *Off The Record: The CCF in Saskatchewan* (Toronto: McLelland and Stewart, 1968), p. 31.
9. Martin Robin, *Shades of Right: Nativist and Fascist Politics in Canada, 1920–1940* (Toronto: University of Toronto Press, 1992), p. 13.
10. Thomas G. Dyer, "Fowler, Charles Lewis," *Dictionary of North Carolina Biography* (Chapel Hill: University of North Carolina Press, 1979–1996).
11. C.L. Fowler, *The Ku Klux Klan: Its Origin, Meaning and Scope of Operations* (Atlanta, Ga.: Author, 1922), p. 7.
12. Ibid., pp. 23–25.
13. Leonard Moore, *Citizen Klansmen: The Ku Klux Klan in Indiana, 1921–1928* (Chapel Hill: University of North Carolina Press, 1991), p. 7.
14. Felix Harcourt, *Ku Klux Kulture: America and the Klan in the 1920s* (Chicago: University of Chicago Press, 2017), pp. 112–13.
15. Tom Rice, *White Robes, Silver Screens: Movies and the Making of the Ku Klux Klan* (Bloomington: Indiana University Press, 2015), pp. 159–60.
16. Robin Winks, *The Blacks in Canada* (New Haven: Yale University Press, 1971), p. 321.
17. Reuben Maury, *The Wars of the Godly* (New York: Robert M. McBride & Co., 1928), pp. 291–92
18. Jack Shafer, "1924: The Wildest Convention in U.S. History," *Politico Magazine*, March 7, 2016, retrieved from https://www.politico.com/magazine/story/2016/03/1924-the-craziest-convention-in-us-history-213708
19. "Editor of Klan Paper Arrested in New York," Jewish Telegraphic Agency n.d. (probably July 1924).

20. Shawn Lay, *Hooded Knights on the Niagara: The Ku Klux Klan in Buffalo, New York* (New York: New York University Press, 1995), p. 55.
21. "Klan Editor Picked the Wrong Man," United Press in *Marshall [Michigan] Evening Chronicle*, June 27, 1924.
22. A.D. Monk. "Knightshirt", p. 31.
23. *Toronto Star*, Feb. 9, 1925.
24. Canadian Great War Project, "Lt.-Col. Harold Arthur Clement Machin," www.kenoragreatwarproject.ca.
25. Adrienne Shadd, *The Long Journey from Tollgate to Parkway* (Toronto: National Heritage Books, 2010), p. 214.
26. Bulletin No. 22, Hutchison Fonds, n.d. (issued between March and May 1926).
27. Gordon Unger, "James G. Gardiner: The Premier as a Pragmatic Politician 1926–1929" (master's thesis, University of Saskatchewan, 1967), p. 96.
28. Calderwood, "Rise and Fall," pp. 14–15, quoting Klan correspondence.
29. Ibid., pp. 15–16.
30. Tyler Cline, "'A Clarion Call To Real Patriots The World Over': The Curious Case of the Ku Klux Klan of Kanada in New Brunswick during the 1920s and 1930s," *Acadiensis* 48, no. 1 (Spring 2019): 101.
31. Greg Marquis, *Saint John as an Immigrant City 1851–1951*, Working Paper No. 30 (Halifax: Atlantic Metropolis Centre, 2009), pp. 33–34.
32. Cline, "A Clarion Call," p. 101.
33. B.J. Grant, *Fit To Print* (Fredericton, N.B.: Fiddlehead Poetry Books / Goose Lane Editions, 1987), p. 164.
34. Arthur T. Doyle, *Front Benches & Back Rooms* (Toronto: Green Tree, 1976), p. 258.
35. "Court Action Against the KKK," *Saint John Globe*, Aug. 18, 1925.
36. James Pitsula, *Keeping Canada British: The Ku Klux Klan in 1920s Saskatchewan* (Vancouver: UBC Press, 2013), pp. 59–60.
37. *Ottawa Citizen*, Aug. 6, 1925; "Klan Has Started Branch at Goderich," *Ottawa Citizen*, Dec. 26, 1925.
38. "Says K.K.K. No Connection With Masonic Order," *Ottawa Citizen*, July 15, 1925.
39. "Klan Fiery Cross Burned at Dresden," *London Free Press*, Aug. 1, 1925; "Fiery Cross of KKK Burned at Wallaceburg," *London Free Press*, Aug. 20, 1925.

40. "Klan Spokesman Outlines Aims," *London Free Press*, Aug. 3, 1925, p. 3.
41. Carolyn Whitzman, *Suburb, Slum, Urban Village: Transformations in Toronto's Parkdale Neighbourhood 1875–2002* (Vancouver: UBC Press, 2009), p. 133.
42. *Toronto Star*, Aug. 10, 1925.
43. Stephen A. Speisman, *The Jews of Toronto: A History to 1937* (Toronto: McClelland and Stewart, 1979), p. 323.
44. "Klan Meeting Breaks Up When Hawkins Declines to Answer Questions," *London Free Press*, Sept. 2, 1925, p. 1.
45. L.N. Bronson, "1925 — Flaming Crosses, Hooded Men Entered Limelight," *London Free Press*, Aug. 5, 1973.
46. Dahn Higley, *O.P.P.: The History of the Ontario Provincial Police Force* (Toronto: Queen's Printer, 1984).
47. See the correspondence in RG4, Series 4-32, Central Registry Files. Ministry of the Attorney General of Ontario. Public Archives of Ontario.
48. Scott Kerwin, "Smith, Janet Kennedy," *Dictionary of Canadian Biography* (Toronto: University of Toronto, 2005), retrieved from http://www.biographi.ca/en/bio.php?BioId=42000
49. "Wong Foon Sing," *Lethbridge Herald*, June 18, 1925, p. 3; Edward Starkins, *Who Killed Janet Smith?* (Vancouver: Anvil Press, 2011), p. 53.
50. Starkins, *Who Killed Janet Smith?*, p. 156.
51. Ibid., p. 188.
52. Ibid., p. 256.
53. Jesse Donaldson, "The Strange and Violent Story Behind Vancouver's Most Racist Street Name," *Vice*, March 13, 2018, retrieved from https://www.vice.com/en_ca/article/wj4vkw/the-strange-and-violent-story-behind-vancouvers-most-racist-street-name
54. "Klan in Vancouver," *Village Chronicler*, no. 4 (Nov. 5, 2010), p. 2.

## Chapter 4

1. P.M. Richards, "How the Ku Klux Klan Came to Canada," *Saturday Night*, June 26, 1926.
2. *Toronto Star*, March 5, 1926.
3. *Northern Advance*, May 27, 1926.
4. *Barrie Examiner*, June 17, 1926.
5. Toronto *Globe*, June 25, 1926.
6. Bulletin No. 32, Hutchison Fonds, Queen's University, Nov. 3, 1926.

7. *Barrie Examiner*, June 24, 1926.
8. Ibid.
9. File 1526, *Rex v. Skelly, Lee and Butler*, Provincial Archives of Ontario (PAO).
10. Letter, Edward Bayly to Peter White, June 25, 1926, File 1526, PAO.
11. Letter, Peter White to the Attorney General, June 30, 1926, File 1526, PAO.
12. Letter, F.G. Evans to Edward Bayly, Sept. 23, 1926, File 1526, PAO.
13. Letter, F.G. Evans to Edward Bayly, Sept. 25, 1926, File 1526, PAO.
14. Letter, Edward Bayly to Peter White, Oct. 8, 1926, File 1526, PAO.
15. *Barrie Examiner*, Oct. 21, 1926.
16. Bulletin No. 31, Hutchison Fonds, Oct, 13, 1926.
17. Frederick H. Armstrong, *Forest City: An Illustrated History of London, Canada* (Windsor, Ont.: Windsor Publications, 1986), p. 177.
18. Ron W. Shaw, *Klan Gathering Yonder: Smiths Falls and the Ku Klux Klan of Kanada* (Perth, Ont.: Perth and District Historical Society, 2018), retrieved from http://perthhs.org/documents/klan-gathering-yonder.pdf
19. *Ottawa Citizen*, May 23, 1925.
20. Shaw, *Klan Gathering Yonder*.
21. *Ottawa Citizen*, May 23, 1925.
22. Gerry Boyce, *Belleville: A Popular History* (Toronto: Dundurn, 2009), p. 196.
23. Canada, Census 1921. George Marshall's personal details available through Ancestry.ca.
24. Boyce, *Belleville*, p. 198.
25. Ibid., p. 198.
26. John Cooper, *Rapid Ray: The Story of Ray Lewis* (Toronto: Tundra Books, 2002), pp. 62–63. The offensive term was spelled out in full in the original.
27. John Terry Copp."The Canadian General Election of 1908" (PhD dissertation, McGill University, 1962), p. 257.
28. *Guelph Evening Mercury and Advertiser*, Oct. 5, 1926.
29. Stephen Thorning, "Ku Klux Klan was operating in Guelph in 1926," *Wellington Advertiser*, March 7, 2003.
30. Toronto *Globe*, Nov. 24, 1924.
31. Telegram, William Templeman to A.G. Nickle, Oct. 7, 1926; Letter, Edward Bayly to William Templeman, Oct. 7, 1926, File 2254, PAO.
32. Bulletin No. 36, Hutchison Fonds, Feb. 26, 1927.
33. Letter, John Blake to Edward Bayly, Feb. 8, 1927, File 116, PAO.

34. Memorandum, Edward Bayly to the Attorney General, Jan. 17, 1928, PAO.
35. Memorandum, Acting OPP Commissioner Alfred Cuddy, Nov. 2, 1928, File 116, PAO.
36. Memorandum, John Miller to Edward Bayly, Nov. 2, 1928, File 116, PAO.
37. Letter, Edward Bayly to John Blake, Police Magistrate, Galt, n.d., File 116, PAO.
38. Claim by Insp. John Miller, CID, n.d.; Memorandum, John Miller to Edward Bayly, Nov. 2, 1928; Memorandum, Acting OPP Commissioner Alfred Cuddy, Nov. 2, 1928; File 116, PAO.
39. George Hutchison and Charlotte Montgomery, "Dr. B.C. Eckardt: Associate of the Great, Famous," *London Free Press*, June 16, 1972; telephone interview with the author, Nov. 16, 1987.
40. Letters from a confidential source, November 1987. This source had first-hand knowledge of Klan activities in the London area during this period. Despite the passage of years, the source's name remains confidential at their request.
41. "Klansmen Balked by Minister," *London Evening Advertiser*, June 29, 1925, p. 1.
42. Minutes of Kloncilium Meeting, Hutchison Fonds, June 6, 1927.
43. Toronto *Globe*, July 13, 1928; Toronto *Globe*, Nov. 4, 1929; Bulletin No. 25, Hutchison Fonds, May 26, 1926.
44. *Regina Morning Leader*, Feb. 19, 1925.
45. Memorandum, Acting OPP Commissioner Alfred Cuddy, Nov. 2, 1928, File 116, PAO.
46. Memorandum, John Miller to Edward Bayly, Nov. 2, 1928, File 116, PAO.
47. Edward Starkins, *Who Killed Janet Smith (Vancouver: Anvil Press, 2011), pp. 257–58.*
48. Lani Russwurm, *History of the Ku Klux Klan in Vancouver (2017), retrieved from https://forbiddenvancouver.ca/blog/kkk-history-vancouver/*
49. David Elliott, "Studies of Eight Canadian Fundamentalists" (PhD dissertation, University of British Columbia, 1989), pp. 79–80, 233.
50. Clement Llewellyn Davies's personal details are found on Ancestry.com; Elliott, "Eight Canadian Fundamentalists," p. 218–19, pp. 227–28.
51. Victoria *Daily Colonist*, Jan. 17, 1926, p. 13.
52. Jennifer Ann Polk, "The Canadian Red Cross and Relief in Siberia, 1918–1921" (master's thesis, Carleton University, 2004), p. 28.

53. Ian Macdonald and Betty O'Keefe, *Canadian Holy War: A Story of Clans, Tongs, Murder, and Bigotry* (Victoria: Heritage House, 2000), pp. 11–12.
54. Ibid., p. 34.
55. Dr. Martin G. Dunlevy, Letter to Superintendent of BCPP, quoted by B.C. Attorney General, GR 1323, File P-130-38-1925, Ku Klux Klan Reel B 2213. Cited by Selkirk College, KCIR Cabinet.
56. Russwurm, *History of the Ku Klux Klan in Vancouver.*
57. Toronto *Globe*, Nov. 16, 1925.
58. Harry McGrath, "Discordant Voices: Vancouver's Scots Community and the Janet Smith Case, 1924" (master's thesis, Simon Fraser University, 2014), p. 38.
59. Ibid., pp. 38, 43.

## Chapter 5

1. "Ku Klux Klan Diminishes in U.S.," *Saturday Night*, Oct. 16, 1926.
2. Bulletin No. 21, Hutchison Fonds, n.d. (issued between March and May 1926).
3. Bulletin No. 31, Hutchison Fonds, Oct. 13, 1926.
4. Address to "All Genii, Kind and Major Kleagles, Kleagles and Citizens of the Invisible Empire," Hutchison Fonds, n.d.
5. Address to "All Genii, Kind and Major Kleagles, Kleagles and Citizens of the Invisible Empire," Hutchison Fonds, Nov. 2, 1926.
6. Bulletin No. 33, Hutchison Fonds, Dec. 9, 1926.
7. Final Klonvocation Bulletin, Hutchison Fonds, Jan. 4, 1927.
8. Special Bulletin No. 36, Hutchison Fonds, Feb. 26, 1927.
9. Ibid.
10. Bulletin No. 35, Hutchison Fonds, Jan. 27, 1927.
11. Bulletin No. 43, Hutchison Fonds, Sept. 29, 1927.
12. Richard V. Pierard, "The Contribution of British Israelism to Antisemitism Within Conservative Protestantism," in *Holocaust and Church Struggle: Religion, Power and the Politics of Resistance*, eds. Hubert G. Locke and Marcia Sachs Litell (Lanham, Md.: University Press of America,1996), p. 50.
13. James Pitsula, *Keeping Canada British: The Ku Klux Klan in 1920s Saskatchewan* (Vancouver: UBC Press, 2013), p. 25.
14. Francesca Brzezicki, "The Ku Klux Klan Rally in Kingston," blog entry, *Spectres of Kingston's Past*, February 14, 2016, retrieved from https://kingstonspast.wordpress.com/2016/02/14/the-ku-klux-klan-rally-in-kingston/#more-1772
15. *Kingston Whig-Standard*, Aug. 1, 1927.

16. "Impressive Parade of Ku Klux Klan," Toronto *Globe*, Sept. 5, 1927.
17. "Firemen Quickly Extinguish Fiery Cross in Ottawa," *Ottawa Citizen*, Oct. 24, 1927.
18. "Letter Sent to Mayor Ellis by Ottawa's K.K.K.," *Ottawa Citizen*, April 29, 1929.

**Chapter 6**

1. John Larsen and Maurice Richard Libby, *Moose Jaw: People, Places, History* (Regina: Coteau Books, 2001), p. 69.
2. The description of how Pat Emmons came to Saskatchewan and flourished is drawn from James Pitsula's defining work *Keeping Canada British: The Ku Klux Klan in 1920s Saskatchewan* (Vancouver: UBC Press, 2013), pp. 28–31.
3. James Gray, *Red Lights on the Prairies* (Saskatoon: Fifth House, 1995), p. 273.
4. Bulletin No. 25, Hutchison Fonds, May 26, 1926.
5. Kevin Anderson,"'This Typical Old Canadian Form of Racial and Religious Hate': Anti-Catholicism and English Canadian Nationalism 1905–1965" (PhD dissertation, McMaster University, 2013), p. 118.
6. Norman Ward and David Smith, *Jimmy Gardiner: Relentless Liberal* (Toronto: University of Toronto Press, 1990), p. 92.
7. Pitsula, *Keeping Canada British*, p. 125.
8. James Gray, *The Roar of the Twenties* (Toronto: Macmillan, 1975), p. 232.
9. Howard Palmer, "Nativism in Alberta, 1925–1930," *Historical Papers* 9, no. 1 (1974): 195.
10. C.H. Higginbotham, *Off the Record: The CCF in Saskatchewan* (Toronto: McLelland and Stewart, 1968), p. 28.
11. *Regina Leader-Post*, Nov. 4, 1931; *Regina Leader-Post*, April 13, 1938.
12. Pitsula, *Keeping Canada British*, p. 42.
13. Higginbotham, *Off the Record*, p. 29.
14. *Warren [Pennsylvania] Times Mirror*, Jan. 24, 1936.
15. J.J. Maloney, *Rome in Canada* (Vancouver: Columbia Protestant Publications, 1934), p. 97.
16. Pitsula, *Keeping Canada British*, p. 150.
17. Maloney, *Rome in Canada*, pp. 146–47.
18. Steven Hewitt, "Old Myths Die Hard: The Transformation of the Mounted Police in Alberta and Saskatchewan 1914–1939" (PhD dissertation, University of Saskatchewan, 1997), p. 202.

19. Hewitt, "Old Myths," p. 201.
20. Kevin Moffitt, "When the Hoods and Burning Crosses Came to Saskatchewan," *Globe and Mail*, June 6, 1989.
21. Ibid.
22. Lloyd Begley, "The Foreign Threat: Nativism in Saskatchewan 1896–1930" (master's thesis, University of Manitoba, 1997), p. 138.
23. Larsen and Libby, *Moose Jaw*, p. 53.
24. Thomas H. McLeod and Ian McLeod, *Tommy Douglas: The Road to Jerusalem* (Edmonton: Hurtig, 1987), p. 52.
25. Maloney, *Rome in Canada*, pp. 150–51.
26. Anthony Waldman, "Daniel Carlyle Grant and the Ku Klux Klan in Winnipeg, 1928," *Manitoba History*, No. 85, Fall 2017. www.mhs.mb.ca.
27. Ibid.
28. Ibid.
29. David Rome. *Clouds in the Thirties: On Antisemitism in Canada, 1929–1939* (Montreal: Canadian Jewish Congress, 1977), 2:86.
30. Lita-Rose Betcherman, *The Swastika and the Maple Leaf: Fascist Movements in Canada in the Thirties* (Toronto: Fitzenhry and Whiteside, 1975), pp. 65–66; Jonathan Fine. "Anti-Semitism in Manitoba in the 1930s and 40s,"*Manitoba History*, No. 32 (Autumn 1995).

## Chapter 7

1. Norman James Fennema, "Remote Control: A History of the Regulation of Religion in the Canadian Public Square" (PhD dissertation, University of Victoria, 2003), p. 94.
2. Candace Savage, *Strangers in the House: A Prairie Story of Bigotry and Belonging* (Vancouver: Greystone Books, 2019), p. 203.
3. Appleblatt, *J.J.Maloney*, p. 46.
4. Gregory S. Kealey and Reg Whitaker, eds., *R.C.M.P. Security Bulletins: The Early Years, 1919–1929* (St. John's, Nfld.: Canadian Committee on Labour History, 1994), pp. 323, 327–28.
5. Dennis Gruending, *Emmett Hall: Establishment Radical* (Toronto: Macmillan, 1985), p. 229.
6. "Prosecution Rests in Libel Case: Defence to Proceed This Morning," *Saskatoon Phoenix*, Jan. 25, 1928.
7. James Pitsula, *Keeping Canada British: The Ku Klux Klan in 1920s Saskatchewan* (Vancouver: UBC Press, 2013), pp. 152–55.
8. "Counsel in Criminal Libel Case Heard in Strong Pleas to Jury," *Saskatoon Phoenix*, Jan. 26, 1928.

9. Gruending, *Emmett Hall*, p. 229.
10. Pitsula, *Keeping Canada British*, pp. 101–2.
11. Norman Ward and David Smith, *Jimmy Gardiner: Relentless Liberal* (Toronto: University of Toronto Press, 1990), pp. 89–90.
12. C.H. Higginbotham, *Off the Record: The CCF in Saskatchewan* (Toronto: McLelland and Stewart, 1968), p. 31.
13. Pitsula, *Keeping Canada British*, p. 101.
14. Cecil Foster, *They Call Me George: The Untold Story of Black Train Porters and the Birth of Modern Canada* (Windsor, Ont.: Biblioasis, 2019), p. 48.
15. Higginbotham, *Off the Record*, p. 31.
16. Pitsula, *Keeping Canada British*, p. 92.
17. "Maloney-Miller," *Ottawa Citizen*, March 9, 1928.
18. Translation from the original French in Savage, *Strangers in the House*, pp. 206–7.
19. Pitsula, *Keeping Canada British*, pp. 241–42.
20. Raymond Huel, "The Anderson Amendments and the Secularization of Saskatchewan Public Schools," Canadian Catholic Historical Association (CCHA), *Study Sessions* 44 (1977): 61–76.
21. Thomas H. McLeod and Ian McLeod, *Tommy Douglas: The Road to Jerusalem* (Edmonton: Hurtig, 1987), p. 52.
22. Appleblatt, *J.J. Maloney*, p. 47, quoting Maloney's autobiography.
23. Heather Robertson, *Grass Roots* (Toronto: James Lorimer, 1973), pp. 324–25.
24. "James Henry Hawkins," Certificate of Death, Commonwealth of Virginia, April 11, 1950, State File No. 8088.
25. "Racial Tensions in the Coronado Neighborhood," Sargeant Memorial Collection, Online Archives, Norfolk Public Library, Norfolk, Va., July 29, 1954.
26. *Saskatoon Star-Phoenix*, Sept. 10, 1949; *Saskatoon Star-Phoenix*, Sept. 27, 1949.
27. McLeod and McLeod, *Tommy Douglas*, p. 62.
28. "Maloney Makes Statement on Room Incident," *Regina Leader-Post*, Jan. 16, 1931.

## Chapter 8

1. Toronto *Globe*, June 23, 1929.
2. John Cooper, *Rapid Ray: The Story of Ray Lewis* (Toronto: Tundra Books, 2002), pp. 29–30.
3. Ibid., p. 31.

4. Gerry Boyce, *Belleville: A Popular History* (Toronto: Dundurn, 2009), p. 197.
5. Jeff Heinrich, "KKK," *Ottawa Citizen*, July 8, 1989; "Klan Holds Its First Field Day Near This City,"*Ottawa Citizen*, Sept. 16, 1929.
6. Toronto *Globe*, March 11, 1930.
7. John Weaver, *Crimes, Constables and Courts: Order and Transgression in a Canadian City 1816–1970* (Montreal and Kingston: McGill-Queen's University Press, 1995), p. 153.
8. Toronto *Globe*, April 17, 1930.
9. "Deny Ku Klux Klan Parade Privileges," Canadian Press, in *Ottawa Citizen*, July 22, 1930.
10. Katherine J. Lennard, "Uniform Threat: Manufacturing the Ku Klux Klan's Visible Empire" (PhD dissertation, University of Michigan, 2017), p. 253.
11. "The Ku Klux Klan," *Canadian Forum*, April 1930, p. 233.
12. Rabbi Maurice Eisendrath, "This Nordic Nonsense," sermon, March 23, 1930, in *The Lost and Found Sermons of Rabbi Maurice Eisendrath*, retrieved from http://eisendrathsermons.blogspot.com /2012/03/march-23-1930.html.

## Chapter 9

1. J.J. Maloney, *Rome in Canada* (Vancouver: Columbia Protestant Publications, 1934), p. 130.
2. Ibid., pp. 134-35.
3. J.A. Huel, "J.J. Maloney," in *The Developing West: Essays on Canadian History*, ed. John Foster (Edmonton: University of Alberta Press, 1983), p. 223.
4. James Pitsula, *Keeping Canada British: The Ku Klux Klan in 1920s Saskatchewan* (Vancouver: UBC Press, 2013), p. 154.
5. Maloney, *Rome in Canada*, p. 79.
6. Toronto *Globe*, Aug. 8, 1924.
7. Toronto *Globe*, Aug. 1, 1924.
8. William Peter Baergen, *The Ku Klux Klan in Central Alberta* (Red Deer: Central Alberta Historical Society, 2000), p. 324. The account that follows of J.J. Maloney's time in Alberta benefits from this work.
9. Howard Palmer, "Nativism in Alberta, 1925–1930," *Historical Papers* 9, no. 1 (1974): 209.
10. *Edmonton Journal*, May 26, 1930, quoted in Baergen, *Central Alberta*, p. 182.

11. *Edmonton Journal,* May 26, 1930 quoted in Baergen, *Central Alberta,* p. 184.
12. Baergen, *Central Alberta,* p. 195.
13. Don Wetherell. "Upholding Social Decency and Political Equality: The *Lacombe Western Globe* and the Ku Klux Klan, 1929-1932," *Alberta History* 54, no. 4 (2003).
14. *Drumheller Mail,* Nov. 14, 1929, quoted in Baergen, *Central Alberta,* p. 135.
15. Baergen, *Central Alberta,* pp. 199–200.
16. Palmer, "Nativism in Alberta," 193.
17. John Irving, *The Social Credit Movement in Alberta* (Toronto: University of Toronto Press, 1959), p. 4.
18. William E. Mann, *Sect, Cult and Church in Alberta* (Toronto: University of Toronto Press, 1955), p. 16.
19. Baergen, *Central Alberta,* p. 112.
20. Kyle Randolph Franz, "Alberta's Red Democrats: The Challenge and Legacy of Blairmore Communism, 1921–1936" (PhD dissertation, Queen's University, 2013), pp. 209–10.
21. Palmer, "Nativism in Alberta," p. 194.
22. Letter, Edmonton Fire Chief to City Commissioners, June 30, 1933. City of Edmonton Archives. RG-11 7-2 77 reprinted in letsfindoutpodcast.files.wordpress.com.
23. *The Liberator,* May 1932, reprinted in Baergen, *Central Alberta,* p. 309.
24. *Saskatoon Star-Phoenix,* Jan. 13, 1933.
25. "Charges Maloney Retained Bonds," *Edmonton Journal,* Oct. 11, 1934.
26. "Morris Baker Gets 18-Month Term," *Edmonton Journal,* June 7, 1937.
27. Maloney, *Rome in Canada,* p. 160.
28. "J.J. Maloney Wanted by Police," *Regina Leader-Post,* Feb. 3, 1940.
29. George Smith. "Klan Ex-Kligraph Sits in Commons, Pouliot Asserts," Toronto *Globe,* March 25, 1931.
30. "Fiery Cross Burns on Hillside Here; Klan Celebrates," *Edmonton Journal,* n.d. (probably July 30, 1930).
31. *Calgary Albertan,* Jan. 6, 1933.
32. Letter, *Calgary Herald,* Jan. 17, 1933.
33. *Calgary Herald,* Jan. 19, 1933.
34. Travel records, Ancestry.com
35. An autographed copy of Maloney's book in the author's possession was presented to an admirer at the Elysium Hotel on May 1, 1935.

36. John Joseph Maloney, Death Certificate, April 7, 1944, Ancestry.ca.

## Chapter 10

1. LiLynn Wan, "'Out of Many Kindreds and Tongues': Racial Identity and Rights Activism in Vancouver, 1919–1939" (PhD dissertation, Dalhousie University. 2011), p. 62.
2. Ibid., p. 64.
3. Fredericton *Daily Gleaner*, Dec, 9, 2018.
4. Ibid.
5. James Lord, New Brunswick Death Certificate No. 057622, Ancestry.ca.
6. "Bill Would Ban Discrimination Against Classes," Toronto *Globe*, March 14, 1933.
7. Cyril Levitt and William Shaffir, *The Riot at Christie Pits*, 2nd ed. (Toronto: New Jewish Press / University of Toronto Press, 2018), pp. 111–12.
8. *Globe and Mail*, Nov, 8, 1937.
9. Lita-Rose Betcherman, *The Swastika and the Maple Leaf: Fascist Movements in Canada in the Thirties* (Toronto: Fitzhenry and Whiteside, 1975), pp. 105–6.
10. Trevor Griffey, *History of the Ku Klux Klan in Washington State* (Seattle: University of Washington, Seattle Civil Rights & Labor History Project, 2007), retrieved from https://depts.washington.edu/civilr/kkk_history.htm; personal data on Luther Powell from Ancestry.com.
11. David Elliott, "Studies of Eight Canadian Fundamentalists" (PhD dissertation, University of British Columbia, 1989), p. 233.
12. Ibid., p. 245.
13. Stanley R. Barrett, *Is God a Racist?: The Right Wing in Canada* (Toronto: University of Toronto Press, 1989), pp. 90–91.
14. "Political Campaign Review," *Ottawa Citizen*, Aug. 18, 1926.
15. Betcherman, *The Swastika and the Maple Leaf*, pp. 104–5.
16. "Attempt to Burn Down Brockville Catholic Church Fails," *Ottawa Citizen*, Oct. 13, 1938.
17. "The Plural of Cluck is Klux," *Calgary Herald*, reprinted in *Hanna Herald*, June 13, 1946.
18. Heather Robertson, *Grass Roots* (Toronto: James Lorimer, 1973), p. 325.

## Chapter 11

1. Cecil Houston and William J. Smyth, *The Sash Canada Wore: A Historical Geography of the Orange Order in Canada* (Toronto: University of Toronto Press, 1980), p. 173.
2. Jean-François Nadeau, *The Canadian Führer: The Life of Adrien Arcand*, trans. Bob Chodos, Eric Hamovitch and Susan Joanis (Toronto: James Lorimer, 2011), p. 300.
3. Graham Reynolds, *Viola Desmond's Canada: A History of Blacks and Racial Segregation in the Promised Land* (Halifax and Winnipeg: Fernwood, 2016).
4. The Government of Nova Scotia granted Viola Desmond a full pardon in April 2010 in recognition of her innocence.
5. Reynolds, *Viola Desmond's Canada*, p. 59.
6. Michael Barkun, *Religion and the Racist Right: The Origins of the Christian Identity Movement* (Chapel Hill: University of North Carolina Press, 1997), p. 48.
7. Ibid., p. xi.
8. Neil R. McMillen, *The Citizens' Council: Organized Resistance to the Second Reconstruction, 1954–1964* (1971; repr. Urbana: University of Illinois Press, 1994), p. 102.
9. Darryl Paulson, "Stay Out, The Water's Fine: Desegregating Municipal Swimming Facilities in St. Petersburg, Florida," *Tampa Bay History* (Fall/Winter 1982): p. 9.
10. Ancestry.ca.
11. Brett Barrouquere, *White Shadow: David Duke's Lasting Influence on American White Supremacy* (Montgomery, Ala.: Southern Poverty Law Center, 2019), retrieved from https://www.splcenter.org/20110228/ku-klux-klan-history-racism.
12. Tyler Bridges, *The Rise of David Duke* (Jackson: University Press of Mississippi, 1995), p. 73.
13. Stanley R. Barrett, *Is God a Racist?: The Right Wing in Canada* (Toronto: University of Toronto Press, 1989), pp. 101–2.
14. Franklin Bialystok, *Delayed Impact: The Holocaust and the Canadian Jewish Community* (Montreal and Kingston: McGill-Queen's University Press, 2000), p. 114.
15. Christie Blatchford, "Hate and Mob Power is as Ugly as Ever, Only Now It's Louder," *National Post*, Aug. 18, 2017.
16. Bialystok, *Delayed Impact*, p. 196.
17. Royal Commission of Inquiry into Certain Activities of the RCMP, *Second Report: Freedom and Security under the Law* (Ottawa: Minister

of Supply and Services Canada, 1981), Part 3, Ch. 9, Paragraph 34, pp. 305–6.

18. Stewart Bell, *Bayou of Pigs: The True Story of an Audacious Plot to Turn a Tropical Island into a Criminal Paradise* (Mississauga, Ont.: John Wiley, 2008), p. 17.
19. Barrett, *Is God a Racist?*, pp. 126–27.
20. Warren Kinsella, *Web of Hate: Inside Canada's Far Right Network* (Toronto: HarperCollins Canada, 1996), p. 205.
21. Bell, *Bayou of Pigs*, pp. 45–46.
22. "Racial Slogans Found, Three Men Charged," *Globe and Mail*, May 26, 1975.
23. Barrett, *Is God a Racist?*, p. 124.
24. Bridges, *Rise of David Duke*, p. 73.

## Chapter 12

1. Patsy Sims, *The Klan*, 2nd ed. (Lexington: University of Kentucky Press, 1996), p. 12.
2. Stanley R. Barrett, *Is God a Racist?: The Right Wing in Canada* (Toronto: University of Toronto Press, 1989), pp. 96–97.
3. Julian Sher, "The Klansman Who Came Calling to Canada," *Globe and Mail*, Nov. 9, 1991.
4. Tyler Bridges, *The Rise of David Duke* (Jackson: University Press of Mississippi, 1995), p. 73.
5. Stewart Bell, *Bayou of Pigs: The True Story of an Audacious Plot to Turn a Tropical Island into a Criminal Paradise* (Mississauga, Ont.: John Wiley, 2008), p. 61.
6. "Klansmen Evicted from Toronto Office," *Globe and Mail*, Nov. 4, 1980.
7. "Klan Actions to be Watched Closely," *Globe and Mail*, June 28, 1980.
8. Kate Cornick, "Roy McMurtry Got a Threatening Letter from the Ku Klux Klan. He Calls it a 'Badge of Honour,'" *CBC News*, Feb. 17, 2019, retrieved from https://www.cbc.ca/news/canada/toronto/roy-mcmurtry-mandela-judge-ontario-attorney-general-1.5008783.
9. "The Ontario Attorney General's Office Has Ordered an Investigation," United Press International, Oct. 17, 1980.
10. Barrett, *Is God a Racist?*, p. 129.
11. "Klan Member is Contesting Mayor's Chair in Toronto," *Globe and Mail*, Oct. 17, 1980.
12. Mark Wigmore, "McMurtry: Politician at WLU," *Cord Weekly*, Oct. 30, 1980, p. 3.

13. Brian Laghi, "Hooded Klansmen Taunt 250 Protesters," *Globe and Mail*, Aug. 17, 1981.
14. Peter Moon, "OPP Licenced Klansman as Security Guard," *Globe and Mail*, May 22, 1981.
15. "Klan Burns Large Cross on Farm," *Globe and Mail*, Nov. 10, 1980.
16. Julian Sher, "White Hoods," *Solidarity Times*, Nov. 9, 1983, pp. 10–11.
17. "Homicide Detectives Have Been Called in," United Press International, May 25, 1981.
18. "Ku Klux Klan Opens Toronto Office," *Globe and Mail*, June 27, 1980.
19. John D. McAlpine, *Report Arising Out of the Activities of the Ku Klux Klan in British Columbia as Presented to the Honourable J.H. Heinrich Minister of Labour for the Province of British Columbia* (Victoria, B.C., 1981).
20. Ibid., p. 4.
21. Sher, "The Klansman Who Came Calling."
22. "The Klan Will Expand into the Maritimes," United Press International, Nov. 24, 1980.
23. Fredericton *Daily Gleaner*, Dec. 9, 2018.
24. "Ku Klux Klan Makes its Mark in Vancouver," Canadian Press, *Globe and Mail*, Oct. 19, 1981.
25. Barrett, *Is God a Racist?*, p. 139.
26. Shelley Banks, "MLA Urges Acts of Racism be Made a Crime in B.C.," *Vancouver Sun*, January 26, 1981.
27. McAlpine, *Report Arising Out of the Activities of the Ku Klux Klan*, pp. 16–18.
28. Sher, "White Hoods," p. 11.
29. Suresh Jain, "Ethnic Groups Turn to the Authorities for Help in Fighting Racism in Canada," *India Today*, March 31, 1981.
30. Ibid.
31. Warren Kinsella, *Web of Hate: Inside Canada's Far Right Network* (Toronto: HarperCollins Canada, 1996), pp. 22–23.
32. Barrett, *Is God a Racist?*, p. 142.
33. Drew Fagan, "Calgarians Plead Guilty in Bombing Conspiracy Involving Trizec Head," *Globe and Mail*, Feb. 28, 1989; Kinsella, *Web of Hate*, pp. 29–31, 25.
34. Carolyn Whitzman, *Suburb, Slum, Urban Village: Transformations in Toronto's Parkdale Neighbourhood 1875–2002* (Vancouver: UBC Press, 2009), p. 187.

35. Zuhair Kashmeri, "Sent Packing by Foes of Klan, Ex-Informer Says He's Genuine," *Globe and Mail,* July 1, 1981.
36. Robert Devet, "Weekend Video: The Legacy of Four the Moment," *Nova Scotia Advocate,* April 15, 2018.

## Chapter 13

1. This narrative is drawn from two main sources: Judy Stoffman, "The Pups of War," *Today Magazine,* Oct. 17, 1981; and Stewart Bell's book on the Dominica plot entitled *Bayou of Pigs: The True Story of an Audacious Plot to Turn a Tropical Island Into A Criminal Paradise* (Mississauga, Ont.: John Wiley, 2008). The title is a play on the ill-fated CIA-inspired 1962 invasion of Cuba at the Bay of Pigs. Also useful were Ken Lawrence's "Behind the Klan's Karibbean Koup Attempt," No. 13 (July–August 1981), pp. 22–27, and "Klan Koup Attempt Part II," No. 16 (March 1982) , pp. 44-50, *Covert Action Information Bulletin.*
2. Bell, *Bayou of Pigs,* pp. 10, 209.
3. Ibid., p. 16.
4. Stoffman, "Pups of War," p. 9.
5. Bell, *Bayou of Pigs,* p. 44–45.
6. Matthew Lauder, "Operation Red Dog: Canadian Neo-Nazis were Central to the Planned Invasion of Dominica in 1981," *Canadian Content,* May 19, 2003, retrieved from https://operationreddog.netlify.app/2017/04/09/operation-red-dog-canadian-neo-nazis-were-central-to-the-planned-invasion-of-dominica-in-1981/index.html.
7. Bell, *Bayou of Pigs,* p. 86.
8. Ibid., pp. 58–59.
9. Kathleen Belew, *Bring the War Home: The White Power Movement and Paramilitary America* (Cambridge, Mass.: Harvard University Press, 2018), p. 86.
10. William P. Barrett. "Bayou of Pigs: A Rag-tag Band of Mercenaries Barely Missed the Boat," *Dallas Times-Herald,* May 10, 1981.
11. Stoffman, "Pups of War," p. 12.
12. Bell, *Bayou of Pigs,* p. 107.
13. Stephen Schneider, *Iced: The Story of Organized Crime in Canada* (Mississauga, Ont.: John Wiley. 2009), p. 321.
14. Julian Sher, "White Hoods," *Solidarity Times,* Nov. 9, 1983, p. 177; Stoffman, "Pups of War," p. 12.
15. Sher, "White Hoods," p. 173.

16. Sher, "White Hoods," p. 171; Stoffman, "Pups of War," p. 12.
17. Sher, "White Hoods," p. 175.
18. Belew, *Bring The War Home*, p. 88.
19. "Missing Man in Canada Once Involved in Plot to Overthrow Dominica Government," *Dominica News Online*, Feb. 3, 2015, retrieved from https://dominicanewsonline.com/news/homepage/news/general/missing-man-in-canada-once-involved-in-plot-to-overthrow-dominica-government.
20. Stoffman, "Pups of War," p. 10.
21. Peter Moon, "The Ku Klux Klan, a Mobster's Money and a Failed Coup," *Globe and Mail*, May 3, 1981.
22. Sher, "White Hoods," p. 11.
23. "Drug Charge Laid Against Klan Director," *Globe and Mail*, Nov. 27, 1981.
24. "Drug Count Dropped Against KKK Head," *Globe and Mail*, Dec, 17, 1981.
25. Peter Moon, "OPP Licenced Klansman as Security Guard," *Globe and Mail*, May 22, 1981.
26. "Sentence Suspended for Murder Plot," *Globe and Mail*, May 17, 1983.
27. Stanley R. Barrett, *Is God a Racist?: The Right Wing in Canada* (Toronto: University of Toronto Press, 1989), p. 149.
28. Sher, "White Hoods," p. 181.
29. "Alleged Member of Ku Klux Klan Charged in Death Conspiracy," *Globe and Mail*, Aug. 17, 1982.
30. "Police Cameras Crack Crime Ring, Murder Scheme," [video], *Fifth Estate*, CBC television, Feb. 19, 1985, retrieved from https://www.cbc.ca/player/play/1742239430.
31. Kirk Makin, "Two Klansmen Jailed for Planning Murder of Third KKK Member," *Globe and Mail*, Feb. 9, 1983.
32. "Alleged Member of Ku Klux Klan Charged in Death Conspiracy," *Globe and Mail*, Aug. 17, 1982.
33. "Stop the Frame-Up by the KKK Union Buster!" *Spartacist Canada*, January 1984, p. 12.
34. *Globe and Mail*, April 30, 1983.
35. *R. v. MacFarlane*, Court of Appeal for Ontario [1988] OJ No. 1310.
36. "Ex-KKK Official Gets Life Term in Beating Death," Montreal *Gazette*, March 2, 1984.

## Chapter 14

1. Stanley R. Barrett, *Is God a Racist?: The Right Wing in Canada* (Toronto: University of Toronto Press, 1989), p. 153.
2. Warren Kinsella, *Web of Hate: Inside Canada's Far Right Network* (Toronto: HarperCollins Canada, 1996), p. 220.
3. Julian Sher, "White Hoods," *Solidarity Times*, Nov. 9, 1983, pp. 184–85.
4. Andrew Mitrovica, "Front Man," *Walrus*, Sept. 12, 2004.
5. This account of Bill Harcus and the Manitoba Ku Klux Klan is based in part on the work of Warren Kinsella and his book *Web of Hate*, pp. 34–49.
6. Barrett, *Is God a Racist?*, p. 172.
7. Kinsella, *Web of Hate*, p. 111.
8. Barrett, *Is God a Racist?*, p. 172.
9. David Bercuson and Douglas Wertheimer, *A Trust Betrayed: The Keegstra Affair* (Toronto: Doubleday, 1985), p. 174.
10. William Peter Baergen, *The Ku Klux Klan in Central Alberta* (Red Deer: Central Alberta Historical Society, 2000), p. 276.
11. *Nealy v. Johnston*, Canadian Human Rights Tribunal, Decision, July 25, 1989.
12. "'Aryan' Group Ordered to Halt Hate Via Phone," Canadian Press, in Montreal *Gazette*, July 26, 1989.
13. Carol Sanders, "Pair Plead Guilty in Stabbing Death of Former Manitoba Ku Klux Klan Leader," *Winnipeg Free Press*, Oct. 22, 2018.
14. Kathleen Belew, *Bring the War Home: The White Power Movement and Paramilitary America* (Cambridge, Mass.: Harvard University Press. 2018), p. 151.
15. Peter Moon, "Few Show up in Buffalo, Neo-Nazi Rally Fizzles Peacefully," *Globe and Mail*, Jan. 16, 1981.
16. Kinsella, *Web of Hate*, p. 168.
17. Ron Bourgeault, "The Killing of Leo Lachance," *Canadian Dimension*, March/April 1994.
18. Kinsella, *Web of Hate*, p. 41.
19. Ibid., p. 337.
20. Cam Stewart, *Combating Hate and Bias Crime and Incidents in Alberta: Current Responses and Recommendations for the Future — July 2007* (Calgary: Alberta Hate and Bias Crime and Incidents Committee, 2007).
21. Kent Roach, *Canadian Justice, Indigenous Injustice: The Gerald Stanley and Colton Boushie Case* (Montreal and Kingston: McGill-Queen's University Press, 2019).

22. Susanne Reber and Robert Renaud, *Starlight Tour: The Last Lonely Night of Neil Stonechild* (Toronto: Random House, 2019).
23. Thomas King, *The Inconvenient Indian: A Curious Account of Native People in North America* (Toronto: Doubleday Canada, 2012), pp. 190–91..
24. Mr. Justice David Wright, *Report of the Commission of Inquiry Into Matters Related to the Death of Neil Stonechild* (Regina, 2004), p. 208.
25. April Lindgren, "Fire Those with Racist Past, Jewish Group Tells Forces," *Ottawa Citizen*, Oct. 7, 1993.
26. David Bercuson, *Significant Incident: Canada's Army, the Airborne, and the Murder in Somalia* (Toronto: McLelland and Stewart, 1996), p. 227.
27. Belew, *Bring the War Home*, pp. 135–37.
28. Bercuson, *Significant Incident*, p. 11.
29. Martha Armstrong, "A Tale of Two Videos: Media Event, Moral Panic and the Canadian Airborne Regiment" (master's thesis, McGill University, 1997), p. 53.
30. David Roberts, "Skinheads Charged in Slaying," *Globe and Mail*, March 2, 1996.
31. "Gays Targeted, Crown Says," Canadian Press, *Globe and Mail*, Aug. 13, 1997.
32. "Jailed Pair May Seek Compensation,"Canadian Press, *Globe and Mail*, Aug. 20, 1997.
33. "Collapsed Murder Case Worries Gay Community," Canadian Press, *Prince George Citizen*, Aug. 21, 1997.
34. Security Intelligence Review Committee (SIRC), *The Heritage Front Affair: Report to the Solicitor General of Canada* (Ottawa: Author, 1994.
35. Salim Jiwa. "Skinhead was Thrown Out of Army: Accused Murderer Nathan Leblanc was 'Unsuitable for Further Service,'" Vancouver *Province*, April 24, 1998.
36. David Pugliese. "Sajjan Taken to Task About White Supremacists in the Canadian Forces — Military Says it's Dealing with the Issue," *Ottawa Citizen*, June 14, 2019.
37. Canadian Military Police Criminal Intelligence Section, *White Supremacy, Hate Groups, and Racism in the Canadian Armed Forces*, Nov. 29, 2018, 2000-1040 (MPCIS) Scribd.
38. SIRC, *The Heritage Front Affair*, Ch. 3.2.4, p. 5.
39. Warren Kinsella, *Unholy Alliances: Terrorists, Extremists, Front Companies, and the Libyan Connection in Canada* (Toronto: Lester, 1992).

40. SIRC, *The Heritage Front Affair*, Ch. 3, p. 6.
41. Andrew Mitrovica, *Covert Entry: Spies, Lies and Crimes Inside Canada's Secret Service* (Toronto: Random House, 2002), pp. 129–30.
42. Mitrovica, "Front Man."
43. Megan Eston, "A Heart of Courage," *University of Toronto Magazine*, Oct. 2, 2019.
44. SIRC, *The Heritage Front Affair*, Part 1–42, pp. 6–9.
45. Rudy Paltiel, "John Ross Taylor: White Supremacist Defied Court," *Globe and Mail*, Nov. 9, 1994.

## Chapter 15

1. Cecil Houston and William J. Smyth, *The Sash Canada Wore: A Historical Geography of the Orange Order in Canada* (Toronto: University of Toronto Press, 1980), pp. 54–55.
2. "Roman Catholic Officials Believe They are Victims of Organized Firebugs," *Ottawa Citizen*, Dec. 7, 1922.
3. "Ku Klux Klan is Entering Montreal," *Ottawa Citizen*, Oct. 3, 1921.
4 "Archives Lost in Oka Church Fire; No Responsibility Incendiary Fires," *Ottawa Citizen*, Dec. 6, 1922.
5. "Says Spontaneous Combustion Cause of Basilica Fire," Canadian Press, *Ottawa Citizen*, April 28, 1923.
6. Albert Nerenberg, "Caricatures Frighten Quebec Ku Klux Klan Leader Larocque," Montreal *Gazette*, Sept. 6, 1991.
7. Manchester (New Hampshire) *Union Leader*, Nov. 9, 1989.
8. Timothy Winegard, *Oka: A Convergence of Cultures and the Canadian Forces* (Kingston, Ont.: Canadian Defence Academy Press, 2008), p. 116.
9. Geoffrey York and Loreen Pindera, *People of the Pines: The Warriors and the Legacy of Oka* (Toronto: Little, Brown, 1991), p. 249.
10. Ibid., p. 320.
11. Michael Orsini, "The Journalist and the Angry White Mob: Reflections From the Field," in *This is an Honour Song: Twenty Years Since the Blockades*, eds. Leanne Simpson and Kiera Ladner , (Winnipeg: Arbeiter Ring Publishing, 2010), pp. 254–55.
12. Warren Kinsella, *Web of Hate: Inside Canada's Far Right Network* (Toronto: HarperCollins Canada, 1996), pp. 292–93.
13. Winegard, *Oka*, p. 157.
14. Montreal *Gazette*, Sept. 4, 1990.
15. Rick Hornung, *One Nation Under the Gun: Inside the Mohawk Civil War* (Toronto: Stoddart, 1991), pp. 254–55.

16. Winegard, *Oka*, pp. 158–59; Craig Maclaine and Michael Baxendale, *This Is Our Land: The Mohawk Revolt at Oka* (Montreal: Optimum, 1990), p. 61; Harry Swain, *Oka: A Political Crisis and its Legacy* (Toronto: Douglas and McIntyre, 2010), pp. 139–40.
17. David Johnston, "Riled Montreal KKK Leader Broke with U.S. Parent," Montreal *Gazette*, April 8, 1992.
18. Lane Beauchamp, "Minister Plots Rise of KKK Camp, Arkansas Site to Hose Klan Meeting in Fall," Oklahoma City *Oklahoman*, Aug. 4, 1991.
19. "Queers Fight Back," *Anti-Racist Action* (Toronto, n.d.) (late 1992 based on dates cited in the article).
20. Dan Hawaleshka, "Sherbrooke Klan leader Convicted of Assault," Montreal *Gazette*, May 27, 1992.
21. André Picard, "Handling Murder with Kid Gloves," *Globe and Mail*, April 13, 1993.
22. Brigitte Noël, "Why Montreal was a Hotbed for Neo-Nazis in the 90s," *Vice*, Jan. 18, 2018; Eric Trottier, "Arrestation des deux principaux leaders du KKK à Montréal," *La Presse*, Jan. 20, 1992, p. 1; Marie-France Léger, "Aucune accusation contre le leader du KKK," *La Presse*, March 7, 1992, p. A3; Yves Boisvert, "Six mois de prison à un sympathisant d'extrême droite porteur de bombes," *La Presse*, March 20, 1993.
23. "Klan Recruiters Get Chilly Reception in Ontario Town," Montreal *Gazette*, Jan. 18, 1993; Peter Small, "Residents Baffled after Klan Shows up in Halton Region," *Toronto Star*, Jan. 18, 1993.
24. Lisa Tallyn. "Two Years: Ex-Mayoral Candidate Sentenced for Racist Attack on Local Shopkeeper," Georgetown (Ontario) *Independent and Free Press*, Oct. 27, 1996.
25. *Warman v. Harrison*, Canadian Human Rights Tribunal, Decision, Aug. 15, 2006 (2006 CHRT 30).
26. Stewart Bell, "Confessions of a Grand Wizard," *National Post*, May 23, 2009.

## Chapter 16

1. Ana-Maria Bliuc, Nicholas Faulkner, Andrew Jakubowicz, and Craig McGarty, "Online Networks of Racial Hate: A Systematic Review of 10 Years of Research on Cyber-Racism," *Computers in Human Behaviour* 87 (2018): 82.
2. *B'nai Brith v. Manitoba Knights of the Ku Klux Klan*, Canadian Human Rights Commission, Decision, Dec. 16, 1992.

3. Warren Kinsella, *Web of Hate: Inside Canada's Far Right Network* (Toronto: HarperCollins Canada, 1996), p. 42.
4. Cheryl Sullivan, "White Supremacists Forge Ahead on Path of Violence," *Christian Science Monitor*, Jan. 19–25, 1987, p. 6.
5. Kinsella, *Web of Hate*, p. 130.
6. Ciaran OMaolain, *The Radical Right: A World Directory* (Harlow, U.K.: Longman, 1987), p. 43.
7. Kathleen Belew, *Bring The War Home: The White Power Movement and Paramilitary America* (Cambridge, Mass.: Harvard University Press, 2018), p. 121.
8. Southern Poverty Law Center, *Louis Beam (n.d.), retrieved from https://www.splcenter.org/fighting-hate/extremist-files/individual/louis-beam.*
9. Kinsella, *Web of Hate*, p. 333.
10. Morris Dees with James Corcoran, *Gathering Storm: America's Militia Threat* (New York: Harper, 1996), p. 40.
11. Barbara Perry and Ryan Scrivens, *Right Wing Extremism in Canada: An Environmental Scan* (2015), retrieved from https://www.researchgate.net/publication/307971749_Right_Wing_Extremism_in_Canada_An_Environmental_Scan_2015.
12. Christopher Garland, "Klan's New Message of Cyber-Hate," *NZHerald*, March 27, 2008, retrieved from https://www.nzherald.co.nz/world/news/article.cfm?c_id=2&objectid=10500415.
13. David Schwab Abel, "The Racist Next Door," *Broward Palm Beach New Times*, Feb. 19, 1998.
14. Stewart Bell, *Bayou of Pigs: The True Story of an Audacious Plot to Turn a Tropical Island Into A Criminal Paradise* (Mississauga, Ont.: John Wiley, 2008), p. 210.
15. Eli Saslov, *Rising Out of Hatred: The Awakening of a Former White Nationalist* (New York: Doubleday, 2018), pp. 56–57.
16. Belew, *Bring the War Home*, p. 96.
17. Sean Hier, "Digital Freedom: The Canadian Right Wing on the Internet" (master's thesis, University of Guelph, 1997), p. 3.
18. See Chapter 15 for a discussion of Craig Harrison's case before the Canadian Human Rights Tribunal.
19. *Hate on the Internet*, issue position paper posted to stopracism.ca (n.d., probably ca. 2001).
20. *Warman v. Harrison*, Canadian Human Rights Commission, Decision, Aug. 15, 2006 (2006 CHRT 30), para 49.
21. *Warman and CHRC v. Marc Lemire*, Canadian Human Rights Commission, Decision, Sept. 2, 2009.

22. Veronica Rhodes, "KKK Revived with Strong Regina Ties," *Regina Leader-Post*, Aug. 25, 2007; *CBC News*, Aug. 27, 2007.
23. Perry and Scrivens, *Right-Wing Extremism in Canada*.
24. Ron Graham, *The Last Act: Pierre Trudeau, the Gang of Eight, and the Fight for Canada* (Toronto: Allen Lane, 2011), pp. 87–93.
25. Canadian Military Police Criminal Intelligence Section, *White Supremacy, Hate Groups, and Racism in the Canadian Armed Forces*, Nov. 29, 2018, 2000-1040 (MPCIS) Scribd., Para 7.
26. Mack Lamoureux and Ben Makuch, "Member of a Neo-Nazi Terror Group Appears to be a Former Canadian Soldier," *Vice News*, Aug. 2, 2018.
27. Canadian Military Police Criminal Intelligence Section, *White Supremacy*, Annex A.
28. Cameron MacLean, "Canadian Military Investigating Whether Winnipeg Member Involved in Hate Group," *CBC News*. Aug. 19, 2019.
29. Barbara Perry, Tanner Mirrlees, and Ryan Scrivens, "The Dangers of Porous Borders: The 'Trump Effect' in Canada," *Journal of Hate Studies* 14, no. 1 (February 2019): 54.
30. Christopher Curtis, Shannon Carranco, and Jon Milton, "Alt-Right in Montreal: How Charlottesville Exposed the Key Players in the Local White Nationalist Movement," Montreal *Gazette*, May 14, 2018.
31. Dagmawit Dejene, "Covering the New Hate," *Ryerson Review of Journalism* (Spring 2018).
32. Melanie Marquis, "Charlottesville: Canadians Who Attended White Supremacist Rally Identified," Canadian Press, *Huffington Post*, Aug. 17, 2017.
33. Kristofer Allendfeldt, "The KKK is in Rapid Decline — but its Symbols Remain Worryingly Potent," *Conversation*, March 1, 2019.

# INDEX

Page numbers in *italics* refer to photographs.